PRESIDENTIAL NOMINATIONS
IN A REFORM AGE

*Praeger Special Studies
in American Political Parties
and Elections*

Gerald M. Pomper, General Editor

*Copublished with the
Eagleton Institute of Politics,
Rutgers University*

PRESIDENTIAL NOMINATIONS IN A REFORM AGE

Thomas R. Marshall

American Political Parties
and Elections

general editor:
Gerald M. Pomper

PRAEGER SPECIAL STUDIES • PRAEGER SCIENTIFIC

Library of Congress Cataloging in Publication Data

Marshall, Thomas R.
  Presidential nominations in a reform age.

  (American political parties and elections)
  Includes index.
  1. Presidents—United States—Nomination. I. Title.
II. Series.
JK521.M37   324.5'0973   81-1684
ISBN 0-03-057678-4   AACR2

Published in 1981 by Praeger Publishers
CBS Educational and Professional Publishing
A Division of CBS, Inc.
521 Fifth Avenue, New York, New York 10175 U.S.A.

123456789 145 987654321

Printed in the United States of America

PREFACE

This book makes two simple arguments. The first is that contemporary presidential nominations are quite unlike nominations before the 1970s. Since 1968, changes in party rules, state delegate selection practices, and federal laws have undone the traditional brokered convention system. The resulting nominations system—herein labeled the system of popular appeal—emphasizes full access and control by the party's grass-roots voters and activists.

A second argument is that presidential nominating politics since 1970 have demonstrated important regularities from one contest to another. Contemporary nominations battles are not just exciting, colorful, unique sets of events. Rather, the six Democratic and Republican nominations between 1972 and 1980 share important similarities. This book emphasizes these recurrent features.

In part, this book is based on my own analysis of the behavior of the media, the candidates, and the public between 1972 and 1980. In part, however, I have also attempted to summarize the rapidly growing literature on presidential nominations now found in many books and monographs, in journal articles and convention papers, in newspaper accounts and public documents. To the many authors of the research cited herein I express my appreciation.

I also express my appreciation to several colleagues for their comments and suggestions—especially to Charles Hadley, John Jackson III, Gerald Pomper, and Frank Sorauf, and, at Praeger, to Betsy Brown. At the University of Texas at Arlington I have appreciated the cooperation of my colleagues, the University's Organized Research Fund, and the academic computing center. For assistance in typing and editing, I am especially indebted to Billie Ann Babb, Michele Bock, Marget Hagen, Frankie Sims, and Denise Parker.

This book is dedicated to my family.

CONTENTS

LIST OF TABLES

LIST OF FIGURES

1

THE NOMINATING OF U.S. PRESIDENTS

Within the last decade, great changes have transformed the presidential nominations contest. Candidates now begin campaigning several years before the first primary. More states hold primaries then ever before. Top party leaders no longer control their party's nomination. New federal laws restrict donors in their giving and candidates in their spending. Taxpayers now match small donations to the candidates. The media trail the candidates from one primary or caucus to another, reporting and interpreting the race. The nominee captures the nomination by trouncing his rivals in openly contested state primaries and caucuses. The national convention now merely confirms the apparent nominee.

To many U.S. residents, the nominations race is at once colorful, exciting, and a bit bewildering. Yet beneath all the drama and confusion lies a new, albeit not readily apparent, order. Since 1970, a new nominations system has emerged. This system is amenable to description, measurement, and empirical analysis. In broadest outline, contemporary nominations resemble a contest played by fixed groups of actors under new rules; the actors' actions, interactions, and reactions collectively decide the nomination.

As several political scientists have argued, the nominations race is as important as the general election itself.[1] In the November general election, voters may usually choose between but two candidates who have any realistic prospect of winning the White House. Before the national conventions, however, the choice is much greater. By law, millions of adult U.S. citizens are eligible to be president. Through the nominations process this enormous number is normally reduced to two serious contenders, one from either major party.

Different societies choose their top leaders in a variety of ways; the current U.S. presidential selection process is but one alternative. Like so many U.S. institutions, the current nominations process has not been widely imitated either in contemporary times or in earlier decades. Indeed, modern methods for nominating and electing the president are relatively unique even for the United States: until the 1970s U.S. presidents won their nominations in ways quite different from those now practiced.[2]

PAST AND PRESENT NOMINATIONS

The first U.S. president, General Washington, was elected without any formal nomination at all. Washington's personal popularity and prestige dissuaded any other aspirants from entering the race and won the reluctant general a unanimous vote from the electors. Yet even as early as Washington's second term, groups of top party leaders began meeting separately to contend for the vice-presidency.

By 1800, political parties coalesced from personal factions; in that year two groups of congressmen met openly in Washington to decide on their respective tickets. By agreeing upon a slate and thereby focusing their energies, each party ensured that its own strength would not splinter. For another two decades, the congressional caucus system usually succeeded in uniting at least one party. In those days, no contender ever won the White House without first gaining the caucus nod.

The caucus system, however, failed to outlive the founding fathers themselves. After 1820, the parties collapsed into regional and personal factions. Only after a decade's interlude did two national parties reemerge; nearly simultaneously, both experimented with the earliest national party conventions. While the first conventions were merely convenient devices to legitimize the ambitions of the leading candidates, state and local party leaders soon gained control of the conventions. These politicos—or "bosses" to their critics—handpicked their own state's delegates, then bargained with would-be nominees and with each other to decide the nomination.

Like the earlier caucus system, the national party conventions usually, but not always, united the party behind a single ticket. Unlike the caucus, the brokered convention system proved remarkably durable. With few changes it endured well over a century, surviving the coming of presidential primaries, the advent of polling, and the rise of nationwide mass communication. As late as 1968, its basic features had remained intact: would-be nominees won the nomination from a handful of state and local party leaders.

By 1972, however, the brokered convention system had collapsed and was replaced by the system of popular appeal. Several factors contributed to the demise of the old nominations system. During the 1950s and 1960s, grass-roots party activists demanded a greater voice in party affairs. A badly divided Democratic convention in 1968 provided a final impetus for reform. Campaign finance scandals led to the regulation of fund-raising and -spending practices. Together, new party rules, state practices, and federal laws undermined the control of top party leaders over delegate selection, and in the 1970s a new system of presidential nominations emerged.

A MODEL OF CONTEMPORARY PRESIDENTIAL NOMINATIONS

The new nominations system is shown as a schema in Figure 1.1. The contest involves three sets of players—or actors—over a series of rounds or stages. The key players include the major news media, the candidates themselves, and the various publics. The stages or rounds include state primaries, caucuses, and conventions.

Before the Primaries

Long before the first state primary or caucus, the key players begin their activities. Candidates and advisors chart a strategy to carry off the nomination, deciding which states to enter and which to avoid, how to raise the needed funds, and in which states to begin building an organization. Candidates also strive to increase name recognition and public support as reflected in the polls, although, in fact, the polls seldom change very much until the early primaries.

Before the early delegate selection races the media describe and label the candidates. While preprimary coverage is short on real substance, it does introduce potential voters to the less familiar candidates. The media declare some candidates "front-runners" and others "underdogs" or "long shots." Columnists and reporters guess

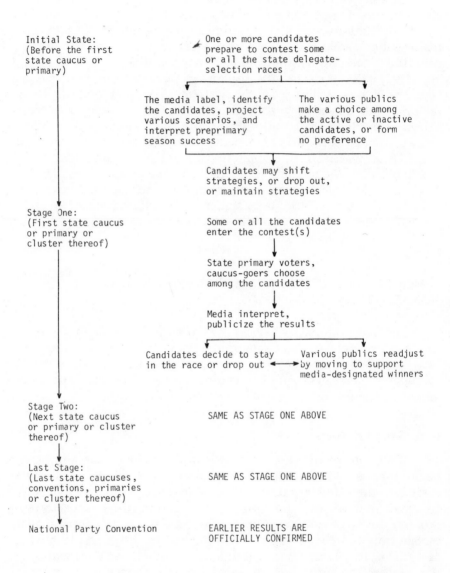

Initial State:
(Before the first
state caucus or
primary)

One or more candidates
prepare to contest some
or all the state delegate-
selection races

The media label, identify
the candidates, project
various scenarios, and
interpret preprimary
season success

The various publics
make a choice among
the active or inactive
candidates, or form
no preference

Candidates may shift
strategies, or drop out,
or maintain strategies

Stage One:
(First state caucus
or primary or
cluster thereof)

Some or all the candidates
enter the contest(s)

State primary voters,
caucus-goers choose
among the candidates

Media interpret,
publicize the results

Candidates decide to stay
in the race or drop out

Various publics readjust
by moving to support
media-designated winners

Stage Two:
(Next state caucus
or primary or cluster
thereof)

SAME AS STAGE ONE ABOVE

Last Stage:
(Last state caucuses,
conventions, primaries
or cluster thereof)

SAME AS STAGE ONE ABOVE

National Party Convention

EARLIER RESULTS ARE
OFFICIALLY CONFIRMED

FIGURE 1.1 - A MODEL OF THE SYSTEM OF POPULAR APPEAL

4

at the probable winning scenario for the candidates; later, they rely on these scripts to judge each candidate's progress throughout the primary season.

The vast, amorphous public also begins to grasp the nominations race. For most U.S. residents, the preprimary positioning holds little of interest, and at this early stage most of them remain uninformed and uninterested. The most politically aware voters may simply learn a little about the candidates and find one or two contenders who appeal to them. A very small number of donors, amateur party workers, and party leaders follow the campaigns more closely, sometimes meeting the candidates personally at receptions or attending fund-raising dinners or parties. These few active adults—probably numbering no more than 2 or 3 percent of all adult U.S. residents—may endorse and actively work for a favorite candidate.

Long before the earliest state caucus or primary, the players begin to interact. The media judge the front-runner by examining public opinion polls, fund-raising success, and the endorsements of prominent politicos. A candidate's meager poll ratings, lack of fund-raising success, or slight media attention may influence potential volunteers to "wait and see" or may even cause a few candidates to drop out in discouragement. No single actors can completely control the contest even at this early stage.

The Early Primaries

When the earliest state caucuses and primaries begin, the nominations race changes markedly. For the first time the candidates submit their bids to state primary voters and caucus-goers. A candidate may enter all or only a few states. At this point, the nominations race begins to dominate the media, and the candidates are thrust to the forefront of public attention.

In each state caucus or primary, eligible adults may choose among the candidates or uncommitted delegates. In most states only a fraction of all adults actually vote or go to a caucus meeting. As Chapter Five later suggests, active adults vary greatly in their motives and in their knowledge about the candidates. Whatever their motives may be, however, primary voters and caucus-goers exert more control over the nominations contest now than in decades past.

As the primary and caucus results are tallied, the media report and interpret the returns. A candidate who receives the most votes or delegates is almost always declared the winner. A candidate who wins fewer votes or delegates is usually declared a loser or simply ignored by the press. The media have developed several rules—some of them fairly complicated—by which to evaluate primary and caucus results. By these rules, described at length in Chapter Three, the press judges which state contests are important and which are not and how well each candidate fared in each state.

For each state primary or caucus, the media interpret the returns, which, in turn, influences both active and inactive adults in other states. Donors, state party leaders, elected office holders, interest group officials, and volunteers all tend to "invest" their efforts in winning candidates. So, too, does the mass public, as reflected in periodic public opinion polls.

A general pattern recurs from year to year and from contest to contest: polls follow primary and caucus results. This tendency need not be especially surprising. Surrounded by confusion about the race's outcome, many undecided and little-committed voters rely on the early primary and caucus returns to spot the probable nominee and then "invest" their emotional energies and votes in that candidate. Most Americans have little in-depth knowledge about the candidates' issue stands and seldom report intense personal feelings about the candidates. As Chapter Five suggests, when a candidate surges, the resulting media attention brings that candidate into the public eye, endowing him with a superficially appealing image. As a result, polls often follow winners.

Momentum

The first two to six primaries and caucuses are usually critical for a candidate, since these will deplete a candidate's initial treasury and exhaust the initial supply of volunteers. To continue the race, the candidate will need to attract new volunteers and donors for the upcoming yet more expensive primaries.

At this point, an unsuccessful candidate is not likely to attract substantial new support and will soon be forced from the race. By contrast, a successful contender will win attention from the media, new funds from donors, and new support from party workers, volunteers, and the polls. As this process continues, candidates who fare poorly will be driven from the race. In multicandidate races the field of hopefuls will begin to dwindle. In most contests, an apparent nominee will emerge after the early or middle primaries. The leader will then be aided by his own momentum through the later contests.

The Later Primaries

The nominations race may effectively be over after the first handful of primaries or caucuses, while in other years the contest may continue through to the last. In all races, however, the nominee is almost certain to emerge before the convention opens. A stalemated race is now unlikely.

The nominee is most likely to emerge after the early or middle primaries in two of three possible situations. A very strong candidate —perhaps an incumbent—who draws only weak opposition may push out his weaker rivals in the early primaries and caucuses. In this case the challengers will have fared so poorly that a few early losses will end their challenge.

Paradoxically, if the initial field is extremely crowded, the nominee is also likely to emerge from the pack—although perhaps not before the middle or late primaries. In this case many hopefuls will drop out after the early primaries and caucuses, and attention will focus on the strongest survivor. Even if one or more challengers continue the race, the probable nominee's momentum is likely to carry him to the nomination.

Prolonged competition is most likely in a third case: when two well-known candidates square off, with each representing a well-organized, regionally strong wing of the party. In these cases the competition may well continue into the middle or late primaries, or even through the last state caucuses and conventions, before the nominee is apparent. When two strong, evenly matched contenders square off, neither is as likely to gather momentum as in the two other situations. By concentrating his resources, even the weaker candidate can produce occasional victories, thereby adding suspense to the race. Even so, a brokered, deadlocked convention remains unlikely.

Confirming the Nomination

The nominations race officially terminates at the national party conventions. In reality, however, the national convention now only ratifies the winner's claims. The real victory results from the earlier competition in state primaries, caucuses, and conventions.

The national convention still does conduct some important business. It demonstrates the national makeup of the parties as well as their diversity. Interest groups bargain with the nominee for their support in the upcoming campaign. Delegates write new party rules that will affect the balance of power within the party as well as the next nominations race four years hence. Local and state politicians attract national media attention. Party factions bargain over the platform. The nominee announces his running mate, seeks to unify the party, and begins the struggle against the other party.

Conventions are colorful spectacles. They are highlighted by parades, demonstrations, lively (or sometimes dull) speeches, bands, banners, balloons, spotlights, and an occasional floor fight. Roll call votes offer at least a little suspense and hint at the possibilities of secret intrigue.

In the new nominations system, though, convention bargaining no longer decides the nomination. Unlike earlier conventions, which featured smoke-filled rooms and secret deals among top party leaders, the conventions of the new era only confirm the nomination. Now the nominee wins the title in openly contested primaries and caucuses. The national party convention, for all its hoopla, only ratifies and legitimizes that outcome.[3]

A New Order

To a casual observer, the special features of each year may obscure the underlying regularities of contemporary nominations. In some years there are only a few contenders, in other years, many. The Democratic and Republican Parties show different internal lines of conflict. Some candidates boast engaging (or demagogic) personalities and appeals. Issues and crises change from race to race. Election rules vary slightly. Assassinations, controversial interviews, and campaign blunders may divert attention from underlying regularities.

Yet contemporary nominations are more than isolated sets of interesting, colorful, and unique events. Beneath all the apparent color and confusion lies a new era in nominating politics. Whatever its virtues or drawbacks, the new system tends to produce a nominee well before the convention. Brokered, stalemated conventions are now unlikely. The new era of popular appeal differs from either the congressional caucus system or the brokered convention system in its key rules, process, and players.

KEY FEATURES OF THE NEW NOMINATIONS GAME

Four key features shape nominating politics in the new era of popular appeal.

First, each player focuses more on his own, individual welfare than on the collective welfare of all the players. Some goals require competition, but others do not.

Second, each player fixes a strategy to achieve his own goals, with each player's strategy designed to manipulate the other players. While strategies are often ineffective and flawed, each player's strategy is an attempt to reduce the contest's tremendous complexities to a manageable level.

Third, no single player, alone, can control the outcome. While each player tries to manipulate other players, each must also react to forces beyond his control. Power and control are now more widely dispersed among the players than ever before. As a result, coordination is difficult if not altogether impossible. By the time coordination is feasible, the nomination outcome is usually readily apparent. The nomination results more from the impersonal interactions of individually oriented players than from any intentional cooperation among the players.

Fourth, the contest produces a high level of momentum. Momentum refers to the contest's tendency to produce a nominee well before the national convention. It also signifies the tendency of polls, activists, delegates, and the media to move behind the eventual nominee. Momentum results both from the players' individualistic behavior and from new election rules and laws.

Individual and Collective Goals

Individual Goals

No one would be surprised that each candidate aims to win the nomination for himself. Yet that same narrowness of vision and individualistic focus is seldom attributed to the media, to voters, or to grass-roots activists. In reality, though, each player must react to a host of unique pressures, and each strives to satisfy individual goals. The media, for instance, must react to several unique pressures: deadlines, competition for readers or viewers, newspaper or network news policy, federal regulations or professional ethic, which stress even-handed treatment, and cost limits. For most editors and reporters, time is short, the workload pressing, and a deadline always at hand. While reporters and editors may very well desire to provide more complete coverage, they must also respond to the immediate demands of their profession.

Donors, campaign staffers, and amateur activists also seek personal, individual goals. Public office holders desire a nominee who will help carry the local ticket or may seek to curry favor with an incumbent. Interest group officials seek a sympathetic nominee, or at least a nominee indebted for their support. Volunteers seek a nominee who reflects their own ideological views or, in other cases, an appealing personality to relieve the humdrum of their lives.

Since players may be searching for numerous separate goals, focusing solely on the candidates themselves cannot adequately explain the new nomination system. Voters, activists, and the media all have goals quite distinct from those of the candidates. Focusing on the candidates' goals alone is an inadequate view of the new nominations race.

The Competitive Nature of Goals

As the players seek to achieve their own goals, they find that while some goals may be achieved with little overt competition, others require it. The candidates are thrust into the most competitive situation, each wanting the nomination for himself, while only one can prevail.[4] In the resulting zero-sum competition,[5] candidates show the greatest incidence of overt conflict and competition and, not infrequently, personal hostility.

Nevertheless, for most players, conflict and hostility are not required to achieve their goals. Reporters may seek to satisfy editors' demands by filing a daily newspaper story or a nightly newscast segment. This requires very little overt competition, since each reporter can satisfy this aim regardless of other reporters' success. Indeed, in many cases sharing information and advice may even prove helpful. Editors and publishers who want accurate, balanced stories may find it helpful to check their own reporter's accounts against those of others. Not surprisingly, the media show more cooperation and less conflict than do the candidates.

Voters may also discharge their sense of civic duty with little competition or conflict. Canvassers and telephone volunteers typically spend more time identifying voters and distributing information than trying to convert supporters of another candidate. Many volunteers immerse themselves in clerical tasks and avoid any overt conflict at all. If activists and donors are seeking to add excitement to their lives or to support a sympathetic candidate, they can usually do so without risking a personal confrontation.

Individual and Collective Goals

In the brokered convention system, top party leaders dominated the race. They focused chiefly on a collective goal: the party's electoral welfare. To be sure, the nation's welfare was probably too abstract, uncertain, and subjective to be much considered. Yet the party's own short-term electoral welfare was usually a key concern in tapping the nominee.

In the new nominations system, control no longer rests with top party leaders; power and control are instead dispersed more widely than ever before. As the number of actors has grown, so each actor's behavior has grown less altruistic, less far-sighted, and less collectively oriented. Now each quests for narrowly defined, personal goals. The media, primary voters, and caucus-goers, donors, volunteers, and inactive adults react mostly to short-term events. The candidates primarily focus on winning enough delegates to gain the nomination. The concept of collective goal-seeking is far too abstract and ephemeral a notion to be of any help in understanding the players' behavior. In the new nominations system, collective goals are vague and illusory, easily lost in the pursuit of very immediate, real, and personal goals. Each actor focuses primarily on achieving his own welfare and individual goals.

The Players' Strategies

Just as goals vary greatly, so, too, do strategies. An actor's strategy focuses both on long-term goals and on short-term pressures. Except for the candidates, most actors appear to respond chiefly to short-range demands.

Candidates focus primarily on a single, long-range objective: winning the nomination. A candidate's strategy is usually detailed long before the earliest primaries; nevertheless, most continually revise their plans throughout the preconvention season to cope with changing circumstances: spending limits, fund-raising success or failure, their own success in key primaries, and the success or failure of their rivals.

For other participants, strategies are less oriented to long-range goals. Reporters and editors, for example, may strive to meet a daily deadline for a colorful and captivating campaign account. For the press, the campaign primarily involves meeting a succession of short-term pressures.

Strategies also differ in their complexity. At one extreme, a potential nominee may build a book-length campaign plan based on weeks of consultation with campaign experts and advisers. At the other, most ordinary Americans have so little interest in the contest that they never participate at all. For most Americans the very notion of a "strategy" is an exaggeration of their interest. Their "strategy" for dealing with nominating politics involves ignoring the race or passively following the primary results via the networks or the headlines just as they may follow sporting events.

Strategies are not always effective. This problem is most serious for the players engaged in zero-sum conflicts: the candidates. Candidate strategies often appear to be based on highly dubious assumptions or on an outright misunderstanding of the game's new features. Some candidates, for example, enter only a handful of little-noticed primary and caucus states, although even a strong showing there is unlikely to win many delegates, publicity, or poll gains. An actor's strategy may be flawed for any of several reasons. Candidates and their advisers see the game in different ways. Their resources vary. Some candidates and their advisers have but a limited understanding of recently changed campaign laws, party rules, and reporting patterns. Many are inexperienced in running a nationwide campaign. Strategic decisions that result from interchanges among many advisers may be flawed by common organizational problems: "group-think," personal ambitions, personal likes and dislikes, individual struggles for power and influence within the organization, and so forth. Future events cannot be predicted with certainty; time is always short; fatigue, human frailties, and the press of events all affect the strategic decisions of the actors.[6]

The Fragmentation of Power

In past decades, during the brokered convention system, a few top party leaders could coordinate their efforts and thereby control the nomination by handpicking their own delegates and then negotiating among themselves and the would-be nominees. In that system a few state and local party leaders decided the nomination.

In the era of popular appeal, however, power and control over the nomination is fragmented among more actors than ever before. No longer can a single actor or a handful of players personally control the nomination.[7] New party rules, national laws, and state delegate-selection practices have fragmented and dispersed power broadly; responsibility and control over the nomination are now shared by so many participants that coordination is difficult, if not impossible.

This is the case for several reasons. Some key actors are engaged in a zero-sum conflict in which confrontation is inevitable. Candidates all aim for the nomination, but since the award may be won only by one candidate, the others must inevitably fail. In this case, the zero-sum conflict among the hopefuls precludes much meaningful coordination. Not surprisingly, there are few apparent instances in which actively competing candidates have coordinated their efforts.

Other participants face basic and probably insurmountable barriers to coordinating their efforts. Primary voters and caucus-goers are too numerous and dispersed, they are of varied social status, and they lack the means of communicating one with another. Most adults in the United States are too uninterested and uninformed to participate actively in primaries or caucuses at all, let alone to co-ordinate their activities.

The glare of the media, public scrutiny, and new norms of fair play also make coordination difficult. At times, several candidates might find it desirable to coordinate their efforts; two weaker candidates, for instance, might benefit from choosing one state apiece during a string of primaries. If each concentrated all his efforts in a single state, the weaker candidates might thereby block a stronger candidate who divided his energies and resources among several states. In this case, collaboration may be a perfectly rational strategy for the weaker candidates. Yet the media and the public (and certainly the front-running candidate) are likely to treat this as a violation of the rules of fair play. Still other efforts at coordination by candidates and their strategists may run foul of Federal Election Commission regulations—such as joint planning of spending between candidates and interest groups or the shifting of delegates from an inactive candidate to an active one. In the new nominations race openness is a priority. "Secret deals" are perceived as unfair and are disparaged and discouraged. Efforts at coordination must usually remain secretive and furtive—to be disavowed in public and probably breached in practice.

Coordination is most difficult precisely at the game's most critical stage: during the early key primaries. At that time, the field of candidates is likely to be most crowded and the outcome the most uncertain. Candidates are all scrambling for an early advantage. Few delegate blocs have yet been assembled. Reporters may be unfamiliar with and mistrustful of one another. Voters have the least amount of information on which candidates are realistic contenders and which are not.

Later, during the last primaries and caucuses, coordination is more feasible. By that time, the field of candidates has probably narrowed. Blocs of delegates have formed. Favorite sons, uncommitted delegates, and inactive candidates can more easily estimate the probability that a shift of some delegates would decide the nomination. Yet by this time the contest's wholly impersonal workings are likely to have produced a probable nominee—a candidate so far ahead of his rivals in media attention, the delegate count, and the polls that his nomination is highly probable if not already a foregone conclusion. In short, when coordination among the players is finally feasible, the eventual outcome of the nominations race is usually no longer in doubt.

The new nominations system is far from completely chaotic. Rather, it demonstrates regular stages and sequences. These regularities, however, do not depend on any careful coordination and collaboration among individual players. Examples of meaningful, effective coordination among elites are less common now than in earlier times. Instead, the system's orderliness and regularity results chiefly from impersonal factors, not from any intended or deliberate coordination by its players.

Momentum

New party rules, campaign laws, and the behavior of the players all produce a high level of momentum. As a result, the competition tends to produce an apparent nominee well before the national convention. The nominee emerges from state primaries and caucuses by gaining far more favorable publicity, media attention, and delegates than any other hopeful. Public opinion polls, donors, delegates, and activists all move toward supporting the eventual nominee. As a result, a nominee wins acceptance based on his successful record in openly contested state primaries and caucuses, not by the consent of top party leaders.

Momentum occurs primarily for three reasons. First, the media provide more than a proportionate amount of coverage to candidates who run well in the primaries and caucuses; candidates who finish second, third, or worse win far less coverage. As Chapter Three later explains, the media also do not deal equally with all the state primaries and caucuses. Instead, they focus attention on a handful of races. The media also judge and interpret primary and caucus returns and emphasize the horse-race aspects of the race. As a result, the press magnifies and reinforces the leading candidate's winning image.

Second, party rules and state law usually provide at least a small delegate bonus for a winning candidate. In recent years, both parties (especially the Democrats) have encouraged the use of proportionality in the awarding of delegates. Even so, many states award the candidate with the most votes a greater share of the delegates than his share of the popular vote.

New campaign laws, especially fund-raising laws, also encourage momentum. Given the restriction on individual donations, few candidates can collect the total amount allowed from their most committed supporters. Once these early funds have been spent in the early primaries and caucuses, a candidate must look for new donations. To attract continued funds, a candidate must appeal to donors who did not initially support his candidacy. Few donors, however, will back an apparently unsuccessful contender. As a result, candidates who fare poorly will quickly find themselves out of funds. Most will soon drop out.

Momentum in the new nominations system was probably neither foreseen nor intended by reformers. To some players—for example, those who hope for a deadlocked convention—momentum may even be undesirable. Yet present rules virtually ensure that momentum will occur, not as the result of planning and coordination among the players, but as a national byproduct of the new rules.

THE PLAN OF THIS BOOK

This chapter has overviewed a new model of presidential nominations: the system of popular appeal. Chapter Two contrasts the new system with two earlier nominating systems: the congressional caucus system and the brokered convention system; it describes the efforts of modern-day reformers to change the brokered convention system and assesses the impact of recent rules changes. As Chapter Two suggests, contemporary party reformers have been markedly successful in achieving their objectives.

Chapter Three examines the behavior of the media; Chapter Four, that of the candidates; and Chapter Five, that of the public. Since 1968, the media have gained more influence over the nominations race than ever before. A review of media behavior shows that most of the national news media have already routinized their campaign coverage. Although their impact is great, the media's behavior is far from arbitrary or capricious.

Chapter Four suggests that candidates now take a more active role in winning their party's nod than ever before. A successful candidate must fashion his campaign by his own efforts, beginning long before the first state primary or caucus. Candidates may pursue several strategies to gain the nomination. Most candidate strategies, though, are seriously flawed and ignore the realities of the new nominations system.

Chapter Five divides the adult public into spectators, voters, and caucus-goers, and activists, donors, and party regulars. Now, power has shifted from the party's top leaders to grass-roots voters and activists. In most cases, U.S. adults are little informed and little interested in the race, and the polls tend to follow primary winners. Although the public's impact is greater than ever before, this does not affect the race's outcome in any simple or straightforward way.

The sixth and final chapter reviews major controversies in the nominations process. The system of popular appeal achieves some values: openness, easy participation, and control by the party's grass roots. Many critics, however, allege that the system also has a variety of faults: a tendency to produce unacceptable nominees, a weakening in the parties' vitality, and an overly independent executive. Although the new system of popular appeal is controversial, it is likely to endure, essentially unchanged, for the foreseeable future.

NOTES

1. William Keech and Donald Matthews, *The Party's Choice* (Washington, D.C.: Brookings, 1977), pp. 14–19.
2. Donald Matthews, ed., *Perspectives on Presidential Selection* (Washington, D.C.: Brookings, 1973); James Ceaser, *Presidential Selection: Theory and Development* (Princeton, New Jersey: Princeton University Press, 1979).
3. For an example, see Richard Reeves, *Convention* (New York: Harcourt, Brace, 1977).
4. As Chapter Four explains, however, some contenders may in fact be aiming to win the vice-presidential spot, to gain publicity, or (in the case of favorite sons) to prevent intraparty feuds from complicating home-state politics. If a candidate is seeking a goal other than the nomination itself, conflict may be significantly reduced.
5. Zero-sum competition includes those controversies in which the participants seek a single, indivisible goal. In such contests only one player can win, and all the others must fail. R. Duncan Luce and Howard Raiffa, *Games and Decisions* (New York: John Wiley & Sons, 1967); James Coleman, *The Mathematics of Collective Action* (Chicago: Aldine, 1973).
6. Anthony Downs, *Inside Bureaucracy* (Boston: Little, Brown, 1966); Herbert Simon, *Administrative Behavior* (New York: Macmillan, 1961); and Irving Janis, *Victims of Groupthink* (Boston: Houghton Mifflin, 1972). For a good description of early candidate planning for the 1976 race, see Arthur T. Hadley, *The Invisible Primary* (Englewood Cliffs, N.J.: Prentice-Hall, 1976); Jonathon Moore and Janet Fraser, ed., *Campaign for President—The Managers Look at '76* (Cambridge, Mass.: Ballinger, 1977).
7. The sole exception may be in a contest in which an initial front-runner—perhaps the incumbent president—is so popular within his own party that little opposition emerges. In the absence of a strong opposition an incumbent will likely have sufficient resources to dominate the nominations contest. See Chapters Two, Four, and Five.

2

THREE PRESIDENTIAL NOMINATIONS SYSTEMS

Consider these four presidential candidates:

In 1789, General Washington won the first of his two presidential terms. The general showed a considerable reluctance to accept the office at all, was never formally nominated, and never actively campaigned. Nevertheless he won a unanimous vote from the presidential electors.

In 1812, James Monroe gained certain election to the White House through nomination by a caucus of his party's congressmen. Assembled at the Capitol, the Democratic–Republican caucus gave Monroe a narrow margin of 64 votes to his now obscure opponent's 55 ballots.

In 1968, Vice-President Hubert Humphrey ignored a challenge by two rivals and bypassed all of that year's presidential primaries. Nevertheless, Humphrey handily won his party's nomination through the support of his party's incumbent president, governors, big city mayors, and Southern politicos.

In 1972, a theretofore little-known senator from South Dakota, George McGovern, astounded his better-regarded opponents by carrying off the nomination. McGovern scored well in several primaries and trounced the hapless party regulars in local caucus meetings and state conventions. By convention time McGovern had collected so many delegates that his party's regular leaders found it impossible to stop him.

Each of these four politicians gained the right to be seriously considered as a presidential candidate in different ways. Since the earliest days of the Republic, many men and women have sought the presidency. Yet, in most years, only two candidates are seriously considered in the general election. Whenever coherent parties have existed, they have usually found some way of choosing a single standard-bearer for their followers. How is the entire field of would-be presidents normally reduced to an effective choice between two candidates?

A review of presidential elections shows three distinct systems by which parties have chosen their nominees. Each system differs from the other two in several respects—the type of candidate favored, the site of the nomination, the role of ordinary voters, party leaders, and the media. Each system has key participants, each of whom holds resources and has goals and strategies. Each system has both formal and informal rules; in each, there are fixed sites and stages for making critical decisions.[1]

The first two nominating systems both failed, through a lack of public confidence, short-range political crises, and divisions among political elites. In the 1820s the congressional caucus system failed; about a decade later, the reemergent national parties turned to national conventions to choose their candidates. In the late 1960s the brokered convention system also collapsed.

In the 1970s, the third nominating system emerged: the system of popular appeal. In this system a candidate gained convention delegates—and thereby, the nomination—in openly contested state primaries, caucuses, and conventions. Only by succeeding in this manner could a candidate gain enough delegates to carry off the Democratic or Republican nomination. By the 1970s, the brokered convention system—so long dominated by the party's top office holders and officials—was dead. The national convention itself survived only to ratify the nomination and to conduct other party business.

THE FIRST NOMINATIONS: 1789–96

Neither in 1789 nor in 1792 did General (respectively President) Washington bother to gain a formal nomination for the presidency. Since he had no opponent in either year, he won the office without challenge. Washington might twice capture the presidency without any special effort—indeed, despite his own reluctance—yet no other politician was so obvious or popular a choice for the presidency or vice-presidency. John Adams, who was chosen vice-president in 1789, owed his office to the efforts of prominent Federalists. Four years later, in 1792, the Federalists in Congress met to recommend Adams to the Federalist electors. In that same year, the Federalists' political opponents in Congress recommended George Clinton of New York for the vice-presidency.

In 1796, Washington refused a third term, but his belated Farewell Address came so late that aspiring candidates were left with little time to organize their campaigns.[2] Once again the congressional parties met. The Federalists once more settled on Adams, and the Democratic–Republicans recommended Thomas Jefferson as their presidential choice. In neither case, however, did the party leaders make a formal nomination; they simply decided among themselves, then counted on their personal influence to hold the electors in line.

In these first three elections, the presidential and vice-presidential nominations were settled by exchanges of letters, private meetings, and informal caucusing by the party's congressmen. But while these informal methods sufficed to recommend the obvious candidates, they failed to command complete loyalty from the electors. In the balloting of presidential electors in 1796, several failed to support both their party's recommended presidential and vice-presidential nominees. As a result, in 1796, Adams won the presidency, while his opponent, Jefferson, gained the vice-presidency.[3]

THE CONGRESSIONAL CAUCUS SYSTEM: 1800–24

The Caucus System

In 1800, both the Federalists and the Democratic–Republicans in Congress met formally and separately to confirm their tickets. That party differences spilled over into presidential politics came as no surprise. By 1800, the Federalists and their foes openly disagreed on the most basic issues in U.S. politics: tariffs, foreign policy, economic and industrial policy, and citizen participation in politics. Each party supported local party committees and correspondents, and each subsidized party newspapers. Each party actively contested local and congressional elections.

When the presidential electors' votes were counted in December of 1800, the success of the caucus as a nominating device was readily apparent. Each Democratic–Republican elector followed the caucus' advice and voted for Jefferson and Aaron Burr. The Federalist electors, too, all-but-unanimously accepted their party leaders' recommendations, balloting for both Adams and Charles Pinckney. By 1800, the caucuses had won a widespread if not quite unanimous acceptance as a nominations technique.[4]

After 1800, the Democratic–Republicans relied on the congressional caucus for another two decades. In 1804, the caucus renominated Jefferson for a second term; in 1808 and 1812, James Madison was chosen; in 1816, James Monroe narrowly won the party's nod and then was renominated in 1820.

The Federalists again relied on a caucus to nominate their ticket in 1804, but after that year the party was too weak to seriously contest the presidency. Although the Federalist leaders still resorted to closed meetings of top party leaders in 1808 and 1812, by then the Federalists were a spent political force, and neither in 1816 nor in 1820 did their dwindling band even bother to nominate a ticket.

Little is known of the caucuses' inner workings between 1800 and 1820. In some years, the parties' congressional leaders agreed on an obvious choice. as in the Democratic–Republican caucuses of 1800, 1804, 1808, and 1812. At other times the vote was closer, as in 1816, when Monroe won by only a narrow vote. Apparently members of Congress met privately before the caucus to sound out the sentiment for their favorites and lobbied their fellow congressmen before the meeting. At times some congressmen refused to attend the caucus, either on principle or for political reasons.[5] Local politicians and party activists often joined the lobbying efforts through private meetings and personal correspondence. Incumbent presidents, too, encouraged their favorites—sometimes subtly, sometimes not. Nor were the candidates themselves above a bit of behind-the-scenes lobbying, through either correspondence or patronage.

Despite its increasingly unsavory reputation, the congressional caucus served the dominant Democratic–Republicans well for two decades. Although several nominations were contested—and the choice of Monroe in 1816 very narrowly decided indeed—most party supporters closed ranks behind the ticket once the nomination had been made. By achieving unity, the Democratic–Republican caucus ensured its electoral success and prevented the Federalists from regaining the White House.[6]

The Decline of the Caucus

Its earlier successes notwithstanding, the congressional caucus system collapsed in the 1820s. Its demise could be traced to several causes: a turnover in the political elite, the westward growth of the nation, increasingly democratic political customs, and two poorly staged caucuses in 1820 and 1824.

By 1820, political leadership in the United States was clearly changing. For nearly three decades after Washington's first election, Revolutionary War heroes and Constitutional signatories dominated Congress and national politics. These leaders could depend on their personal friendships and public prestige to win the nomination for one of their own, then to gain public acceptance of that choice. By the end of Monroe's presidency, however, most members of that closely-knit elite were either dead or in retirement; they had been replaced by another generation of ambitious politicians, most of whom rose to prominence as regional spokesmen. Among this new breed of politicians, none commanded a broad national following either in Congress or among the nation's voters. Nor would these new politicians willingly defer to a rival of no greater prestige. Under these circumstances, there was little prospect that a caucus nominee could pressure his presidential rivals to step aside.

Not only had the nation's original leaders passed from the scene, but its political habits and geography were changing as well. By 1820, the original 13 states numbered 24 as westward migration to the Ohio and Mississippi Valleys had led to the settlement, organization, and admission of new states. In the West, mass political rallies and a nearly universal white manhood suffrage had replaced the old oligarchies of merchants, bankers, and planters. In the nation's cities and towns, and even in New England, the suffrage grew even broader.[7] To many new voters the congressional caucus in far-off Washington, D.C., must have seemed remote and oligarchical indeed.

In 1820 and 1824, two poorly-staged caucuses sank the congressional caucus system forever. In 1820, President Monroe's supporters called a caucus to renominate him for a second term. Monroe's own popularity and the absence of any formidable opposition, however, made his nomination and reelection a foregone conclusion. Accordingly, few congressmen bothered to attend; and those who did adjourned without taking any formal action. To many observers the increasingly unpopular "King Caucus" seemed finished.[8]

Four years later, Monroe prepared to leave the White House without settling on a political heir. Several candidates maneuvered for the presidency, and none had any intention of allowing a congressional caucus to dash his hopes. The early field included John Calhoun from South Carolina (who eventually withdrew from the vice-presidency), Henry Clay of Kentucky, John Quincy Adams of Massachusetts, and Andrew Jackson from Tennessee. Each was primarily a sectional favorite, although Jackson enjoyed some fame as a military hero.

A fifth candidate, William Crawford of Georgia, then serving as Secretary of the Treasury, enjoyed more support in Congress than any of the others, but he, too, failed to dominate the field. Worse yet, Crawford apparently suffered one serious stroke, and then a second, during the precaucus maneuvering and the campaign. As a result his health was always in question, and he failed to rally his supporters and woo uncommitted politicians to his candidacy.

None daunted, Crawford's supporters in Congress called another caucus, but only 66 of 216 Democratic-Republican congressmen attended. The others stayed away, either because they disapproved of the caucus itself or because they supported another candidate. The poorly attended caucus only exposed its dwindling appeal and further blackened its reputation as undemocratic. Crawford's nomination did not deter either Adams, Clay, or Jackson from running and won Crawford little if any additional support. Each of the other candidates chose to be nominated by state legislatures.[9] In the subsequent balloting of the electors, Crawford ran a weak third behind Jackson and Adams. By now the caucus, widely viewed as undemocratic, unpopular with voters, and now (worse yet!) a political failure, was finally finished.

THE BROKERED CONVENTION SYSTEM: 1832-1968

The Interlude: 1824-28

After the congressional caucus system collapsed in 1824, would-be presidents turned to state legislatures and local conventions to secure a nomination. In 1824 and 1828, Jackson was nominated by the Tennessee legislature. In 1824, Clay entered his bid through state legislative caucuses in Missouri, Ohio, Kentucky, and Louisiana. Caucuses in Maine and Massachusetts forwarded Adams in 1824. Four years later, Adams chose to be nominated by several state conventions. In 1824, South Carolina's legislature first nominated one favorite son, Congressman William Lowndes; when Lowndes died, they forwarded another, Senator John Calhoun. Mass meetings, too, were sometimes held. One citizens' convention in November 1823, at Steubenville, Ohio, recommended DeWitt Clinton. A party convention, held in March of 1824 at Harrisburg, Pennsylvania, nominated Jackson for the presidency.

Nomination by state legislatures or local conventions proved necessary since the party system was in disarray throughout the 1820s. By 1820, the Democratic–Republican coalition encompassed virtually the entire political spectrum and soon disintegrated. Not until the 1830s did politicians coalesce into two broad national parties. In this interim period prominent politicians, such as Adams, Clay, Calhoun, Jackson, and Daniel Webster, dominated the political scene.

Without a party coalition to narrow the field, the number of hopefuls could easily expand. Any number of aspiring politicians might be flattered to accept a presidential nomination, or, if one was not forthcoming, could try to engineer one. As a result, the number of candidates could swell considerably, as happened in 1824. A multitude of contenders, though, could easily fragment a coalition's strength, and, as a result, the election might go to the House of Representatives, as it did in 1824. Later, in 1836, the newly formed Whigs abandoned a national convention to offer three regional candidates. Though the Whigs' chances were none too bright, that year in any case, dividing their efforts among three candidates further weakened the party's already dim prospects.

The First Conventions

During the 1830s, two nationally organized, broadly based party coalitions reemerged. Jackson's followers organized themselves into the Democratic Party; his several opponents combined to form the National Republicans or, shortly thereafter, the Whigs. Almost simultaneously, both parties moved toward a national convention to nominate the ticket and to conduct other party business.

A national party convention appealed to party leaders for several reasons. First, conventions were already familiar features at the state and local level. A convention attended by local party supporters appeared democratic enough to satisfy the critics of the old, now defunct, congressional caucus. A national convention could concentrate attention, excitement, and publicity on a single ticket. Finally, at least in 1832, the leading candidates found a convention both safe and useful. By then Jackson had quarreled with his vice-president, John Calhoun, and wanted to replace the South Carolinian on the ticket. Henry Clay, the apparent choice of the National Republicans, favored a convention as a means of uniting Jackson's diverse opponents around his own candidacy. The newly formed (and ultimately short-lived) AntiMasons could capture national attention and publicize their distaste for secret elite societies.

The AntiMasons were the first to convene, meeting in Baltimore on September 26, 1831. One hundred and sixteen delegates from 13 states crowded into a street-corner saloon, and after a long although disorganized meeting, the delegates drafted a former attorney general, Willard Wirt, as their nominee.

Three months later, on December 12, the National Republicans convened in the same saloon. Numbering 155 delegates from 18 states, the delegates unanimously nominated Clay and used the occasion to whip up support for the National Bank. The delegates apparently decided that if one convention was good for the party, two would be better yet; in May of 1832 they held a second convention in Washington, D.C., so that their young supporters could renominate Clay.

Finally, the Democrats, too, assembled in Baltimore in May 1832 to rally their party behind President Jackson. Equally important to Old Hickory, the convention obligingly dumped vice-president Calhoun in favor of New York's Martin ("The Little Magician") Van Buren. No formal vote was taken on Jackson's renomination; the convention simply concurred in Jackson's previous nomination by several state legislatures.

By modern standards these early conventions were informal affairs. At the time, formality mattered very little, since it was a foregone conclusion who were to be the nominees: both Jackson and Clay were the obvious choices of either party. Unlike modern conventions, the number of delegates was not clearly fixed. States near the convention sent more delegates than they had votes to cast. States far distant from the convention site were sometimes not represented at all or sent only one or two delegates to cast the state's convention votes.

Their informality notwithstanding, the first conventions proved forerunners for later conclaves. The number of delegate votes to be cast by each state was fixed before the convention—at first on the basis of each state's number of electoral votes. The state party organization chose delegates to cast the state's votes. The delegates established convention rules and wrote simple policy statements, which, in time, were to become long and elaborate party platforms.

The convention system apparently proved satisfactory to the leading candidates and to the party's leaders. After 1832, the Democrats continued to rely on a convention to choose their nominee. The Whigs temporarily abandoned the convention in 1836 and forwarded three regional candidates; when that strategy failed, they returned to a convention in 1840, won that year's contest, and met again every subsequent election year until their decline in the 1850s. The Republicans, who replaced the Whigs by 1856, also relied on conventions to choose their ticket, as did most of the minor parties, one-time parties, and "bolters" of later years.

By the 1840s and 1850s, the conventions began to perform activities beyond simply nominating a national ticket. The delegates wrote more complete platforms, sometimes provoking bitter battles over their content. Divided state party factions spawned credentials disputes, forcing the national party to designate which faction could officially represent the state. Local, state, and congressional party leaders found the convention could gain them national recognition through eloquent speech-making or hard-nosed bargaining. State politicos traded the delegates for favorable platform stands or promises of patronage. State and national candidates bolstered their appeal through convention bargains and appeals.

Within a decade of their origin, the national conventions and the party system itself underwent a critical transformation. The first conventions had been mere legitimizing forums for the front-running candidates. Soon, though, state party leaders assumed control of the conventions and forced aspiring nominees to bargain with them to win the party's nod. At the convention, the party's top managers could confirm their preconvention bargain or, if no candidate had been agreed upon, strike the necessary deals.

As a result, power within the parties moved from prominent candidates to the party's managers. The first example of this shift came in 1840, when the National Republican's politicos decided that General William Henry Harrison would run a better race than the ever-willing Henry Clay. At that year's convention party, leaders dumped Clay in favor of "Tippecanoe and Tyler Too"—an alliterative and (more importantly) winning ticket. Four years later the Democrats underwent a similar transformation. In 1844, the Democratic convention abandoned former president Van Buren, the early front-runner, and settled on the first "dark horse" nominee, James Polk.

Presidential Primaries

From the 1830s until the early 1900s, rank-and-file party supporters enjoyed little if any input into presidential nominating politics. The party's governors, senators, high-ranking party officials, and mayors normally controlled the conventions. Ordinary party voters could influence the party's nomination neither through primaries, nor through public opinion polls (which were as yet almost unknown), nor through participation in state and local party committees and conventions.

By 1900, populists and progressives were demanding that the power of top party leaders be curbed. The reformers' overall agenda was a broad one: improved social services and working conditions, a civil service and merit system for government employees, antitrust legislation, and a host of other reforms. Reformers particularly singled out the conventions, which by 1900 suffered from an unsavory reputation for political chicanery, as well as from an almost unbroken line of little-distinguished nominees and presidents.[10]

To weaken the party "bosses" and "machines," reformers urged that voters directly choose the candidates through primary elections. In state and local primaries, voters could either choose their state's convention delegates or, alternatively, they could vote for a favorite presidential candidate, and the winning candidate would take the delegates.

Robert LaFollette's progressives in Wisconsin took the lead. In 1905, that state enacted a primary providing for the direct election of national convention delegates. LaFollette hoped that the primary would allow him to outmaneuver Wisconsin's conservative party regulars. Reformers elsewhere took his lead, and by 1908 a handful of states chose their delegates through a presidential primary. Four years later, in 1912, Oregon voters cast their ballots directly for the presidential candidates themselves.[11]

The primaries' first real test came almost immediately. In 1912, former president Theodore Roosevelt challenged the GOP incumbent, William Howard Taft. Roosevelt handily demonstrated his popularity with rank-and-file Republicans by defeating Taft in nine state primaries. LaFollette took two contests, and the beleaguered Taft won but a single race. Taft, however, controlled the party's patronage and retained the support of most of its leaders. By overwhelming Roosevelt in the nonprimary states, Taft won renomination at a bitterly divided party convention.

Although Roosevelt failed in his effort to unseat Taft, for a time more and more states adopted a presidential primary. By 1916, 26 states had enacted some type of a primary. After 1916, however, the trend reversed. Party regulars charged that the primaries were too costly and divisive and were often uncontested; in many states the regulars repealed or restricted the primary. By 1935, the number of primaries had dwindled to 18, and that number remained almost constant until the 1970s. In most states the parties returned to choosing their delegates through caucuses and conventions or by committee.

The Primaries' Limited Impact

Before the 1970s, a candidate might, at most, use the primaries to demonstrate a broad voter appeal, provide a solid base of delegates, or expose the weakness of a rival. Through a strong primary showing a candidate could reassure the party's regulars and convince them to provide the rest of the necessary delegates.

For a candidate with perceived liabilities, the primaries could convince party leaders to take his candidacy seriously. In 1960, for example, by winning in heavily Protestant West Virginia, John Kennedy convinced party pros that his Catholicism did not render him ineligible. That win also pressured Minnesota Senator Hubert Humphrey to drop out, leaving Kennedy without any active competition in the other primaries. Eventually the party's leaders backed Kennedy for the nomination.

Former contenders could also reaffirm their support by winning the primaries. In 1956, former Democratic nominee and ex-Illinois governor Adlai Stevenson bested Tennessee Senator Estes Kefauver in the late, contested primaries. Thus reassured of Stevenson's appeal, the party's managers renominated Stevenson at the convention. In 1968, former vice-president Richard Nixon swept most of that year's GOP primaries and thereby gained momentum for his nomination bid.

A successful primary record could aid an aspiring nominee. Yet in political reality a string of primary victories was seldom sufficient to transform an obscure candidate into a front-runner. Until the 1970s, neither was any apparent nominee ever eliminated solely on the basis of his poor primary showings.

The key to understanding the primaries' limited impact lay in the successful efforts of state party leaders to repeal their state's primary or at least to limit its impact. In some states the primary was abolished; in others, it was legally separated from delegate selection; in still others, it was rendered politically irrelevant.

Until the 1970s, the primary states chose only about a third of the convention delegates. The other two-thirds were chosen in nonprimary states; those delegates were appointed by party chieftains or chosen by party caucuses and conventions or by committee. In the nonprimary states there was seldom much opportunity for a meaningful challenge to the party regulars.

Further, no candidate could realistically expect to win all the primary state delegates without the aid of top party leaders. In some states the primary was only "advisory." Here, a candidate could run in the presidential preference contest—sometimes dubbed the "beauty contest"—but the actual delegates were chosen elsewhere, usually by party conventions or committee.

"Favorite sons" and uncommitted slates were another peril to a primary-oriented candidate. A favorite son was usually a home-state governor or senator who could expect support from the local party machine. Uncommitted slates—usually delegate slates composed of a state's leading party figures—achieved the same result: preventing an outsider from winning delegates. In several primary states—Ohio, West Virginia, Illinois, California, and New Jersey—strong party machines maintained a tradition of running favorite sons or uncommitted slates.

State party leaders could further complicate an unwanted outsider's prospects by imposing high filing fees, raising the number of petitions required for a candidate to be listed on the primary ballot, setting the filing date long in advance of the primary, requiring petitions to be gathered in several different districts, and relying on other rules to prevent access to the ballot. They might also rely on winner-take-all provisions to divide the delegates or impose a unit rule to thwart an unwanted outsider. Only a very determined candidate could challenge a hostile party organization in very many states. Until the 1970s, few did.

The presidential primary states were so widely scattered that an insurgent stood little chance of winning them all. Before the 1970s, most major primaries were in a few Northern and Western states: New Hampshire, Wisconsin, Oregon, and California. Several primary states, though, were in the South (Florida) or in the mountain states (Montana, South Dakota). Of the large primary states, many relied on the uncommitted slates or favorite-son slates just described.

A few candidates found that even a string of primary wins *and* a strong poll showing was not enough to win the nomination. In 1952, for example, Estes Kefauver upended incumbent president Truman in New Hampshire's primary, then went on to win almost all that year's Democratic primaries. Kefauver also handily led the popularity polls among Democratic identifiers. All this notwithstanding, Kefauver collected few delegates, and he lost the nomination. The party's nod went to Illinois' reluctant governor, Adlai Stevenson, who had entered no primaries and who did not announce his candidacy until the convention itself.[12]

Although winning the primaries did not guarantee the nomination when the regulars were hostile, a string of primary failures might end a candidate's hopes. Even a single well-publicized loss might stop a candidate's psychological momentum and prevent a "bandwagon" effect gathering speed. In 1944, Wendell Wilkie aimed at his second GOP nomination. Never tested in the primaries, Wilkie staked his claim on a strong primary showing. A poor finish in Wisconsin, however, only confirmed the suspicion that he was unpopular with party voters, and it finished Wilkie's chances for renomination. Four years later, in 1948, supporters of General Douglas McArthur aimed for the Republican nomination. The absent general ran second in Wisconsin and was not thereafter considered a serious contender by party pros. Later that year, Minnesota's Harold Stassen won a string of primary wins but lost the Oregon primary to New York's Thomas Dewey. Dewey, trying for a second GOP nomination, later won the convention's nod.

To avoid embarrassment, some candidates bypassed the primaries altogether and counted on state party leaders for the nomination, or a candidate might run in only a few primaries where success seemed ensured. In fact, until the 1970s seldom were more than a handful of primaries seriously contested. As late as 1968, Vice-President Hubert Humphrey ignored all that year's primaries and still won the Democratic nomination. Incumbents, too, could skip the primaries, relying on home-state favorite sons to do their battles. In 1964, for example, Lyndon Johnson avoided the primaries and relied on stand-ins to skirmish with Alabama's governor, George Wallace. Johnson ran only in Oregon (where he was automatically entered) and in Florida (where he was unopposed).

Nominations in the Brokered Convention System

For well over a century, candidates won their nominations from the party's top leaders. Not until the 1970s could a candidate be sure that a grass-roots campaign would secure the nod.[13] Until the 1970s, the nominee more often emerged by assembling a core of committed supporters, then winning over other sympathetic or like-minded party leaders and uncommitted politicos. When a candidate had expanded his delegate base to a near-majority of the delegates, a "bandwagon effect" would be likely to carry him to victory.[14]

Superficially, the national conventions varied greatly. Some conventions were brief and harmonious, others were prolonged and rancorous. The conventions were often wracked by disputes over credentials or platform issues. Because both parties were broad, nationally oriented, loosely bound coalitions, they could seldom escape being torn by divisive issues. Disputes over slavery, "cheap" versus "sound" money, prohibition, isolationism, war and peace, and civil rights all reverberated through the party conventions.

Nor did the brokered convention system always succeed in producing unity behind the ticket. Whenever the party itself was badly split, harmony seldom prevailed at the convention. In 1860, for example, the Democrats splintered into three separate tickets. In 1864, the peace Republicans, on the one hand, and the war Democrats, on the other, each bolted their parties' respective tickets. Later, in 1872, liberal Republicans abandoned General Grant and were later joined by the then-dispirited Democrats. In 1896, "gold" Democrats bolted and nominated a "sound money" candidate after the regular convention had chosen silver-tongued (and silver-standard) William Jennings Bryan. That same year, the "silver" Republicans, too, bolted their party's convention. In 1912, a disgruntled Theodore Roosevelt and his backers nominated their own Bull Moose ticket after the GOP convention had chosen incumbent Taft. In 1948, the Democratic nominee, Harry Truman, was abandoned both by his party's left wing and by the conservative Southern Dixiecrats. Like the earlier congressional caucus system and the later system of popular appeal, the brokered convention system could seldom produce an artificial harmony when there was none in the party.

National party conventions varied in their length and in their ability to achieve unity behind the ticket. In all these conventions, however, the key to the nomination lay in successful coalition formation. Few candidates, other than incumbents, could dominate the convention through primary wins or by their own personal popularity. Instead, a hopeful might gain the nod by winning over top party regulars through platform promises, policy stands, patronage bargains, or personal friendships.

Until the advent of the primaries, most of the necessary bargaining was conducted at the convention itself. As a result, early conventions were often protracted, drawn-out affairs. Many delegations arrived pledged to favorite sons who, in turn, bargained with the leading candidates or convention brokers. After the primaries and with the spread of nationwide communications, the sorting-out of coalitions began even before the convention opened, and, with the leading coalitions often well formed by then, the number of convention ballots required grew fewer and fewer. The last multiballot convention occurred in 1952.[15]

Before the convention, the aspiring nominees began with a core of uncommitted delegates. Often these delegates came from a candidate's own home state or region. Each coalition then sought to add to its strength by winning over the most sympathetic of favorite sons or uncommitted delegations. The core coalition usually expanded by first winning over delegates from states in a candidate's home region. By this process the coalition grew in size. A candidate could try to convince uncommitted politicians to join his bandwagon by a variety of campaign techniques: a test of strength on a platform issue, a credentials battle, personal lobbying and deals, or policy and patronage bargains. Each candidate would, of course, try to dissuade delegates from joining an opponent's camp or to pry loose parts of opposing coalitions.

In many cases several ballots were necessary before a winning coalition began to emerge. On early ballots favorite sons might hold their delegates until the ballot shaped up more clearly or until a candidate offered better terms. In some years a coalition would surge, then falter, before it achieved the required majority. Then another coalition would begin emerging, or the coalitions might reshape themselves behind a "dark horse" candidate. The bargaining often occurred amidst much uncertainty and confusion; rumors, demonstrations, and newspaper accounts often swept the convention floors as candidates sought to stampede the delegates.

Finally, some candidate would approach the required threshold for victory. At Republican conventions a simple majority sufficed; until 1936, the Democrats required a two-thirds majority. As the winning candidate's coalition grew, a "bandwagon effect" took hold. As one candidate edged closer to the required tally, a hold-out politician could most easily estimate whether his support could decide the nomination and bring an expected payoff. Previously undecided delegates were tempted to join the bandwagon, fearing that the leading candidate would win the nomination even without their support; if that nominee was elected, he would then owe them nothing. The bandwagon effect seems to have been a regular phenomenon of earlier conventions. One convention scholar, William Gamson, suggested that a candidate with over 40 percent of the delegates could probably expect his momentum to carry the nomination. If the convention relied on a two-thirds rule, then 60 percent of the delegates was usually enough to ensure victory.[16]

The nominations contest during the brokered convention system was played out between the candidates themselves and a handful of state politicians. Even with the advent of the primaries, ordinary party voters and the media seldom played any significant role in deciding the outcome. To be sure, the party's managers were seldom foolish enough to reject an overwhelmingly popular candidate in favor of one with limited appeal. Yet until the rules changes of the 1970s, the party's rank-and-file voters had no way of participating in the key convention or preconvention bargaining.

THE SYSTEM OF POPULAR APPEAL: 1972–PRESENT

During the 1960s, the brokered convention system faced its most serious challenges. Within but a few years it was replaced by a new method of making nominations: the system of popular appeal. Like the earlier congressional caucus system, the brokered convention system was undone by long-range pressures, short-term crises, public pressure for reform, and by a division among party leaders themselves.

Pressures for Change

The Rise of the Amateurs

The most serious threat to the brokered convention system developed during the 1950s and 1960s in the growing organization of amateur party activists. These amateur politicians—then mostly liberal Democrats—challenged their party's top leaders (or regulars) for control of the party. Their challenge came not only in reform-prone states such as Wisconsin, Minnesota, California, and Oregon, but even in the bastions of "machine politics" in Chicago and New York City.[17]

The amateurs agreed with the regulars neither on what a party should be nor what it should do. The regulars preferred ethically and geographically "balanced" tickets—those with the widest appeal to the Democratic Party's traditional coalition of working-class, ethnic, and minority voters. To the regulars, balanced tickets, party loyalty, and patronage were the key to a political party. The details of a candidate's policy promises or ideology were of lesser concern.

Amateur activists, on the contrary, cared more for a candidate's policy ideas than patronage and more for a candidate's ideology than his ethnic background or residency. To the amateurs, unwavering loyalty to the party, regardless of its candidates' credentials, was not a highly desirable attribute. Unlike the regulars, the amateurs were not exclusively concerned with office holding and patronage; rather, principles were the key reason for supporting a candidate.

The amateurs often proved formidable political foes. Vocal, articulate, and skilled in organizing, the middle- and upper-middle-class reform Democrats demonstrated that they could compete with the increasingly outclassed party regulars and with the weakened urban party machines. In middle-class urban and suburban neighborhoods the amateurs often wrested control over nominations and over party affairs from the latter. By the mid-1960s, liberal, reform, and amateur Democrats (all usually synonymous) had established themselves as serious challengers to the regulars, at least in Northern urban and suburban districts.

The Goldwater Amateurs

During the 1960s, liberal Democratic amateurs captured most academic and journalistic attention. Ironically, however, theretofore little-noticed conservative Republican amateurs were the first to demonstrate convincingly the clout of well-organized, enthusiastic volunteers in a presidential nominations race. Organized to back conservative Arizona Senator Barry Goldwater, in state after state GOP amateurs out-organized and out-maneuvered the party's more moderate regulars. In nonprimary states conservative amateurs packed local caucuses and state conventions to elect right-wing delegates. In the primary states they canvassed the precincts and brought their voters to the polls. The amateurs were aided by Goldwater's narrow upset victory in the California GOP primary, by the inept performance of top Republicans (who divided their efforts among a succession of candidates), and by considerable support for the Arizona senator among conservative party chieftains in the South and the West. Despite his eventual electoral disaster, Goldwater's nomination showed that a well-organized albeit narrow groundswell of spirited amateurs might outmaneuver the ever thinner ranks of the party's regulars if opportunity allowed.[18]

Participation for the Democrats

During the mid-1960s, the Democratic Party itself took a small step toward undermining the brokered convention system. For generations segregationists in the one-party South had excluded blacks from Democratic Party affairs. In 1964, however, the Democratic National Convention interrupted its otherwise harmonious renomination of Lyndon Johnson to warn Southern Democrats to stop excluding blacks. While the warning applied only to future conventions, to many Democrats the action affirmed the principle that *all* Democrats, not only the top party leaders, should participate in the party. If Southern blacks could participate in party decision making, why should outsiders be excluded anywhere?

The Polls and the Primaries

Polls and primaries offered an alternative to the party regulars' control over nominations. Through polls and primaries, the public's wishes could be directly measured and expressed. In state and local nominations control by party regulars was an anachronism. If voters could express their preferences in polls or through primary elections, what justification had the regulars for controlling presidential nominations?

Admittedly the feeling was a vague one. Most voters did not seem intensely committed to participating more actively in presidential politics.[19] Yet throughout the 1950s and 1960s, the brokered convention system seems steadily to have lost public support. At best the regulars' claim was a subtle one; to many, the regulars' claim to control appeared blatantly undemocratic.

Vietnam and the Antiwar Movement

Well-established political systems seldom collapse from long-term pressures alone. If these long-range strains had alone been at work, the brokered convention system might well have survived with only minor changes. Yet in 1968 an intense political crisis exploded within the Democratic Party's ranks.

By 1968, the Vietnam conflict had escalated into a full-blown war and so had the domestic opposition to the U.S. war involvement. After a long search for a candidate, antiwar Democrats convinced Minnesota Senator Eugene McCarthy to challenge Lyndon Johnson for the nomination.[20] McCarthy's candidacy seemed quixotic at first. After all, no incumbent who had wanted to be renominated had been denied his party's standard during this century.

Political history notwithstanding, McCarthy's candidacy attracted hundreds, then thousands of dedicated volunteers, including an unprecedented turnout of students. By contrast, Johnson's renomination efforts were handicapped by the sporadic, often inept efforts of his supporters and by Johnson's own growing unpopularity. As the votes from New Hampshire's early primary were counted, the party's regulars received a rude jolt. Johnson was humiliated, barely escaping an electoral defeat by his theretofore little-known and little-regarded challenger.[21] After New Hampshire, Johnson was faced with an apparent defeat in the upcoming Wisconsin primary and with a long and bitter struggle for renomination, at the same time that Vietnam peace negotiations were opening. Shortly after New Hampshire's primary, Johnson withdrew from the race.

The 1968 Democratic Convention

New Hampshire's results, Johnson's withdrawal, McCarthy's newly credible candidacy, and Robert Kennedy's subsequent entry into the race spurred on antiwar activists, party dissidents, and liberal amateurs. Yet the remainder of the preconvention season brought few political comforts for the insurgents. In the handful of primaries, the insurgents experienced little difficulty. There, the party's regulars (who overwhelmingly backed Vice-President Hubert Humphrey) simply abandoned the field to McCarthy and Kennedy, who trounced a series of ineffectual favorite sons.[22]

Johnson's designated successor, Humphrey, ignored all that year's primaries and counted on the regulars to provide the needed delegates. His strategy succeeded. In 1968, most states still chose their convention delegates in caucuses and conventions, by party committee, or through appointment. In these states the regulars dominated the delegate-selection race, and the insurgents made little headway. Even in some primary states, such as Pennsylvania, the voting for presidential candidates had no impact on the actual choosing of the delegates. Almost everywhere, it seemed to the insurgents, the pro-Humphrey regulars were entrenched behind their procedures and rules, immune to the challenges of McCarthy, Kennedy, and the antiwar activists.

The August 1968 convention in Chicago capped one of the most prolonged and divisive nominations battles of recent decades. The death of Robert Kennedy, the frustration and rage of antiwar activists and insurgents, and the stubbornness of party regulars all produced a convention whose rancor spilled over both onto the convention floor and into the streets of Chicago. From the early credentials disputes to the Vietnam platform plank to the presidential nomination balloting, the well-televised convention foundered between the outraged insurgents and the beleaguered regulars.[23] To the insurgents, the party's regulars had won an unfair and undeserved victory by manipulating the rules.

Sparked by an ad hoc reform committee headed by Iowa Governor Harold Hughes, reformers and insurgents pressed for changes in the party's delegate-selection rules. They aimed to undo the regulars' control over future conventions by giving ordinary voters and party activists more power over the choice of delegates. On a close (and apparently confused) roll-call vote, the convention voted to establish a commission to study and revise those rules before the 1972 convention.

Democratic Party Reforms

The McGovern–Fraser Commission

Shortly after the 1968 convention, Democratic Party Chairman Fred Harris appointed South Dakota Senator George McGovern to chair the rules reform commission.[24] Later, when McGovern resigned to announce his presidential drive, Minneapolis Congressman Donald Fraser headed the group. After lengthy public hearings, the McGovern–Fraser Commission produced 18 "guidelines" for state parties to follow in delegate selection. In so doing, the commission effectively abolished the brokered convention system.

The 18 guidelines focused on three recurring aims of reformers, and together these three goals formed the core of the reform agenda throughout the 1970s. First, reformers urged that more rank-and-file party identifiers be allowed to participate in delegate selection. Second, reformers encouraged more convention representation for groups who had been underrepresented at past party conventions— particularly members of racial minorities, women, and young voters (those under 30). Third—and most important—reformers sought to allocate a state's convention delegates according to the wishes of ordinary party voters and caucus-goers; by so doing, reformers sought to eliminate the party regulars' control over delegate selection.

Ensuring Public Access. The commission's public hearings clearly established that in many states rank-and-file Democrats had little if any chance to influence delegate selection in 1968. In a few states, such as Georgia or Louisiana, most or all the delegates were simply appointed by the governor or the state party chairman; here, ordinary party supporters had no opportunity at all to choose the delegates. In many caucus–convention states Democrats were discouraged from attending caucus meetings by the absence of published party rules, dates, times, or places of the local meetings, or by fees charged to attend or to serve as delegates. In some presidential primary states voters found that the delegates were not identified by their presidential preference on the ballot, that the delegates were not bound to vote for the candidate indicated, or that no delegates were chosen in the primary at all and were instead chosen by other means. All these restrictions confused and frustrated many voters.

The commission moved to ensure that ordinary Democrats would have an opportunity to participate easily and meaningfully. It required that fees be reduced, that petition requirements be simplified, and that written rules and adequate public notice be given for caucuses and conventions. Delegates were to be selected on uniform dates and times, and the competition was to be held in places open and accessible to the public. Democratic state parties were urged (but not required) to go yet further by removing all fees and costs, by easing the financial burden for delegates and alternates, and by making "all feasible efforts" to change state laws that made participation difficult.

Prohibiting Discrimination. The commission charged both that state parties discouraged participation generally, and that women, young persons, and racial minorities were often particularly discouraged. Before 1972, relatively few blacks, women, or young persons managed to win seats as convention delegates or alternates at either party conclave.

The commission required state Democratic parties to bar discrimination based on race, color, creed, national origin, age, or sex. Unlike earlier years, the commission then went further by requiring state parties to "overcome the effects of *past* discrimination by affirmative steps to encourage representation on the national convention delegations of minority groups, young people, and women *in reasonable relationship to their presence in the population of the state*." Although the commission added that this was "not to be accomplished by the mandatory imposition of quotas," Affirmative Action programs later provoked considerable confusion and controversy. To some party regulars and party conservatives this requirement seemed to constitute little less than a quota.

Encouraging Grass-Roots Control. Although disputes over Affirmative Action drew most of the criticism about the new guidelines, the brokered convention system might have weathered that requirement if party leaders had simply appointed the required number of blacks, women, and young persons. It was in the third area that the commission took its most far-reaching action. By tying the dividing and naming of delegates to grass-roots sentiment, the commission effectively eliminated the control formerly exercised by top party leaders.

The commission reported that in 1968 there had been little connection between the grass-roots support shown for a candidate (at local caucuses or in primary voting) and the number of delegates a candidate received at the national party convention. In some states there was no opportunity at all for party supporters to indicate their preference. In other states winner-take-all rules and the unit rule were applied to gain the leading candidate more than a proportional share of the delegates. In some primary states the appointed delegates had simply ignored the primary results.

In this area the guidelines prohibited the untimely choice of delegates—such as for instance, the selection of delegates before the year of the convention. The commission also permitted no more than 10 percent of a state's delegation to be chosen by a party committee. No party official or office holder could serve automatically, or ex officio, as delegate. The filling of vacancies for delegates and alternates was regulated, the unit rule was prohibited at any stage of delegate selection, and the apportionment of delegates was tied to a one-Democrat (or one-voter), one-delegate basis. In addition, the commission urged (but did not require) that proportional representation be used at all stages of delegate selection.

The new guidelines restricted the authority and control of party regulars as never before. Never had the regulars been required to share so much power over delegate selection with the amateurs or with the party's grass-roots supporters. Now the regulars were forced to compete for their delegate seats in open competition with any and all challengers. The party's officials and its top-ranking elected office holders could no longer rely on automatically being chosen as delegates, nor could they choose more than a few delegates by party committee. The old practice of meeting in private to bargain over an official slate was banned. Neither the regulars nor their opponents could apply the unit rule or resort to closed caucus meetings. Failing to represent young persons, women, or minorities adequately might well bring a challenge. In nonprimary states at least three-quarters of the delegates were to be chosen from districts no larger than a congressional district, thereby increasing the chance that insurgents would gain at least a few delegates.

Challenge and Compliance

The State Parties' Response.   Few state Democratic parties would have met the new guidelines without changing their rules and customs. Yet by 1972 40 state parties and the District of Columbia achieved full compliance, and the other 10 state parties were judged in "substantial compliance." In many states the Democratic party achieved compliance by acting alone—by giving public notice and publishing rules, dates, times, and places for the primary, or caucuses and conventions.

The new guidelines, perhaps unexpectedly, prompted another

change that further limited the regulars' power. Several state parties and legislatures complied by adopting a presidential primary. In fact, the McGovern–Fraser commission had not required that a state adopt *any* form of primary at all. Some Democratic state leaders, however, felt that delegates chosen in a primary would be less likely to face challenges than those selected through the more complicated caucus–convention route. Other Democrats argued that a primary would allow more opportunity for participation. As a result, more states used a presidential primary in 1972 than in 1968, and still more states later adopted a primary (see Table 2.1).

The Daley Challenge.   While most Democratic state parties complied, a few party regulars either misunderstood or ignored the new rules. In Chicago, the party machine loyal to Mayor Richard Daley won 59 convention delegates in the 1972 primary, but in so doing it violated several of the new rules. Anti-Daley insurgents challenged the mayor's delegation, charging that the regulars had not published written rules describing the delegate-selection process, had failed to include enough women, young persons, and blacks on the slate, and had filled the delegate slate without public input. Despite McGovern's attempts to compromise, the convention's credentials committee and then the full convention ousted the mayor's delegates and seated the insurgents.

Daley, for years a power at every convention, did not take his rejection lightly. When the credentials committee ousted his slate only days before the convention opened, the mayor went to court to plead his case. His basic argument was that his state's election law (with which he had complied) should supersede the party's new rules (with which he had not). Although Daley won in a lower court, the Supreme Court overturned that ruling and permitted the credentials committee decision to stand. In so doing, the Court added at least a

TABLE 2.1: Numbers of States and D.C. Holding a Presidential Primary to Select Convention Delegates, 1968–80

(In percentages)

	1968	1972	1976	1980
Democrats	17	23	30	33
Republicans	16	22	29	34

tentative approval of the party's right to apply its own rules. The Court's decision indicated that the new rules could be enforced by the party even if they conflicted with a state's primary election laws.

A New Status Quo.   At the 1972 Democratic convention, George McGovern, liberal insurgent and reformer exemplary, gained the nomination but overwhelmingly lost the fall election. Disgruntled opponents of the new reforms lost no time in opening their drive to revise or undo the new guidelines. To many regulars 1972 had proved a bitter experience, as they had lost their delegate seats to amateur McGovernites. To them, McGovern's November fiasco was no mere coincidence. Rather, his unprecedented loss could be traced directly to the party's failure to heed the judgment of its governors, mayors, senators, and party officials. Joining the drive to turn back the new rules were conservatives, leaders of federated labor, supporters of losing candidates, and some party regulars and academics. Their efforts focused on a second party commission, first chaired by Leonard Woodcock of the United Auto Workers, then by Baltimore Councilwoman Barbara Mikulski.[25]

The Mikulski Commission modified a few of the McGovern–Fraser guidelines but retained their substance. Delegate slates could now be formed in private, but no slate could enjoy any special preference or "official" party sanction. As many as 25 percent of a state's delegation could be appointed, but appointed delegates were to be divided according to the same ratio as publicly chosen delegates. The Mikulski commission also allowed floor privileges to Democratic governors, senators, and U.S. representatives but did not given them voting status as delegates.

In other areas the Mikulski commission generally pleased reformers. The commission required proportional representation in caucus–convention states for any group winning at least 10 percent at local meetings or at later conventions. Statewide winner-take-all primaries were banned, that practice being permitted only in districts no larger than a congressional district. These rules approximated, but did not quite achieve, proportional representation—a long-standing reform goal. Finally, new rules for 1976 required that a presidential candidate be allowed to approve any delegate running on that candidate's behalf.

The commission's decisions did not satisfy critics who wanted to roll back the recent reforms. Opponents of the new rules battled at commission hearings, and then both sides took their dispute to the 1974 Kansas City mid-term convention. By this time, however, the battle had lasted for six years, and many party moderates were ready to accept the new rules, if only to preserve party unity and to preclude further divisiveness. At the Kansas City gathering, a number of party moderates and governors joined reformers to turn back the conservatives' challenge. As a result, the once-radical new rules became the new status quo.

Still later, the Democrats continued to make minor changes for the 1980 contest. In part these slight changes consolidated past efforts, and in part they reflected maneuvering among party factions for an advantage in the 1980 presidential contest. For 1980, Democratic rules required an equal division between men and women on state delegations. A second change banned winner-take-all primaries, even for districts smaller than a state; proportional representation was mandated instead. To accommodate backers of incumbent president Jimmy Carter, the length of the primary season was shortened, and the threshold for proportional representation was "floated" from 15 percent (in the early primaries) to 25 percent (in the late contests).[26] Despite these minor revisions, the McGovern–Fraser guidelines were continued, ensuring that the party's grass-roots activists and voters would control the delegate-selection process.

Republican Party Reforms

After 1968, the Republicans examined their own nominating practices. At this point, GOP delegate-selection procedures were nearly as exclusionary as those of the Democrats. Over the next six years, the GOP followed the Democrats' direction: opening the party to ordinary party supporters and including more women, members of minorities, young persons (as well as senior citizens and ethnic groups) at the national party convention.[27]

The Republicans' reform efforts took the same direction as the Democrats' did, although the GOP's changes were neither as stringent nor as controversial. For one reason, insurgents, reformers, liberals, feminists, racial minorities, and young persons were less commonly found in GOP ranks. As a result, rule changes were less stridently demanded, and their impact was less likely to alter the Republican Party's conservative character. Also, the GOP had not permitted some practices (such as the unit rule) that divided their Democratic counterparts, and the Republicans had won the 1968 election and would win again in 1972. Although national polls showed a steady decline in the percentage of Republican identifiers, the national party was in sound shape, both financially and organizationally. For all these reasons GOP reforms proceeded with less open conflict than the Democrats.

Spurred on by a committee comprised of national committee officials, the 1972 GOP National Committee accepted several changes. Among these were a requirement that all delegates be publicly selected at open meetings and a ban on automatic or ex officio delegates, on proxy voting, and on fees that exceeded state law. The convention also barred discrimination in the choosing of delegates and urged—but never required—each state party to take "positive action" to encourage more involvement by women, racial and ethnic minorities, senior citizens, and young persons. Unlike the Democrats, however, a failure to comply with the positive action program could not lead to a state delegation being unseated, and different state parties enforced the new standards with varying seriousness.[28]

State Republican parties and their would-be nominees were also caught up in several changes not originating with the national GOP's new rules. Of these the most significant included the move toward presidential primaries, the use of proportional representation in dividing delegates, and campaign finance reforms. The Republicans, like the Democrats, were affected by the move toward more and more primaries; in most states a newly enacted primary applied to both parties. Second, the national Republican Party never required state parties to use proportional representation (PR) in allocating convention delegates. Yet in most states (notably excepting California) the Republicans approximated PR more closely in 1976 and 1980 than ever before. In a third area, both Republican and Democratic contenders were forced to comply with post-Watergate fundraising and -spending reforms. As a result of all these changes, GOP nominating politics after 1968 closely paralleled the Democratic Party's process.

Reforms in Campaign Finance

Until the 1970s, the financing of American elections was, at best, loosely and ineffectually regulated. Exposes of fund-raising and -spending scandals and stories of influence-buying in President Nixon's 1972 reelection, however, prompted major campaign finance reforms. Between 1971 and 1974, Congress passed several provisions to further regulate campaign spending, both in preconvention and general election races.[29]

In 1976, the new legislation for the first time seriously regulated presidential nomination and general election races. By then the reforms had withstood a major Supreme Court test (*Buckley* v. *Valeo*), the hasty formation of a new regulatory agency, the Federal Election Commission (FEC), and continued infighting by presidential hopefuls, the White House, and Congress. The new legislation resulted in four major changes: first, the federal treasury would match small donations to qualified candidates; second, large donations were banned; third, any candidate accepting matching funds was limited in preconvention spending; fourth, all candidates were forced to report donations, decline large donations in cash or donations from foreigners, and meet several other requirements.

First, qualified candidates could receive matching funds. A candidate could qualify for this by raising $5000 in each of 20 states, in contributions of up to $250 each. Once a candidate had qualified, all donations of or under $250 would be matched, up to the total spending ceiling. The federal matching funds, established by a taxpayers' checkoff, were first available in 1976. For most candidates matching funds became an important source of campaign revenue. By the mid-primary season in 1980, most candidates were receiving 20 to 30 percent of their total revenues from the federal matching funds.[30]

The second provision barred donations of over $1000 from individuals, or over $5000 from political action committee (PAC) funds. In years past, many candidates had relied heavily on a few large donors, or "fat cats," to finance their nomination bids.[31] These funds could be raised quickly through a candidate's or campaign manager's personal efforts. Influence-buying allegations in Nixon's 1972 reelection campaign, however, led Congress to ban large donations. As a result, a candidate could no longer rely on a few major donors but was forced instead to seek larger number of small ($1000 or under) donations.[32]

Candidates who qualified for and accepted matching funds had their total preconvention spending restricted. In 1976, a candidate could spend up to $10.9 million before the convention, plus an additional $2.2 million for fund-raising expenses. In 1980, the spending limit was raised to $14.7 million, with another $2.9 million allowed for fund-raising costs. A candidate who accepted matching funds was not only limited in total spending, but also in spending in each state. No candidate was forced to accept either the spending ceiling or the matching funds; a candidate who did not was then free to spend any amount, subject only to other FEC rules. Several candidates explored the possibility of rejecting matching funds, but eventually all except

Texas' Democrat-turned-Republican John Connally accepted the matching funds and spending ceilings.

The fourth set of provisions closed a variety of earlier loopholes or scandals. The new laws required a public reporting of all donations and expenditures; cash contributions of over $100 were prohibited; all donations from foreign citizens were banned. The practice of accepting either loans or "in-kind donations" (such as airplanes or free campaign offices) was sharply restricted and regulated. Candidates who accepted matching funds were restricted to $50,000 in personal or family gifts to their own campaign. Each restriction was aimed at correcting perceived flaws in existing campaign practices.

The new campaign finance legislation brought both intended and unintended results. As intended, the new regulations ended many disputes raised in 1972: influence peddling, "laundering" of campaign monies, illegal donations, and the sale of ambassadorships and public offices in return for donations. The new rules forced candidates to control campaign spending more strictly than ever before and to seek a broad base of small donors. Perhaps unintended were still other results: the problems of operating a nationwide campaign on increasingly tight budgets, the discouraging impact on late-entering candidates and on favorite sons, the lengthening cycle of fund raising, the greater impact of primary victories and losses on fund raising, the tendency of candidates to seek free publicity and to schedule media events, and the rise of "uncoordinated" spending by individuals and interest groups in support of a candidate's bid. These and other changes are discussed at greater length in the final section of this chapter.

The Impact of Reform

The effect of each separate reform is difficult, if not impossible, to untangle. Between 1968 and 1976, multitudinous new reforms were enacted, among them new rules regarding participation and convention representation, the choosing of delegates, the use of primaries, and campaign finance. Most had a similar aim: correcting perceived abuses in the nominations process. Together, the changes had a profound effect: ending the brokered convention system and creating a new system of popular appeal.

Initially, reformers began with a narrow list of objectives, and not all the reformers may have foreseen the eventual results of their labors. The initial goals for Democratic Party reformers simply addressed a set of complaints from 1968. Other reformers added campaign finance reforms after the Watergate revelations. The immediate goals of reformers, then, simply addressed a piecemeal series of immediate grievances. Only as those goals were achieved did the reforms prove to have even broader results.

The success of reformers in achieving their immediate goals was apparent by 1972. More women, members of minorities, and young persons could be found at the national conventions; more persons participated in preconvention primaries and caucuses; top party regulars (at least in the Democratic Party) lost control over delegate selection. These results were sudden and dramatic.[33]

That the nomination system itself had been transformed, however, was not so immediately apparent. At first the 1972 Democratic race was merely treated as a peculiar but temporary deviation from the pattern of brokered conventions. Not until after another nominations round in 1976 did academics, candidates, party leaders, or (perhaps) even the reformers themselves realize that their efforts had brought about a new system of nomination.[34]

The impact of reform can be divided into the direct, intended results and long-term results. The first objectives were openly sought by reformers—the second set, not so clearly intended. By achieving their immediate goals, reformers undid the brokered convention system and brought about the new system of popular appeal.

Intended Results of Reform

Democratic party reformers aimed particularly to make three changes after 1968; the Republicans either followed their lead or were brought along when states changed their laws to accommodate the Democrats.

Representation at the National Conventions.   In both parties women, members of minorities, and young persons were better represented after 1968 than in earlier years. In the Democratic Party the largest gains came between 1968 and 1972; after this, the proportion of members of minorities and young delegates leveled off, as did the proportion of women until new rules in 1980 mandated equal division of delegates by sex. Table 2.2 cites the percentage of recent convention delegates who were women, blacks, or young persons.

The Republicans, too, witnessed gains, albeit smaller ones, by women, blacks, and young persons at their national party conventions. The GOP depends far less on blacks and young voters for electoral success, but, even so, small gains in convention representation were registered for those groups. For women the proportion of delegates doubled between 1968 and 1972, then leveled off at about

TABLE 2.2: Women, Young Persons, and Blacks Serving as Delegates at Democratic and Republican National Conventions, 1968–80

(In percentages)

	Blacks	Women	Under 30
	Democrats		
1968	7	13	4
1972	15	40	22
1976	11	33	15
1980	15	49	11
	Republicans		
1968	2	17	1
1972	3	35	7
1976	3	31	7
1980	3	29	5

Source: Data are taken from official party records.

a third of the total convention. Apparently even the GOP's less demanding positive action programs succeeded in raising the numbers of these three groups, although blacks and young persons were still infrequently found at the GOP meetings.

More Public Participation. By 1972, the numbers of adult U.S. residents who participated in preconvention politics rose dramatically. By 1976, the turnout of voters and caucus-goers more than doubled from 1968, and the turnout rose yet further in 1980. In part the rise could be attributed to changing rules—especially those regarding the new primaries and more accessible caucuses; in part it also resulted from voters' greater familiarity with preconvention politics.

Table 2.3 documents the rise of preconvention participation. In 1968, only about 13 million U.S. adults participated actively in preconvention nominating politics. By 1972, this number rose to almost 24 million; in 1976, nearly 30 million people participated; in 1980, about 32 million primary voters and caucus-goers turned out.

One explanation for the gains in participation lay in the increasing number of states that adopted a presidential primary after 1968. Apparently attendance at a political meeting, such as a precinct

TABLE 2.3: Total Number of U.S. Citizens Participating in the Presidential Nominations Contests, 1968–80

Year			Total
1968	Republicans:		
	16 primary states	4,571,000	
	35 nonprimary states	105,000	
	Democrats:		
	17 primary states	8,247,000	
	34 nonprimary states	219,000	13,142,000
1972	Republicans:		
	22 primary states	5,887,000	
	29 nonprimary states	256,000	
	Democrats:		
	23 primary states	16,715,000	
	28 nonprimary states	771,000	23,629,000
1976	Republicans:		
	30 primary states	9,724,000	
	21 nonprimary states	546,000	
	Democrats:		
	31 primary states	18,884,000	
	20 nonprimary states	639,000	29,793,000
1980	Republicans:		
	36 primary states	12,835,000	
	15 nonprimary states	365,000	
	Democrats:		
	34 primary states	18,668,000	
	17 nonprimary states	523,000	32,391,000

Notes: Numbers indicated in the table are the maximum numbers of U.S. residents actively participating in party primaries or caucuses. Data were taken from official party or state records where possible; elsewhere, turnout was estimated with regression procedures from information based on party rules, state population and party competitiveness, and known turnout rates. Estimates were usually necessary only for small, nonprimary states; errors of estimation should not greatly affect the totals.

Primary states include those with any form of primary, whether advisory or binding. Also included are party-run primaries and states with a primary in some but not all districts. Numbers of states include D.C.

caucus, is too demanding for most U.S. residents, no matter how easily accessible the meeting may be. On the other hand, more adults are familiar and comfortable with the simpler act of voting. As more states adopted a presidential primary, more adults voted than had ever attended local caucuses. Overall, in presidential primary states about 28 percent of all voting-age adults voted, and by another count, about 43 percent of registered voters participated.[35] In those states that used a primary continuously over several presidential elections, turnout also rose. As voters became familiar with their state's primary and accustomed to voting, more and more voters began to participate regularly.[36]

Even in the nonprimary states participation rose. New rules in both parties mandated that their caucus–convention meetings be open and accessible to interested party supporters. As a result, turnout in nonprimary states increased after 1968, although on the average only about 5 or 6 percent of all party supporters attended a local caucus meeting in these states.

When the 1980 primary and nonprimary state turnout figures are combined, about 21 percent of all adult U.S. residents participated actively in preconvention politics. By comparison, in 1968 only about 10 percent of all adult U.S. residents participated actively by voting in a primary or by attending a causus.

Grass-roots Control and Proportional Representation.   New rules in both parties required that virtually all the delegates be chosen and committed through an open competition in the primaries or caucuses. As a result, top party leaders lost their previous right simply to name the delegates without any popular input.

New rules in both parties approximated, but never completely achieved, proportional representation (PR), a related goal of many reformers. In the Democratic Party, caucus–convention states were required to use PR, with a minimum cutoff varying between 10 and 15 percent. In primary states the Democrats required that delegate allocation be based on popular preferences but still allowed the winner-take-all format in 1972. By 1976, Democratic rules permitted winner-take-all practices only for districts no larger than a congressional district, and in 1980 some form of proportional representation was mandated.[37]

The GOP never banned the statewide winner-take-all primary, although after 1972 only the California Republicans continued to use it.[38] The Republicans also permitted nonprimary states to use winner-take-all practices. In most states, however, state law or GOP party rules crudely resembled proportionality, or, at a minimum, ensured that the more popular candidate won the largest share of delegates.

Despite the movement away from winner-take-all practices and toward proportionality, reformers never fully achieved that goal. Substantial deviations from PR were still found in both parties, especially among the Republicans.

The major exceptions to PR result from "loophole" primaries, "beauty contest" primaries, and a variety of complicated ballot access rules. "Loophole" primaries are those in which winner-take-all procedures are used at a district level, usually for a congressional district. In this case a candidate might win only a slight majority of the votes (in a two-candidate race) or even a plurality (in a multi-candidate race) but could still capture all the district's delegates. One of the most dramatic examples occurred in the 1976 Texas Democratic primary, where Carter won only 48 percent of the vote but still took 92 of 98 available delegates.

In a "beauty contest" primary voters can vote for their favorite candidate but must vote again to pick the actual delegates. Sometimes the delegate's preference may not even be listed on the ballot. As a result the delegates selected might prefer a different candidate to the one with the most popular votes. Yet another variety of this primary is the delegate-selection primary, in which voters choose only the delegates and do not vote on the potential nominees at all.

Complicated ballot access rules may also limit proportionality in delegate allocation. In some primaries (such as the 1980 New York Republican contest), candidates had to file delegate slates district by district. If a candidate did not gain enough petitions or otherwise failed to meet the complex filing deadlines and procedures, his delegates might be dropped from the ballot. Some states continued to rely on complicated ballot access rules or else required that candidates file long before the primary date.[39]

Because of these primary rules, proportional representation in delegate selection was seldom achieved. In many primaries the more popular candidate won a larger-than-proportionate share of the delegates. In 1980, for example, Carter won 65 percent of the popular vote in the Illinois primary but took 165 of the 179 separately elected delegates. In the 1980 Texas Republican loophole primary, Reagan won only 51 percent of the popular votes but still gained 61 of the 80 delegates. The front-runner's "bonus" amplified both Reagan's and Carter's lead in 1980.[40]

The movement to grass-roots control of delegate selection and the absence of complete proportionality hastened the momentum of the nomination race. A candidate with the most popular votes generally won additional delegates, sometimes in sizeable numbers. Other contenders seldom won as many delegates as their share of the popular vote and as a result were further pressured to drop out of the race.

Other Results of Reform

Aside from the several clearly intended changes already discussed, reforms in the 1970s had still other results. Two major changes are particularly important: the unforeseen impact of campaign finance reforms and the virtual elimination of the influence of top party regulars.

Campaign Finance. New campaign finance laws greatly affected nominating politics after 1972. On one hand, new regulations had their intended effect: eliminating large donations, averting major scandals, and reducing the disparity in candidate spending; on the other, reforms also brought many results that had not been so clearly foreseen or, perhaps, even intended.

For would-be nominees the new spending limits seriously complicated campaign planning. The spending limits were originally set at $10 million, plus an allowance for fund-raising expenses. That original figure, later adjusted for inflation, was close to what McGovern spent to win his 1972 Democratic nomination.[41] During the 1970s, however, two unexpected trends developed: a growing number of state primaries and a fast-rising inflation.

More and more primaries forced the serious contenders to campaign openly in an increasing number of states. Unlike caucus–convention states, the larger voter turnout in presidential primaries encouraged candidates to seek a broader exposure and visibility through increased media spending. As candidates ran in more states, they bought more newspaper ads, radio spots, and television ads. Campaign costs soared. So, too, did other costs of campaigning: rental cars, airfare, telephone bills, and hotel rooms. Adjustments for inflation failed to keep pace with rapidly-rising costs.[42]

In effect, a candidate's campaign budget shrank steadily. Even if a candidate lasted through the entire primary season (which few did), his campaign budget was, at best, inadequate to run a nationwide campaign. Nor were the state-by-state spending limits particularly generous. By 1976 and 1980, no candidate could effectively contest all the state primaries and caucuses.

In response to shrinking budgets, most candidates focused on the large states, the most favorable states, and on the early contests, then counted on momentum to carry them through the rest. Few except the best-prepared of candidates were able to run truly nation-wide campaigns. In 1980, for example, Senator Howard Baker focused on the early Republican primaries in New England and the Midwest, writing off most of the South, his home region. Senator Edward Kennedy spent little time, money, or personal effort in the South, the Midwest, or the Plains states, but focused instead on the large industrial states. California Governor Jerry Brown ran in only a handful of states before dropping out.

Reduced campaign budgets limited the candidates in their media exposure. Few candidates could purchase much national net-work air time; instead, they focused on state and local market advertising just before each targeted state primary. In 1980, only Republican John Connally (who refused federal matching funds and was thereby exempted from the spending ceiling) tried to buy much national media exposure.[43]

Tighter spending limits and declining real campaign budgets encouraged candidates toward low-cost or even "no-cost" campaign-ing. One way to cut costs and gain exposure is to schedule campaign events at times that capture free news time. Understandably, candi-dates are now more likely to schedule rallies, speeches, and events to meet television deadlines and to seek free coverage through talk shows and interviews. Increasingly, as campaign budgets grow more inadequate, candidates adjust their campaign strategies to the media's demands. Not surprisingly, broadcast policies regarding free time, equal time coverage, and the availability of advertising time have become more and more controversial.[44] This trend seems likely to continue, since unpaid media exposure will almost certainly play an increasingly important role in preconvention campaigning.

Dwindling campaign budgets coupled with rising costs also put an added premium on campaign volunteers. A major preconvention campaign might have several hundred staff members, but paying full salaries to these workers would quickly consume a candidate's budget. For most candidates, unpaid volunteers or workers who receive only expenses are the only solution. Some candidates rely primarily on unpaid or poorly paid workers from the start, but even those who do not are eventually forced to do so, simply to save money for media exposure.

In 1980, this trend was especially apparent. The Kennedy cam-paign, for example, early consumed a large share of its treasury on staff salaries. Not surprisingly, after a few early setbacks it soon found itself in trouble.[45] The Reagan and Connally campaigns, too, were forced to quit paying staff salaries, to lay off paid workers, and to rely instead on volunteers.[46] By contrast, the 1980 Carter campaign showed a better understanding of the new campaign realities by minimizing staff salaries, even for the campaign's top operatives.[47]

A successful campaign must restrain not only staff salaries but other campaign costs as well. Most candidates spend heavily on their first few efforts to gain enough momentum for the remaining state contests. Still, spending must be carefully controlled to stay within state-by-state spending ceilings and to leave some money for later media advertising. Spending too much on attractive headquarters, airplanes, or other routine campaign expenses quickly depletes a candidate's budget. In 1980, just as in 1976 and 1972, several candidates spent too freely, only to be forced to cut back later. Senator Kennedy's 1980 campaign, for example, began as a relatively lavish effort but soon ran into trouble. Reagan's spending soared so quickly that a major campaign shake-up was required after New Hampshire to curtail costs.[48] Although the 1980 Carter renomination campaign was a model of early, strict cost control, Carter, too, eventually was tightly pressed by the spending ceilings during the last round of primaries.[49]

New fund-raising rules also affected the nominations race by lengthening the cycle of raising monies. Under the new campaign laws, candidates cannot raise donations in amounts larger than $1000 from individuals of $5000 from political action committees. They must, instead, raise ever larger numbers of small donations. Most candidates do so through a direct mail campaign, or by personal solicitations by key supporters or by campaign aides. Assembling a mailing list, however, may require a year or even longer, since the list is usually compiled from lists of previous backers, then added to by sampling lists of magazine subscribers, past political donors, or sympathetic interest group members.[50] Volunteer fund-raisers must be contacted and convinced, and they, in turn, must have time to organize fund-raisers.[51] All these activities can be extremely time-consuming and pressure a serious contender to begin fund-raising efforts long before the first primary.

The new campaign finance laws discourage favorite sons and late entrants. Most favorite sons are home-state governors or senators who run only in their own state to win a bloc of uncommitted delegates with which to bargain with the leading contenders. Under the new finance rules, a favorite son's chances are greatly complicated by his inability to raise large donations in his home state and by his limited fund-raising appeal elsewhere. While the demise of favorite-son candidacies might also be traced to unfavorable voter attitudes, new fund-raising rules, by presenting serious problems for a potential favorite-son candidate, also lessen the chances of a deadlocked, brokered nominations race.

New campaign finance laws also discourage latecomers. Even a candidate with a very broad appeal would now experience difficulty in meeting reporting requirements and in raising funds without advance preparation. No contender could hope to raise enough money for a serious nationwide race by waiting until the primary season was underway. In 1980, only former president Ford toyed with the notion of a late bid, but he was eventually dissuaded both by fund-raising problems and by other difficulties such as filing deadlines, the dwindling numbers of delegates still available, and the lack of enthusiasm among top Republicans.

Federal campaign finance regulations have been ambivalent toward "draft" movements—unapproved efforts by supporters aimed at encouraging a presently inactive candidate to run for the nomination. In 1976, Federal Election Commission rules virtually banned these efforts by limiting draft movements to a low spending limit of only $1000. As a result, 1976 draft-Humphrey efforts were effectively curtailed. For 1980, the FEC not only allowed unauthorized draft movements to spend more money on behalf of a candidate but to accept individual donations of up to $5000. Also, money spent by unauthorized groups was not counted against the candidate's own spending limits if that candidate later did organize a bid. In 1979, active draft-Kennedy groups organized in Iowa and for Florida's nonbinding caucuses. The Florida groups reported laying out at least $250,000 on behalf of Kennedy.[52] A draft-Ford group also explored the former president's chances but disbanded after its soundings were not sufficiently encouraging to tempt Ford to make a race.[53] Otherwise there were no major draft movements in 1972, 1976, or 1980, and neither the draft-Ford nor the draft-Kennedy efforts proved particularly successful.

Tighter spending limits for candidates encouraged a new style in campaigning: uncoordinated expenditures on behalf of a candidate by that candidate's supporters. Federal law allows such expenditures, provided these efforts are not coordinated with a candidate's own efforts. In 1980, several individuals or interest groups took out advertisements or spent heavily on behalf of a favored candidate. For the Massachusetts primary Norman Lear, a prominent television producer, took out a full-page ad in the *Boston Globe* on behalf of moderate Republican hopeful John Anderson.[54] Later, for New York's primary, liberal activist Stewart Mott sponsored full-page ads backing Edward Kennedy (in the Democratic race) and Republican John Anderson.[55] In New Hampshire, conservative groups reportedly laid out at least $60,000 on behalf of Ronald Reagan who, by then, was already bumping up against his own spending ceiling.[56]

Campaign finance laws also added momentum by pressing candidates who fared poorly in their early primary or caucus races to drop out, thereby reducing the field of contenders. A candidate who failed to win at least 10 percent in a contested primary was cut off from federal matching funds 30 days later and could requalify only by winning at least 20 percent in a later primary. The cutoff did not force out any successful candidates, but it may have hastened the departure of several unsuccessful ones.

Indirectly, too, the new laws reduced the field of contenders. Since few if any candidates could raise all their money before the primaries, they hoped to attract continued funds through a strong primary showing. As Chapter Four explains, a candidate with a poor primary record is not likely to attract more funds and will probably soon drop out of the race.

New campaign laws brought several temporary disruptions, especially in 1976. In that year, the Federal Election Commission's activities were disrupted by a major court suit (*Buckley* v. *Valeo*), and for several weeks during key 1976 primaries the commission could not make matching fund payments. While the delay probably did not change the nominations contest, it did disrupt the campaigns of several candidates.[57] After 1976, other snafus continued. In the 1980 GOP New Hampshire primary, a highly publicized debate between Bush and Reagan involved questions of campaign funding.[58]

Taken together, the new campaign finance rules, in reducing the field of contenders by discouraging favorite sons, late entrants, and draft movements, and in narrowing a large field of hopefuls to fewer contenders, then to a single nominee, made it likely that the party's nominee would emerge from the primary and caucus competition.

When declining real spending limits for candidates interact with the media's behavior and with low levels of voter information, the nominations race is destabilized. This occurs in part because candidates can do little national advertising to present themselves and their issues to the voters and because the national media itself provides very little issue information about the candidates. As a result, voter attitudes toward most candidates are little informed until just before the state primaries. Then, when candidates begin their local advertising, voter information about the candidates increases quickly, and preferences may shift rapidly. Voter learning in the primaries is largely short-term learning, and opinion polls may shift suddenly.

When this happens, and "upset" may occur. Upsets are especially likely during the early primaries or when one candidate spends heavily in statewide advertising but the opponent spends very little.[59] In short, the often unstable nature of the race can, in part, be traced to the new finance laws operating in conjunction with routine campaign behavior of candidates, voters, and the media.

Eliminating the Party Regulars.   Reformers clearly intended to reduce the control of top party leaders over delegate selection. New party rules and campaign laws, however, virtually *eliminated* any meaningful role for the regulars. It is doubtful that all the reformers intended their changes to go this far; it is almost certain that the regulars never understood how completely their influence would be eroded.

Unable simply to name the delegates, top state party leaders and elected office holders sought other strategies to control the nomination. These tactics included favorite-son bids, uncommitted slates, and endorsements. In few instances did the regulars succeed.

Some party regulars sought to retain their influence by backing a favorite-son candidate, just as in earlier years. Yet after 1968 favorite sons fared poorly when matched against any major candidate, since primary voters showed little interest in supporting them. In North Carolina's 1972 Democratic primary, for instance, former governor Terry Sanford challenged George Wallace. Despite Sanford's home-state background and the support of most Tar Heel Democratic leaders, Sanford was soundly defeated by Wallace. Four years later, in 1976, Texas Senator Lloyd Bentsen ran as a favorite son, promising to take an independent delegation to the Democratic national convention. Although Bentsen's slates were loaded with prominent Texas Democrats, he was humiliated by Carter.[60]

The favorite-son strategy worked only where a local party leader was unopposed by a serious contender. In West Virginia's 1976 primary, Senator Robert Byrd won his home state's primary, but he was challenged only by George Wallace, who had, by then, dropped out as an active candidate. By 1980, governors and senators had evidently learned the futility of favorite-son bids. Then, not a single serious favorite-son candidacy was raised in either party, even by governors or senators disenchanted with the major contenders. Republican Governors Rhodes (in Ohio), Thompson (Illinois), and Clements (Texas), Democratic Governor Carey, and Senator Moynihan (both of New York) were all mentioned as potential favorite-son candidates, but none organized a bid.[61]

Some party regulars tried a second tactic: running uncommitted delegate slates. This tactic, however, usually worked only when the regulars were aided by complicated primary ballot rules, when a major candidate was not on the ballot at all, or where the local party machine was unusually strong. Uncommitted Democratic delegates did win in 1976 in a few upstate New York cities, in Mayor Daley's Chicago, and in New Jersey. Similarly, uncommitted GOP slates won in New York and New Jersey, although most of these were, in fact, Ford backers unchallenged by Reagan slates. In the caucus–convention states a few uncommitted delegates have won seats, usually as a reward for past party work or as leaders of interest groups. Overall, though, uncommitted delegates fared poorly both in the primary and the nonprimary states.

Supporters of major candidates were seldom very interested in sending state or local party leaders as uncommitted delegates to the national party conventions. Often they balked at sending the regulars at all unless the regulars endorsed their preferred candidate. In 1980, for example, long-term New York Senator Jacob Javits was pressed to endorse Reagan in return for a GOP convention seat.[62] When party leaders refused to endorse the winning candidate, they were likely to be refused a delegate post.

If favorite-son or uncommitted strategies failed, party regulars might turn to a third plan: endorsing a candidate in return for being named as delegates. Most presidential hopefuls were more than willing to place prominent party leaders on their delegate slates. However, this plan tied the party leader closely to the endorsed candidate and left little leeway for bargaining. Worse yet for the regulars, if the endorsed candidate faltered, local politicians might fail to win a delegate seat at all. In 1972, many Democratic regulars decided that Maine Senator Edmund Muskie would be their party's nominee, and they hurried to endorse him. As a result, Muskie's slates were loaded with state and local politicos. Muskie, however, faltered badly in the early primaries and then dropped out, leaving his slates "headless." Thus abandoned, his slates were usually trounced by other candidates, often by McGovern.

Nor were voters apparently much swayed by the endorsements of local party leaders. In 1980, for example, Chicago Mayor Jane Byrne endorsed and campaigned for Edward Kennedy. Despite her efforts, Kennedy was trounced by Carter, both in down-state Illinois and in Chicago. Only a week later, New York City's Democratic mayor and many other prominent state Democrats endorsed Carter, but Kennedy's late surge carried the New York primary. The 1980 nominations race is replete with similar examples. Only in a few states did a candidate clearly benefit by an endorsement—as did George

Bush in the 1980 Michigan primary by the support of that state's popular governor, William Milliken. In most instances voters focused on the candidates themselves, disregarding endorsements.

After 1968, state and local party regulars were unable to find any sure strategy to retain their influence. Neither primary voters nor caucus-goers were eager to allow uncommitted local politicians to take the delegate posts. Party regulars were forced to scramble, as best they could, onto a presidential hopeful's coattails.[63]

SUMMARY

After 1968, reformers were remarkably successful in achieving their agenda for change. Through a combination of party rules changes, state delegate selection practices, and new federal laws, reformers abolished the brokered convention system. The new system of popular appeal, unlike earlier nominating systems, emphasized openness, easy access by ordinary party supporters, and control over delegate selection by the party's grass roots. Table 2.4 summarizes differences in the three U.S. nominating systems.

The new reforms ended the tight control over nominating politics once exercised by the regulars. Perhaps unforeseen by reformers, the reforms went even further, virtually eliminating any significant role for top party leaders. The new reforms ensured a high level of momentum and, as Chapters Three, Four, and Five later explain, affected the behavior of the media, the candidates, and the public.

NOTES

1. For accounts of each presidential nomination through 1968, see Arthur M. Schlesinger, Jr., ed., *History of American Presidential Elections 1789–1968* (New York: Chelsea House, 1971), Vol. I–IV.
2. Washington's Farewell Address came on September 17, 1796. Presidential electors cast their ballots in December of that year.
3. Before the Twelfth Amendment, electors cast two votes apiece. The candidate with the most votes became president; the candidate with the second-highest total became vice-president. This practice encouraged each side to shave votes from the vice-presidential candidate to ensure that the intended candidate would reach the presidency. In 1796, however, there was considerable confusion, accounting for the outcome.
4. Unlike 1796, the electors of 1800 followed their party caucus' advice so well that every Democratic–Republican elector cast one vote apiece for

TABLE 2.4 A Comparison of Three Nominating Systems

Features	I. The Congressional Caucus System	II. The Brokered Convention System	III. The System of Popular Appeal
Years:	1800–1824	1832–1968	1972–present
Site of nomination:	Congressional party caucus meetings	National conventions and preconvention bargaining	Conventions formally ratify state primaries, caucuses, and conventions
Critical time period:	During and immediately before the congressional caucus meeting	During and before the national party convention	During the state primaries, caucuses, and conventions
Critical resources for successful candidates:	An appeal to congressmen and to the national political elite	Popularity with state and local officials and major office holders	Popularity with the party's voters and grass-roots activists

Role of the party's grass-roots voters and activists:	Minimal	Minimal	Controlling
Role of the party's regular leaders and office-holders:	Party congressmen control the nomination	Regular party organizational leaders and major office-holders control the nomination	Minimal
Role of the media:	Minimal	Minimal	Very substantial
Principal reasons for the transition from this system:	Population growth, movement to the West, more democratic political customs; the death of the Founding Fathers	The rise of the amateur activists, the mass media, the anti-Vietnam movement, the 1970 Democratic reforms	

Jefferson and Burr, thereby producing a tied vote. The House of Representatives eventually decided the tie in favor of Jefferson. Later, the Twelfth Amendment separated electoral college voting for the presidential and the vice-presidential candidates. For one dissent against the caucus, see John Randolph, "Protest Against the Caucus," in Schlesinger, *American Presidential Elections*, pp. 229–231.

5. In 1816, supporters of William Crawford called a caucus for March 12, but it was boycotted by Monroe's friends and by several members of Congress who opposed the caucus in principle. When the second caucus met on March 16, Monroe had won over a narrow majority of those attending and gained the nomination by a vote of 65 to 54, with 22 party members not attending. *The Niles National Register*, March 23, 1816, pp. 59-60.

6. In a few instances the defeated candidate refused to accept the caucus verdict. In 1808, George Clinton won the vice-presidential nod from the Democratic–Republican caucus. Not satisfied with second place, Clinton tried to bargain with Federalist leaders for their party's presidential nomination. Federalist leaders, however, were convinced that Clinton could not win and decided to nominate a Federalist. Four years later, in 1812, Clinton's nephew, DeWitt Clinton, bolted the party after Madison was renominated. The younger Clinton was nominated by a state legislative caucus in New York. He also won the Federalist nomination in a closed convention. Both the elder and the younger Clinton, however, failed in their presidential bid.

7. William Crotty, *Political Reform and the American Experiment* (New York: Thomas Y. Crowell, 1977).

8. *The Niles National Register*, September 16, 1823, pp. 2-4; November 1, 1823, p. 134; December 13, 1823, p. 225; January 17, 1824, pp. 305-307; and February 7, 1824, pp. 353-355. See also Charles S. Thompson, *The Rise and Fall of the Congressional Caucus* (New Haven: Yale University Press, 1902).

9. Ironically, Crawford had apparently agreed to step aside on behalf of Monroe in 1816. For an account of the 1824 election, see James F. Hopkins, "The Election of 1824," in Schlesinger, *American Presidential Elections*, pp. 229–231.

10. James Ceaser, *Presidential Selection: Theory and Development* (Princeton, N.J.: Princeton University Press, 1979), pp. 170-212.

11. For an account of the earliest presidential primaries, see Louise Overacker, *The Presidential Primary* (New York: MacMillan, 1926).

12. Schlesinger, *American Presidential Elections*. In the last preconvention (Gallup) poll of 1952, Kefauver led Stevenson, 45 percent to 12 percent. See George H. Gallup, ed., *The Gallup Poll* (New York: Random House, 1972), Vol. 2, pp. 1075-1076. Kefauver shared the misfortune of Thomas Dewey. In 1940, Dewey led in most of the contested Republican primaries but lost the nomination to late-starting Wendell Wilkie, who had entered no primaries at all.

13. The Republican nomination in 1964 of Arizona Senator Barry Goldwater is a possible exception. Goldwater supporters mounted a spirited, ultimately successful grass-roots effort. Goldwater, however, received the backing of many Southern and Western party officials.

14. For efforts to model the nominations process during the brokered convention system, see Steven Brams, *The Presidential Election Game* (New

Haven: Yale University Press, 1978); William Gamson, "Coalition Formation at Presidential Nominating Conventions," *American Journal of Sociology* 68 (1962): 157-171; and James Zais and John Kessel, "A Theory of Presidential Nominations with a 1968 Illustration," in *Perspective on Presidential Selection,* Donald Matthews, ed. (Washington, D.C.: Brookings, 1973), 120-142.

15. For an argument that the brokered convention system was already in its decline by the 1950s, see William Carleton, "The Revolution in the Presidential Nominating Convention," *Political Science Quarterly* 72 (1957): 224-240.

16. Gamson, "Coalition Formation."

17. The term "amateur" was first widely publicized by an account of Democratic club politics in Chicago, New York City, and Los Angeles. See James Q. Wilson, *The Amateur Democrat* (Chicago: University of Chicago Press, 1962). For discussion of amateur party activists and their efforts in several states, see Francis J. Sorauf, "Extra-legal Political Parties in Wisconsin," *American Political Science Review* 49 (1954): 692-704; Currin Shields, "A Note on Party Organization: The Democrats in California," *Western Political Quarterly* 8 (1954): 673-683; Donald Blaisdell, *Democrats of Oregon* (Eugene, Oregon: University of Oregon Press, 1970); and Francis Carney, *The Rise of the Democratic Clubs in California* (New York: Holt, Rinehart and Winston, 1958).

18. John Kessel, *The Goldwater Coalition* (Indianapolis: Bobbs-Merrill, 1968); Aaron Wildavsky, "The Goldwater Phenomenon: Purists, Politicians and the Future of the Two-Party System," *Review of Politics* 27 (1965): 386-413.

19. Public opinion polls have shown a majority favoring a national primary for many years. See "Two in Three Back Nationwide Presidential Primary Plan," *The Gallup Opinion Index,* Report No. 174, January 1980, pp. 19-20.

20. For a description of the search for an antiwar candidate to challenge Johnson, see Lewis Chester et al., *An American Melodrama* (New York: Viking, 1969), pp. 51-67.

21. Johnson led in the vote tallies, winning 27,520 write-in votes. McCarthy won 23,262 votes. Since Johnson had been expected to fare much better than he did, however, McCarthy's support startled most observers.

22. After the New Hampshire primary, either McCarthy or Kennedy (or their slates), or sometimes both, outpolled Humphrey, Johnson, their slates, or stand-ins in the District of Columbia, California, Illinois, Indiana, Massachusetts, Nebraska, New Jersey, Pennsylvania, Oregon, South Dakota, and Wisconsin. In Florida, Ohio, and West Virginia favorite sons or uncommitted slates won. In some primaries only a few delegate seats were contested, and in many states delegate selection was conducted separately from the presidential preference poll. See *Presidential Elections since 1789* (Washington, D.C.: Congressional Quarterly, 1975), pp. 149-151.

23. For a journalist's description of the Chicago convention, see Norman Mailer, *Miami and the Siege of Chicago* (New York: World Publishing, 1968); see also Chester, *An American Melodrama.*

24. For a full commission report, see George McGovern, *Mandate for Reform— A Report of the Commission on Party Structure and Delegate Selection* (Washington, D.C.: The Democratic National Committee, 1970). See also

William Crotty, *Decisions for Democrats* (Baltimore: John Hopkins University Press, 1978).

25. Barbara Mikulski, *A Report of the Commission on Delegate Selection and Party Structure* (Washington, D.C.: The Democratic National Committee, 1973).

26. "Democrats to Adopt Final Rules for 1980," *Congressional Quarterly Weekly Review*, June 3, 1978, pp. 1392–1396.

27. For a review of Republican party changes, see John Bibby, "Party Renewal in the National Republican Party," in *Party Renewal in America*, Gerald Pomper, ed. (New York: Praeger, 1980). Bibby notes that the GOP changes focused more on electoral success than on intraparty democracy. See also Crotty, *Political Reform*, pp. 255–260.

28. *Elections '76* (Washington, D.C.: Congressional Quarterly Press, 1976), pp. 36–37.

29. Herbert Alexander, *Financing Politics* (Washington, D.C.: Congressional Quarterly, 1976).

30. "Candidates Must Adjust to Spending Lid," *Congressional Quarterly Weekly Report*, May 10, 1980, pp. 1244–1247.

31. Alexander, *Financing Politics*, pp. 61–90. For a recent description of the efforts of big donors, see "Despite Tight Campaign Spending Laws, Former 'Fat Cats' Have a Role to Plan," *National Journal*, February 9, 1980, pp. 229–231.

32. Alexander, *Financing Politics*.

33. For a description from 1972, see Denis G. Sullivan et al., *The Politics of Representation* (New York: St. Martin's Press, 1974). For trends in the the Democratic Party, see Morley Winograd, *Openness, Participation and Party Building: Reforms for a Stronger Party* (Washington, D.C.: Democratic National Committee, 1978), p. 18.

34. See, for example, the discussion of William Keech and Donald Matthews, "Patterns in the Presidential Nominating Process, 1936–1977," in *Parties and Elections in an Anti-Party Age*, Jeff Fishel, ed. (Bloomington, Indiana University Press, 1978), pp. 203–218.

35. Austin Ranney, *Participation in American Presidential Nominations, 1976* (Washington, D.C.: American Enterprise Institute, 1977), p. 20.

36. Richard L. Rubin, "Presidential Primaries: Continuities, Dimensions of Change, and Political Implications" (Paper delivered at the 1977 annual meeting of the American Political Science Association, Washington, D.C.). The increase in turnout noted by Rubin evidently did not continue from 1976 to 1980; see "Carter, Reagan Exhibit Similar Assets in Preference primaries," *Congressional Quarterly Weekly Report*, July 5, 1980, pp. 1867–1879, especially p. 1874.

37. A few state Democratic parties won exemptions from party rules when they were unable to change state laws to comply with party rulings. In 1980, for example, Wisconsin Democrats continued to hold an "open" primary, permitting any voter to cast a ballot in the Democratic race.

38. Opponents of the California Republican winner-take-all primary attempted to gather petitions and submit the issue to California voters but failed. Later, their efforts to end the winner-take-all primary in a court challenge also failed. See "California May Abolish GOP 'Winner-Take-All' Primary," *Washington Post*, January 3, 1980, p. A4. See also, "Campaign Notes," *New York Times*, April 19, 1980, p. A9.

39. To prevent states from enacting early filing deadlines, the Democratic Party required that primary states set their filing deadlines 30 to 90 days before the 1980 primary. See "Democrats to Adopt Final Rules for 1980," *Congressional Quarterly Weekly Review*, June 3, 1978, pp. 1392–1396.

40. For estimates of the front-runners' bonus in 1980, see "Primaries' Popular Vote Fails to Reflect Lead in Delegates," *New York Times*, April 16, 1980, p. B8; and "Carter, Reagan Exhibit Similar Assets in Preference Primaries," *Congressional Quarterly Weekly Report*, July 5, 1980, pp. 1867–1875.

41. McGovern reportedly spent about $12 million to win the Democratic nomination in 1972. See Alexander, *Financing Politics*, p. 39. For a review of campaign finance legislation, see The Institute of Politics, John F. Kennedy School of Government, Harvard University, *An Analysis of the Impact of the Federal Election Campaign Act, 1972-78* (Cambridge, Mass.: Harvard University, 1979).

42. "It's More Expensive to Run for President As Inflation Takes to the Campaign Trail," *National Journal*, February 23, 1980, pp. 311–313.

43. "Connally Is Dropping His TV Drive for Primary Contests with Reagan," *New York Times*, December 16, 1979, p. 36; "Connally Is Scrambling to Keep Troubled Presidential Bid Afloat," *New York Times*, February 7, 1980, p. A18; and "The Best Roadshow in Politics Ends," *Washington Post*, March 10, 1980, p. A1.

44. For an example, see "F.C.C., 4-3, Upholds the President in Bid for Prime Time on Television," *New York Times*, November 21, 1979, p. A17.

45. "Kennedy Camp Starts to Lay off Some of Its Staff," *New York Times*, January 24, 1980, p. B8; "Funds Depleted, Kennedy Juggles Campaign Plans," *Washington Post*, January 25, 1980, p. A1; "Kennedy's Decision to Stay in the Race—After Iowa, the Agonizing Overhaul of a 'Cadillac' Campaign," *Washington Post*, February 5, 1980, p. A1; "The Fundraising Tally," *The New Republic*, February 23, 1980, pp. 11–13; and "Kennedy Problems: At Top and Afield," *New York Times*, March 11, 1980, p. B11.

46. For descriptions of the Connally campaign, see "Connally Is Scrambling," *New York Times*, February 7, 1980, p. A18; "Campaign Notes," *Washington Post*, February 20, 1980, p. A3; and "Connally Drive Short on Money, to Close Offices in Many States," *New York Times*, February 21, 1980, p. B11. For descriptions of the Reagan camp's funding problems, see "Reagan Is Buoyed by Victory As His Campaign Enters a Difficult Period," *New York Times*, February 28, 1980, p. A19; "Reagan Plans Layoffs in His Campaign Staff," *New York Times*, March 4, 1980, p. B8; "Reagan Cash Flow Becomes a Trickle," *Washington Post*, March 7, 1980, p. A1; "Reagan Nearing Spending Limits," *New York Times*, March 9, 1980, p. 32L; and "Reagan Striving to Heed Spending Law," *New York Times*, March 15, 1980, p. B16.

47. "The Campaign," *Washington Post*, June 8, 1980, p. A1; and *National Journal*, February, 1980, pp. 311–313.

48. *New York Times*, "Reagan Is Buoyed," February 28, 1980, p. 19; and "Sears Details Disorder in Reagan Camp," *Washington Post*, February 29, 1980, p. A1.

49. "Carter Campaign Approaching Its Spending Limits," *New York Times*, April 22, 1980, p. B10.

50. Alexander, *Financing Politics.*

51. See "It's the Fund Raisers—Not the Fund Givers—Who Count," *National Journal*, February 9, 1980, p. 230; and "Robert Strauss—The President's Supersalesman," *The New York Times Magazine*, February 24, 1980, pp. 24-27+.

52. "Straw Presidential Polls Gain Early Notice," *Congressional Quarterly Weekly Report*, November 3, 1979, p. 2473. Later, however, the Federal Election Commission filed suit to determine whether the Florida for Kennedy Committee had coordinated its activities with other pro-Kennedy groups. "U.S. Election Panel Sues for Draft-Kennedy Data," *New York Times*, December 28, 1979, p. A19; "The Legal Tangle Over Donations to Kennedy," *National Journal*, September 15, 1979, p. 1535.

53. "Ford Still Has Time to Try for Majority of Delegates," *New York Times*, March 5, 1980, p. A22; and "Ford Is Again Edging to Brink of Running," *New York Times*, March 16, 1980, p. A30.

54. *The Boston Globe*, March 3, 1980, p. 20.

55. *New York Times*, March 23, 1980, pp. E6, E7.

56. "Surge in Independent Campaign Spending," *Congressional Quarterly Weekly Report*, June 14, 1980, p. 1639.

57. "Ford Delays Swearing in of Election Unit Members," *New York Times*, May 19, 1976, p. 46; and "Election Agency Operating Again," *New York Times*, May 22, 1976, p. 1.

58. "Reagan Opens Debate to All Republicans," *New York Times*, February 24, 1980, p. 14.

59. Examples often occurred in the 1980 GOP race, when Reagan's early spending forced him to cut back on media outlays in later campaigns. Bush, however, was still able to spend more freely. Rapid poll changes under these circumstances occurred in Pennsylvania and Michigan. See "Bush Found Gaining in Big Drive to Win Pennsylvania Test," *New York Times*, April 20, 1980, p. A1.

60. "Two Reagan Shocks: Suddenly Ford is Behind," *Congressional Quarterly Weekly Report*, May 8, 1976, pp. 1079-1081.

61. "Presidential Delegate Count," *Congressional Quarterly Weekly Report*, June 28, 1980, p. 1801.

62. "Javits to Support Reagan Candidacy," *New York Times*, April 18, 1980, p. B4.

63. To increase the numbers of party leaders attending the 1980 convention, Democratic Party rules allowed each state delegation to add 10 percent more delegates. State party officials and elected officeholders received priority. These delegate seats, however, had to reflect the preferences of publicly selected delegates and were chosen by vote of state party conventions, committees, or the publicly chosen delegates. As a result, more party officials were represented, but they gained little leeway for independent action. See *Congressional Quarterly Weekly Review*, June 3, 1978, p. 1392.

3

THE MEDIA

THE NEW IMPORTANCE OF THE MEDIA

Reforms in the 1970s stripped party regulars of their control over nominating politics and allowed ordinary voters and party activists more influence than ever before. At the same time, the reforms increased the role of the media.

Unlike top party leaders and office holders, voters could not know the candidates personally. While they might have turned to the regulars for advice, apparently few did. Instead, most people learned of the candidates through the media: television, radio, newspapers, and campaign advertising. And, conversely, through pollsters the candidates searched for the moods and feelings of the voters.

Neither the candidates, academics, party reformers, nor the journalists themselves failed to note the increased role of the media. One commentator wrote:

> As the old parties founder, the role of mediating among factions and building up one or another of the candidates has been shifting elsewhere, principally to the press. . . . A generation ago, a power broker like Illinois' Colonel Jake Arvey could "make" an Adlai Stevenson. Now a good interview with Barbara Walters might mean fifty delegates. The press . . . may be taking over the process.[1]

Or:

> Nowadays when a man sets out to be President, his first plan is a
> media strategy. . . . (T)he primary task a Presidential candidate faces
> today is not building a coalition of organized interests, or developing
> alliances with other candidates or politicians in his party, or even
> winning over the voters whose hands he shakes. If he has his modern
> priorities straight, he is first and foremost a seeker after favorable
> notice from the journalists who can make or break his progress.[2]

Most political observers viewed the media's new role with considerable suspicion. Some critics argued that the press acted in arbitrary, erratic, even biased ways. For losing candidates the press
became a scapegoat. For frustrated party reformers the media became
a rival influence. Liberals and conservatives alike saw the media as
employing their powers to aid the opposition. Even journalists
engaged in self-criticism.

These arguments, assumptions, and criticisms jointly constitute
the "Myth of the Press." The Myth assumes that the media are some-
how responsible for the success of some candidates and for the
failure of others. The Myth assumes not only that the press determines candidate success, but that it uses its influence capriciously
and arbitrarily.

The Myth pervades discussion of the role of the media in presidential nominations. For at least four reasons the argument seems
plausible. First, presidential candidates themselves often fashion their
campaigns to attract media attention. Candidates and their managers
plan campaigns around "media events," time announcements to meet
press deadlines, and schedule the candidate into each major media
market. Pollsters, ad agencies, media consultants, press agents, and
even joke writers have permanently joined the inner circle of campaign
advisers.[3]

Second, critics assume that the press is biased. Former vice-
president Spiro Agnew, for example, voiced conservative suspicions
that journalists, commentators, and reporters secretly preferred
liberal candidates and causes. Liberals, in turn, suspect the conservative biases of publishers and station owners.[4] Journalists themselves
have documented instances of biased coverage during presidential
nominations campaigns.

Third, the media have greatly expanded their role as observers
and arbiters of the nominations contest. Networks, wire services,
journals, and newspapers now spend millions of dollars and the time
of hundreds of reporters, technicians, and analysts to follow the
candidates up to and through the national conventions.

Finally, the press does act as a self-appointed judge of each
candidate's progress. Reporters offer analyses of each campaign, not

just "straight" reporting of the candidates' campaign speeches and appearances. At some points an article or expose may seem to damage some candidate's campaign, at least temporarily. After each primary, the media judge who has "won" and who "lost."

Like most myths, the "Myth of the Press" is neither wholly true nor wholly false. The Myth is partly correct in assuming that the media play a major role in the nominations race. On the other hand, the Myth is wrong to assume that the press behaves erratically or capriciously. By the mid-1970s, the press had already established several routine procedures, or "rules," for covering the nomination race. These "rules"—described at length later in this chapter—concern preconvention coverage, routine campaign reporting, evaluating candidate success in the primaries and caucuses, and deciding which states are important and which are not.

It is no coincidence that the news media settled on these rules; they reflect the media's first priority: to interpret the nomination race's tremendous complexity and uncertainty in light of their own institutional norms and their own needs. These priorities include, chiefly, the need to simplify complex events for readers or viewers, the need for timeliness in coverage, the need for drama and excitement, and the norm of evenhanded coverage. These constraints, which are wholly impersonal and common to the whole news industry, dictate coverage patterns.[5]

WHO ARE THE MEDIA?

The Columnists, the Papers, the Networks

In the loosest sense, the term "the press" or "the media" might include all the print or broadcast media of the country (or indeed, of the world) that cover the nominations. By this estimate, the press includes even small-town weeklies that report the briefest of political news (often taken directly from the wire services) and occasionally make editorial endorsements. In this loose sense, the media also include local radio stations that air news bulletins on their obligatory newscasts and even gossip or fashion papers that print personal tidbits about candidates or their families.[6]

More narrowly, though—and probably more accurately—the term "media" refers to the major nationally oriented opinion leaders and news analysts. Included are the wire services—the UPI and AP—whose reports are widely reprinted, as well as the dozen or so major columnists and writers—such as David Broder, Haynes Johnson,

Hugh Sidey, Rowland Evans, and Robert Novak—whose articles reach a national audience and the top reporters for the most influential newspapers, such as the *New York Times, Washington Post,* or *Los Angeles Times.*

The major television networks—NBC, ABC, CBS—must be included for their massive audiences and nationwide exposure. By the same standard, major news weeklies—*Time, Newsweek,* and *U.S. News and World Report*—may also be counted. Finally, a few smaller but serious journals can be added for their impact on a small but politically attentive and active audience; examples include *The New Republic,* the *Atlantic,* and *Harper's.* While the press includes these two or three dozen newspapers, syndicates, networks, journals, columnists, and writers, the term admits of no simple, fixed, clearcut definition. By the last primaries or for a front-runner the press corps may swell to several busloads of reporters.

"Pack Journalism"

One view of the press assumes that reporters are a fiercely competitive group, always struggling for a startling and incisive "scoop." Doubtlessly this image has been bolstered by a few crusading newspapers and writers who, from time to time, reveal a major expose. More often, however, the scheduling and coverage of presidential campaigns leads to another pattern: "pack journalism." While covering the campaign week after week, reporters remain in close personal and physical contact. They are bused together to the same campaign stops, handed the same press releases, housed and fed together, and left mostly to each others' company. From this continued, intense personal contact, pack journalism is born.[7] As a result, campaign reporters tend to turn in similar stories, giving them a roughly similar slant and interpretation.

Pack journalism also refers to the editors' habit of confirming their own reporters' stories by checking them against the wire services, other newspapers, or networks. If a reporter's story is similar to other accounts, it is assumed to be reliable. A story that differs markedly may be held, rechecked, or even rewritten.

Pack journalism ensures that whatever major news source a U.S. voter depends upon, the story will be likely to be similar to coverage offered by most other major newspapers or networks. Differences in reporting are usually found in nuances and subtleties, not in the basics. Similarities in coverage include the number, length, location, slant, and content of campaign stories.[8] As a result, Iowa readers receive a similar version of the campaign as readers in Oregon. The politically attentive public receives similar versions of which candidates are serious contenders and which are not, how well each candidate is faring, and what crises have recently occurred on the campaign trail.

The Pollsters

Through its campaign coverage the press informs the voters about the candidates. The press also performs the reverse activity: discovering the public's mind for candidates and for the voters themselves through public opinion polling.

Polling in presidential elections is an old practice. Polls originated at about the time of the collapse of the congressional caucus system. Unsystematic polls were reported by newspapers and by supporters of candidates as early as the election of 1824. These polls strove more to generate enthusiasm for a favorite candidate than to measure voter attitudes accurately.[9]

Scientific public opinion polling originated in the 1930s with the Gallup organization, which correctly predicted Franklin Roosevelt's reelection in 1936. By the 1950s and 1960s, preconvention polling became widespread; by the 1970s, the floodgates for polling were wide open, and major networks, newspapers, periodicals, and sometimes even columnists all reported their own polls, as did virtually all the major candidates.[10]

Preconvention polling may take several forms. Among the simplest but most unsystematic and unreliable polls are informal "man-on-the-street" polls. These polls interview only a few supposedly typical respondents at shopping centers, on street corners, or in selected neighborhoods. Conclusions from these polls lack scientific validity and may seriously misrepresent voter sentiment. Nonetheless, man-on-the-street polls are often reported, since they provide colorful, easily collected stories for columnists or reporters.

A second type of poll interviews political activists or leaders. The Gallup Poll, for example, sometimes samples Republican and Democratic Party leaders for their opinions. Less systematic polls may ask the preferences of party activists at fund-raising dinners, party conventions, or other gatherings. A notable example occurred before the 1976 Iowa caucuses, when party loyalists attending an annual Democratic dinner in Des Moines were polled and their preferences reported. Carter supporters learned of the straw poll in advance and worked to turn out their supporters. As a result, Carter led his opponents with 23 percent of the straw votes and won national publicity as the front-runner in the upcoming Iowa caucuses.[11] By 1980, numerous state parties conducted such polls.[12]

The most systematic polls design their sampling procedures to ensure that the results provide an accurate cross-section of a specified population, usually of a state or the national electorate. Among the best-known of these in 1980 were the *New York Times* CBS Poll, the Gallup Poll, and the ABC-Harris Polls. Almost all the major presidential contenders in recent years, too, have hired their own pollsters.

Polling in presidential primaries is a risky business, and the pitfalls of preconvention polling are well documented. Since few U.S. adults vote in primaries or attend caucuses, pollsters need to take very large and very costly samples to provide reliable results. Early polls are often based on too few voters to provide accurate results.[13] Early polls may also measure little more than name recognition. As some candidates run well in the early primaries and others drop out, the polls may swing up and down erratically. Large shifts in the polls just before a primary are a frequent occurrence.[14] All these problems have led many reputable pollsters, such as George Gallup and Burns Roper, to caution against taking most preconvention polls too seriously.[15]

If preconvention polling is so perilous, why do so many reporters, columnists, editors, and candidates invest so much time, money, and confidence in the polls? Simply answered: polls, for all their problems, are still considered among the best information available. For candidates, polls offer insights into voter attitudes and help to suggest which issues to emphasize and which to avoid. For editors, polls supplement the impressions of weary and skeptical reporters. Polls also provide one standard by which journalists can evaluate candidate success in the primaries. For volunteers, donors, and voters, the polls offer a way of deciding which candidates have a serious chance of winning the nomination and which do not.

WHAT THE PRESS DOES

The media influence the nominations outcome in several ways. Before the earliest primary or caucus, the media begin to identify and label the candidates. Later, most journalists emphasize the horse-race aspects of the contest or the candidates' personal qualities, not issue differences between the candidates. Attention is focused on primary and caucus returns, with some contenders being declared "winners" and others "losers." Journalists single out a few primaries and caucuses for special attention but virtually ignore most of the rest.

Preprimary Coverage

Several months before the first presidential primary or caucus, the media begin to sort out and identify the candidates. Early news coverage usually takes one of two approaches. First, journalists may briefly present and compare several candidates, giving each no more than a paragraph or two in a short article. These articles are often engagingly written, providing a lively account of the early field of candidates. Pictures and text often do no more than briefly identify each of the serious contenders. Frequently these stories label or stereotype the candidates; one article in early 1972, for example, labeled George McGovern as "the mad professor."[16]

The other type of article commonly found before the primaries is the full-length analysis of a single candidate. These pieces vary in length from a few paragraphs to longer features that run over several pages. A typical article might begin with a personal and political profile of the candidate, then describe his coalition and general issue stands, and conclude by outlining a possible scenario for winning the nomination.

Political scientists may scoff at the importance of these articles. True, most focus on a candidate's personality and on catchy writing at the expense of issues. Yet these early articles ought not be discounted entirely; for many voters they provide a first exposure to the candidates. Early labeling or stereotyping may establish an enduring image for a candidate. In 1975 and 1976, articles often described and sometimes photographed Alabama Governor George Wallace as physically unable to cope with the strains of the presidency.[17] In 1979 and 1980, early coverage described former Texas governor John Connally as a wheeler-dealer and recounted his past legal difficulties.[18]

While the best-known candidates win most of the early coverage, even little-known contenders receive some attention. Since journalists cannot predict the nominations outcome any longer by early fund-raising success or poll support, the press apparently feels obliged to cover almost any candidate with respectable credentials and some discernible strength. In late 1979 and early 1980, for instance, neither Jerry Brown, nor George Bush, nor John Anderson ever fared well in the early polls; nonetheless, each received several articles analyzing his prospects.[19]

Routine Campaign Coverage

From the time of the first caucuses and primaries, background stories give way to a different style of reporting, typically focusing on three types of stories: the first reports a candidate's campaign style; the second focuses on human interest stories; and the third recaps primary and caucus results. By contrast, issue stories are less frequently found.[20]

Many stories simply report a candidate's daily campaign stops, speeches, and appearances. These stories—sometimes described as "whistle-stop" journalism—report the candidate's schedule, the size of the crowd and its enthusiasm, and the routine mechanics of the campaign. Reporting is often enlivened with photos of the candidate greeting well-wishers, or the story may be enlivened (à la Teddy White) with anecdotes or behind-the-scenes descriptions of the campaign staff.

This routine campaign coverage does not, however, fulfill the media's desire for drama and excitement. From time to time reporters enjoy a break in their routine when the candidate makes a gaffe or offers a controversial view, or when a reporter uncovers some newsworthy incident in a candidate's past. Then, the newspapers and newscasts may be filled with that incident for several days. In 1976, Jimmy Carter was forced to clarify his "ethnic purity" remark to reassure blacks that he had intended no slight. In 1980, Edward Kennedy criticized the former Shah of Iran during the hostage crisis and then spent several days clarifying his comments. On the eve of the New Hampshire primary, George Bush had to confront allegations that he had accepted "laundered" campaign money in a Senate race some years earlier. By focusing on these occasional dramatic incidents, the media adds drama to an otherwise unexciting routine.

A second type of reporting focuses on the candidate's personalities, personal backgrounds, or families. These stories aim to add human interest to the campaign. Such stories are quite common for all the major candidates during the preconvention season. If a candidate has some troubling or controversial background, they may appear very frequently throughout the campaign. In 1980, Governor Brown and Senator Kennedy, on the Democratic side, each found his personal life featured throughout the primary season.[21]

The third type of reporting finds the media analyzing primary and caucus vote totals—"horse-race" or "winners-and-losers" journalism. Horse-race journalism is discussed at greater length in the next section.

Relatively few news stories, either in the networks, in journals, or in newspapers, discuss in depth the candidates' issue stands. Even fewer stories compare the issue stands of different candidates.[22] Seldom will the media discuss issue differences between the candidates until the field has dwindled and a front-runner emerged. In 1972, for example, few of McGovern's proposals were much covered until the McGovern–Humphrey showdown in California's late primary. In 1980, GOP nominee Reagan's issue stands were covered very little at all at any time during the nominations race.

Perhaps the candidates' positions on major issues are too complicated, too convoluted, or too vague to describe in a readable article. Perhaps reporters are too caught up in the exhausting campaign schedule of a particular candidate to compare the issue stands of various candidates. Or editors may assume that readers will not suffer through lengthy articles on the subtleties of complex issues. Whatever the reason, stories delving into issues are relatively rare, even in the major nationally oriented media. Among metropolitan and small-town dailies or on local radio and television stations issue stories are seldom found.

The media's focus on campaign style and technique, human interest stories, and vote totals helps to explain why most voters are unclear, at best, on the candidates' issue positions. If a voter relies on network news or on a typical metropolitan daily, that voter is not likely to learn much about the candidates' issue stands. A typical television viewer or newspaper reader will learn a great deal about the candidate's mannerisms, personal appearance, background, campaign schedule, family, and track record in the primaries or caucuses. About a candidate's stand on the major issues, however, the voter will learn relatively little.

Picking Winners and Losers

Perhaps the single most important role of the media involves reporting and interpreting the results of primaries, caucuses, and state conventions. "Horse-race" journalism accounts for a large share of preconvention reporting and has a considerable impact on donors, activists, volunteers, voters, and the candidates themselves.

In most cases the media simply name as the winner the candidates with the most votes (or delegates) in a primary or caucus.[23]

However, the media also evaluate the magnitude of the winner's victory and interpret the showings of the other candidates. By the mid-1970s, the media apparently settled on several "rules" by which to evaluate primary and caucus results; some of these are described below.

The first rule usually applied by the media is that the candidate with the largest number of votes (or delegates) has "won." Even if a candidate wins less than an absolute majority of votes and only a handful more votes than the second-place rival, that candidate will usually be declared the winner. While a handful of exceptions occur —the most notable being Senator Muskie's first-place finish in the 1972 New Hampshire Democratic primary—the media will almost invariable apply this rule to judge the primary or caucus results.

The media also judge the magnitude of the first-place candidate's showing and evaluate the showings of candidates who place second, third, or lower. To do so, the media also use several other criteria, each relying on the notion of *relative success*. By this standard, a candidate succeeds by gaining *more* votes or delegates than expected, and he runs poorly if he wins *fewer* votes or delegates than expected. The concept of relative success requires journalists to calculate the difference between how well a candidate *should* have done and how well that candidate *actually* fared. A prediction about how well a candidate should fare is made before the primary or caucus, and it is then compared to the outcome. Recent news coverage suggests at least five ways in which a candidate's relative success may be evaluated.

Public Opinion Polls

Public opinion polls offer an obvious way of determining how candidates are running before the primary. Reporters use early (pre-primary or precaucus) polls to predict how well a candidate will run. If a candidate slips from preprimary polls, then that candidate has fared worse than expected and should be so judged.

A prominent example occurred in the 1972 Democratic New Hampshire primary. There, an early poll put Muskie's support at 65 percent, with McGovern at only 18 percent. When Muskie finally captured 48 percent of the primary vote in a crowded field, the result was labeled a disappointment for Muskie.[24]

Candidates who do not place first may also be judged to have run well if they exceed their preprimary poll standings. In the 1980 Republican primary in Massachusetts, for example, John Anderson placed second, with 31 percent, but ran ahead of his preprimary poll standings of 17 percent.[25] Anderson won considerable publicity and soon surged in the national polls and on the fund-raising circuit.

Other examples occurred in 1980. In the early Maine caucuses, President Carter came in first, with 43 percent of caucus-goers, which was slightly lower than his precaucus polls. His challenger, Senator Kennedy, placed second, slightly exceeding his precaucus expectations with 38 percent. California Governor Brown placed third, but he also exceeded his precaucus poll standings. As a result, the media declared the results a standoff.[26]

Admittedly this practice is fraught with perils. As noted earlier in this chapter, preprimary polls may measure little more than name familiarity; as candidates begin their canvassing and media advertising, the polls may change considerably. Primary polls are often small and statistically unreliable, leaving large margins for error. Many candidates and their managers evidently understand the notion of relative success and set impossibly high standards for their rivals while claiming that a low percentage of the vote would be a victory for their own candidate.[27] These problems notwithstanding, polls are, in fact, widely used as a standard to judge primary and caucus results.

Previous Success

A second standard holds that a candidate should run as strongly in a primary or caucus as the previous time. This standard applies only to a few candidates who have previously contested their party's nomination. A candidate who slips from an earlier primary showing, especially from a first- to a second-place showing, is likely to be declared a loser.

In 1972, for example, George Wallace won pluralities in Florida (with 42 percent) and in North Carolina (50 percent). In 1976, however, Wallace fell to 31 percent in Florida, placing second to Jimmy Carter. In North Carolina, Wallace again placed second, winning 35 percent to Carter's 54 percent. Press coverage was replete with the obvious comparison: Wallace was doubly a loser—firstly, by winning fewer votes than before, and second, by placing second, not first. One newspaper account of the North Carolina setback read:

> Wallace's stunning defeat was reflected in some of the eastern Tidewater counties of the state where he always commanded solid backing. In New Hanover County, Carter was beating Wallace by more than 20 percent. By contrast, the Alabamian had won that county

four years ago by almost 2 to 1 over former North Carolina Governor Terry Sanford.[28]

Shortly after the North Carolina primary, Wallace ceased his active national campaign for the Democratic nomination.

The Home-State Standard

A third standard, although not one that is always applicable, holds that a candidate should win in his home state or region. By this test the voters most familiar with a candidate should like him best. Any candidate unable to win his home state (or region) is not likely to be taken seriously by the press.

Former governor Terry Sanford's 1972 home-state loss to George Wallace, for example, finished Sanford's dark-horse race. In the same year, Muskie's poor showing in neighboring New Hampshire was doubly damaging to the Maine senator, since Muskie not only failed to match his preprimary polls standing but did so in his native New England. Senator Kennedy's setbacks in the 1980 Maine caucuses and in the New Hampshire and Vermont primaries badly damaged his already floundering campaign.

Incumbent Presidents

A fourth test holds that no sitting president should lose a primary. This rule is apparently applied no matter how little time or resources a President might have invested nor how unlikely it is that he would have won were he not the incumbent. In 1976, the press speculated that President Ford would be forced from the race should he suffer two early losses in New Hampshire and Florida. A loss by an incumbent president, while not necessarily fatal, is always newsworthy.[29]

Time, Endorsements, and Money

The media may also judge a candidate's primary showings by comparing the share of the vote to the time and personal efforts a candidate had invested, to the endorsements collected, money spent, or the size and enthusiasm of crowds. Presumably, a candidate who pours much more money and time into a state than his opponents should outpoll those opponents. If he does not, then the results are likely to be described as a loss.

This test is especially important for little-known candidates who hope to fare well in a state and thereby win publicity and attention for their bid. In 1976, for instance, Texas Senator Lloyd Bentsen spent heavily in the early Mississippi and Oklahoma caucuses. Despite his time, personal efforts, money, and the support of many local political leaders, Bentsen won few delegates. After the Oklahoma caucuses, one newspaper account read:

> Senator Lloyd Bentsen is seriously considering abandonment of his campaign for the Democratic Presidential nomination, political associates of the Texas millionaire reported today. Mr. Bentsen finished a weak third yesterday in the Oklahoma Democratic caucuses after an intensive and lavishly financed campaign, barely defeating Governor George C. Wallace of Alabama, who made no appearances in the state.[30]

Bentsen dropped his national bid shortly thereafter, returning to Texas to continue as a favorite son.

Four years later, another Texan, former governor John Connally, spent heavily in the South Carolina GOP primary and won the endorsement of Republican Senator Strom Thurmond and a former Republican governor. Connally also concentrated much of his own time in South Carolina. When Connally placed only a weak second, he, too, dropped his presidential bid.

The reverse of this standard is also applied. If a candidate spends little or no time, money, or effort in a state, even a very meager primary showing will not necessarily be counted as a setback. A poor showing on the part of a candidate who completely ignores a state primary or caucus is seldom even much acknowledged in reports of the primary or caucus results, especially if his name was involuntarily entered on the primary ballot.

Understanding this "rule" can help a candidate avoid being tagged a loser in unfavorable states. In 1972, for example, Senator McGovern ignored Florida's crowded Democratic primary. Subsequently, most news stories omitted him from the list of losers, although McGovern polled only 6 percent of the Democratic vote and finished sixth among seven major candidates. In 1980, Senator Kennedy avoided most Southern primaries, apparently hoping to avoid being tagged a loser in states where he had slight prospects.

These several rules seem to be widely applied in judging candidate success (or failure) by major newspapers, journals, wire services, and broadcasters. As a result, most of the major American press agrees on how the race is progressing and which candidates are the front-runners. As Appendix A suggests, leading newspapers agreed on the performance of major Democratic and Republican hopefuls in 1972, 1976, and 1980.

Other Key Rules

Candidates as Individuals

The press also treats candidates as individuals, not as representatives of party factions. This rule has broad implications for the nominations race. If one faction of a party divides its support among several candidates but a rival faction produces only one candidate, then the latter may see its candidate surge to the front-runner status on the basis of pluralities. By the time the opposing wing of the party reduces its multiple candidates to a single contender, it may be too late to stop the front-runner's momentum.

For this reason, each party faction is under constant pressure to produce one and only one candidate. To delay in arriving at a single choice until mid-primary season (or even later) is likely to mean that another faction's candidate will win the front-runner label.[31]

This rule is readily apparent in the multicandidate races of 1972, 1976, and 1980. In 1972 conservative and centrist Democrats failed to unite around a stop-McGovern candidate until after the Ohio primary. Then, Hubert Humphrey, too late, eliminated his centrist rivals and squared off against McGovern. By then McGovern had gained momentum, the active support of liberals, and a larger-than-proportionate share of delegates.

In 1976, liberal Democrats fell into the same trap. In Iowa's early caucuses Carter ran virtually alone from the center-right of the Party, while Udall, Harris, and Bayh all competed for liberal support. Carter "won" in Iowa with 28 percent of the first-round delegates and gained early attention. Udall, Harris, and Bayh split 29 percent of the delegates. Later, in New Hampshire's primary, Carter won 29 percent of the vote, while Udall, Harris, and Bayh split 51 percent. Again the media awarded Carter the winner's label, and Carter emerged as the front-runner. Only a few small journals tallied the vote by faction, not by individual candidates.

In 1980, the non-Reagan, centrist wing of the GOP failed to unite on a single challenger until it was too late to stop the former California governor. By fragmenting their votes and support among Bush, Baker, and Anderson throughout the early, key primaries, moderate and liberal Republicans lost whatever chance they may have had to block a Reagan nomination.

Pluralities, Majorities, and Victories

By applying these standards, the press judges how well the candidates have fared in the state primaries, caucuses, and conventions. In judging vote returns, the media also simplify the results. In most cases the media apportion headlines, photographs, and news stories disproportionately to the winner. Candidates who place second, third, or lower in a primary or caucus win far less favorable attention than their share of the vote. Unlike the two parties—who more closely approximate proportionality in allocating delegates— the media use a winner-take-all norm to distribute its rewards—front-page news stories, cover articles, and interviews. A candidate who wins only narrow pluralities in key primaries may still leap to the forefront of public attention. A front-runner usually emerges more quickly from news coverage than in the actual delegate count or vote totals.

This practice is clearly apparent in headlines, photographs, and news stories. In the first two Democratic primaries of 1976, for example, Carter won 29 percent of the New Hampshire vote, followed by Senator Jackson's 23-percent plurality win in Massachusetts. In both cases the bulk of news coverage simplified the returns, emphasizing first that Carter, then that Jackson had won. The narrowness of their victories was less readily apparent.

The same practice recurred on the GOP side in 1980. George Bush first captured media attention by winning a narrow plurality, with 31 percent in the Iowa caucuses; Bush then won heavy press attention. Later, Reagan won 50 percent of the New Hampshire vote and recaptured the media's designation as front-runner. The other hopefuls—Baker, Anderson, Dole, and Crane—all won a share of media coverage far smaller than their votes.

By focusing attention on the first-place candidate, the media simplify vote returns. As early as the first primaries, the media begin to concentrate attention on one or two candidates per party, ignoring most of the others. In 1976, for example, over two-thirds of all news stories that mentioned presidential qualities, issues, or events focused on Gerald Ford, Ronald Reagan, or Jimmy Carter. The other candidates were virtually ignored.[33]

Picking Key Primaries and Caucuses

In addition to picking winners and losers, editors and columnists also determine which state primaries and caucuses are newsworthy and which are not. A few states, most notably New Hampshire, receive enormous press coverage. Other states with many more convention delegates than New Hampshire receive very little media attention.[34]

Editors might use a variety of rules to decide which primaries and caucuses deserve extended coverage and which do not. Some criteria for allocating coverage might be completely subjective; a biased editor, for example, might decide that only states in which a favorite candidate runs well deserve much coverage. Other criteria may be less obviously biased but still peculiar to a given paper or station. Some editors, for example, might award additional coverage to primaries or caucuses in their own state or region.

In 1972, 1976, and 1980, the major nationally oriented media apparently followed several rules in allocating coverage. Most states won virtually no coverage of their primary or caucus results. A few states won extended coverage. More coverage usually went to the larger states. Front-page newspaper space was more likely to go to states whose primaries have historically been important in deciding nominations. When two candidates squared off against each other, or when one candidate faced a make-or-break test, then the press devoted more space to reporting and analyzing the outcome. Primary states usually received more attention than caucus–convention states. In 1980, states holding early contests received more coverage.

Table 3.1 lists the most covered state primaries and caucuses in 1972, 1976, and 1980. Appendix B further analyzes the procedures by which editors assign coverage.

Just as in determining winners and losers of state primaries and caucuses, the media appear to follow rational, even "democratic," principles. States with larger delegations and more diverse electorates

TABLE 3.1: States Winning the Most Coverage, 1972–80

1972	1976	1980
California	New Hampshire	New Hampshire
Wisconsin	Illinois	Pennsylvania
New Hampshire	Florida	Illinois
Florida	Michigan	New York
Illinois	Nebraska	Puerto Rico
Ohio	Pennsylvania	South Carolina
Michigan	Maryland	Massachusetts
Pennsylvania	North Carolina	Iowa
Nebraska	Indiana	Maine
Maryland	Massachusetts	Michigan

Note: States listed are those winning the most front-page, postprimary or -caucus coverage in the *New York Times* and the *Washington Post*. States are listed in descending order.

(most notably excepting New Hampshire) usually dominate news coverage. So do states holding presidential primaries rather than caucus states. By contrast, the media seldom award much coverage to states with little-attended caucuses, those with confusing ballot access rules, those with small or homogeneous electorates, or those whose primaries are not strenuously contested.

The Verdict

By deciphering and simplifying primary and caucus results, the media determine which candidates "win" and which "lose." By lavishing broadcast minutes and front-page column inches on some primaries and caucuses but not on others, the press determines which events capture public attention.

Combining these two terms produces the media's "verdict"— their judgment on how each candidate is faring. Expressed as an equation:

$$
\begin{array}{l}
\text{The relative success,} \\
\text{per candidate}
\end{array}
\times
\begin{array}{l}
\text{The amount of} \\
\text{coverage for each} \\
\text{state primary,} \\
\text{caucus, or} \\
\text{convention}
\end{array}
= \text{The Verdict}
$$

The verdict comprises two dimensions: direction and magnitude. First, the verdict for any candidate may be either positive or negative, depending on a candidate's success in primaries and caucuses. A candidate who "wins" a primary enjoys a positive verdict; a candidate who "loses" a primary or caucus suffers a negative verdict. Second, the verdict may be either small (if the primary or caucus wins very little attention) or large (if the primary or caucus results are well reported).

Combining these two dimensions, the media's verdict for any candidate may range from large and negative, to zero, to large and positive. If a primary is well-covered and a candidate runs well, that candidate's verdict will be large and positive. If a candidate fares poorly in a well-covered primary, then the verdict will be large and negative. If the primary or caucus wins no coverage at all, then the verdict will be zero, regardless of how well the candidate fared.

The verdict can be computed separately for each candidate in every primary, caucus, or state convention and for every newspaper, journal, radio station, or television station. As a shortcut, the verdict was computed for major Democratic and Republican candidates, from 1972 through 1980, for two major newspapers, the *New York Times*, and the *Washington Post*.[35] The number of front-page column inches devoted to reporting the outcome of each state's primary, caucus, or convention was measured. Each candidate's success was measured on a scale ranging from +2 (highly favorable) to a −2 (highly unfavorable). Multiplying the number of front-page column inches by the relative success score yielded a verdict for each candidate in each primary or caucus.

The verdict may be compared across candidates. The 1980 New Hampshire primary results, for instance, received 38 front-page column inches in the *Times*, and incumbent president Carter won a +1 for his performance, yielding Carter a verdict of +38 from the *Times*. By contrast, Senator Kennedy won a 0 (denoting neither success nor failure in the *Times'* view), for a verdict of 0. Governor Brown also received a verdict of 0.

The verdict may also be summed across primaries, caucuses, and state conventions. In the 1980 Iowa caucuses, Carter scored a verdict of +25 in the *Times*, with a +1 for relative success against 25 postcaucus front-page column inches. Then, in Maine's caucuses, Carter received a verdict of 0 (score of 0 against 19 inches). In New Hampshire, Carter won a verdict of +38, thereby totalling a cumulative verdict of +63 from the *Times*. By contrast, Senator Kennedy had a verdict of −25 at that time, and Governor Brown 0.

To compute an overall verdict for each candidate in each year, the separate verdicts of the *Times* and the *Post* were added together. The media's verdict for several contenders in 1980 is indicated in Figure 3.1. Figure 3.2 reports the verdict for Democrats and Republicans in 1976. Figure 3.3 indicates the media's verdict for the 1972 Democratic field.

A candidate's verdict is not always closely related to the actual number of votes received or delegates won. Although it has few delegates, New Hampshire is usually much better covered than Texas or California. By winning New Hampshire's primary, a candidate can gain a large, positive verdict. A similarly strong showing in Texas or California might bring more delegates but would capture less public attention. By running well in a handful of well-covered early primaries, a candidate can surge to the forefront, acquiring considerable momentum while still winning only a few delegates.

The verdict suggests what impression a politically attentive adult might gather from following campaign news. The media verdict helps to suggest why candidates who are judged poorly tend to drop out and why donors, activists, and public opinion polls follow the primaries. In 1972, for example, Hubert Humphrey was judged to

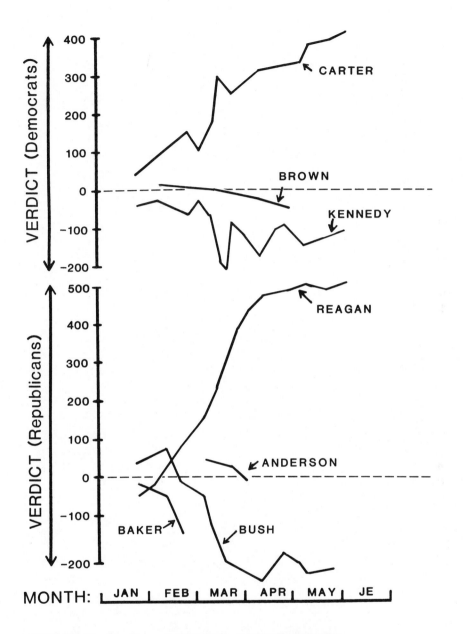

FIGURE 3.1 - MEDIA VERDICTS
FOR MAJOR CANDIDATES, 1980

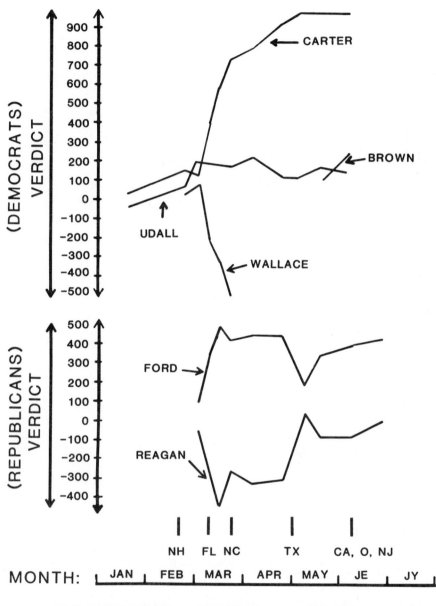

FIGURE 3.2 - MEDIA VERDICTS FOR
MAJOR CANDIDATES, 1976

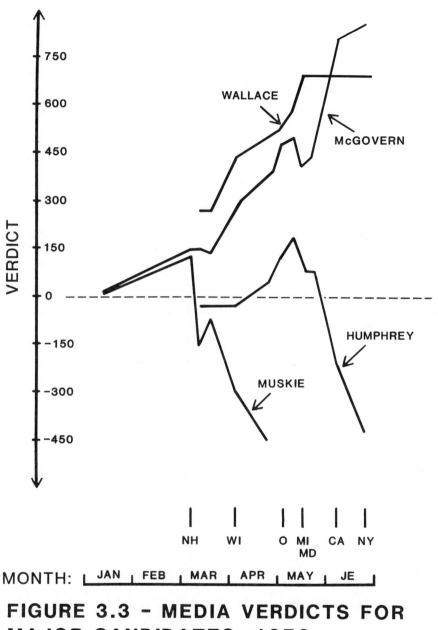

FIGURE 3.3 - MEDIA VERDICTS FOR MAJOR CANDIDATES, 1972

have run very poorly by the end of the primary season although he actually won more popular votes in the preference primaries than either McGovern or Wallace. Humphrey, however, fared poorly in the verdict (and in the delegate tallies), and he had difficulty winning credibility in his stop-McGovern convention efforts. In 1976, Ford's slight lead over Reagan in the early primaries was magnified by the verdict as were Carter's slight pluralities over Udall.

SUMMARY

During the 1970s, the media readjusted their preconvention coverage to meet the new demands of a lengthy, open competition. Now, the media focus on the candidates' personalities, on dramatic campaign incidents, and on the horse-race aspects of the campaign. These patterns may not provide much issue information for voters, but they do meet the media's own needs for simplicity, drama, reader interest, timeliness, and a superficial evenhandedness toward the candidates.

The media's coverage helps explain, in turn, the behavior of voters and of the candidates. Because voters are provided little issue information—but much information on campaign trivia and on the candidates' win–loss records—they are prone to follow primary voters. As Chapter Five explains, the verdict is often a good predictor of changes in public opinion polls as well as of the behavior of donors and volunteers.

The media's behavior also encourages the emergence of a nominee well before the convention. Candidates who fare poorly are likely to drop out after a few primaries or caucuses. The front-running candidate acquires so much favorable publicity—and so many delegates and funds—that his nomination is virtually assured. Together with new campaign laws and the public's behavior, the media encourage a race prone to high levels of momentum.

NOTES

1. "The New Campaign Journalism," *Columbia Journalism Review*, March/April 1976, p. 11. See also Timothy Crouse, *The Boys on the Bus* (New York: Random House, 1973), p. 37.
2. James David Barber, *The Pulse of Politics* (New York: W. W. Norton, 1980), pp. 8–9.

3. For recent examples see "The Art of Selling Politicians Like Soap on TV," *New York Times*, March 9, 1980, p. 1; "You Can't Be Elected with TV along, but You Can't Win without It Either," *National Journal*, March 1, 1980, pp. 344-348. For examples from 1976 see "GOP on TV," *The New Republic*, March 6, 1976, pp. 9-10; "Packaging Politicians," *The New Republic*, February 28, 1976, pp. 11-14; and "The Selling of a Candidate," *The New York Times Sunday Magazine*, March 28, 1976, p. 164.

4. "The Fruits of Agnewism," *Columbia Journalism Review*, January/February 1973, pp. 9-21.

5. Doris A. Graber, *Mass Media and American Politics* (Washington, D.C.: Congressional Quarterly Press, 1980), pp. 57-88; "Covering the Presidential Elections—Despite the Cost, the Press Is Ready," *National Journal*, February 2, 1980, pp. 192-197. For other descriptions of media coverage, see James Perry, *Us and Them: How the Press Covered the 1972 Election* (New York: Clarkson N. Potter, 1973); David Broder, "Political Reporters in Presidential Politics," in *Inside The System*, ed. Charles Peters and Timothy Adams (New York: Praeger, 1970); and Crouse, *Boys on the Bus*.

6. Even nonpolitical publications occasionally carry campaign-related news stories. In December of 1971, for instance, *Women's Wear Daily* carried a breezy article about Jane Muskie. Later the New Hampshire *Union Leader* reprinted a shorter version of the article, prompting her husband, Maine Senator Edmund Muskie, to respond angrily. The resulting "weeping incident" further damaged Muskie's chances in the New Hampshire Primary. See "William Loeb and the New Hampshire Primary: a Question of Ethics," *Columbia Journalism Review*, May/June 1972, pp. 14-15.

7. For a more complete discussion, see Crouse, *Boys on the Bus*. For an account from 1980, see "The Pack Aboard the Plane," *Washington Post*, January 21, 1980, p. 1.

8. Crouse, *Boys on The Bus*; Robert Meadow, "Cross Media Comparison of Coverage of the 1972 Presidential Campaign," *Journalism Quarterly* 50 (1973): 482-488; Doris Graber, "Press Coverage Patterns of Campaign News: The 1968 Presidential Race," *Journalism Quarterly* 48 (1971): 502-512; Dru Evarts and Guido Stempel, "Coverage of the 1972 Campaign by TV, news magazines, and major newspapers," *Journalism Quarterly* 51 (1974): 645-648; and Graber, *Mass Media*.

9. James Tankard Jr., "Public Opinion Polling by Newspapers in the Presidential Election Campaign of 1824," *Journalism Quarterly* 49 (1972): 361-365.

10. "1980 Brings More Pollsters Than Ever," New York *Times*, February 16, 1980, p. A10; "The Pollsters Gear Up for the 1980 Campaign," *National Journal*, December 15, 1979, pp. 2092-2095; "The Almanac of Political Pollsters: 1980," *Public Opinion*, February/March 1980, pp. 50-52; "The New Campaign Journalism"; and "Were Polls Overemphasized," *Columbia Journalism Review*, January/February 1973, pp. 29-30+.

11. "The Perils of Polling," *The New Republic*, January 17, 1976, pp. 13-16.

12. Straw polls were held in late 1979 or early 1980 for one or both parties in Iowa, Maine, Florida, Mississippi, California, and New York. "Straw Presidential Polls Gain Early Notice," *Congressional Quarterly Weekly Report*, November 3, 1979, p. 2473.

13. "1980 Brings More Pollsters," New York *Times*. For an example of a poll based on small numbers of respondents, see "The New Hampshire Out-

look," *Newsweek*, February 25, 1980, p. 31, and "New Hampshire: Giant Slalom," *Newsweek*, February 23, 1976, pp. 20–21.

14. Marcus Felson and Seymour Sudman, "The Accuracy of Presidential Preference Primary Polls," *Public Opinion Quarterly* 39 (1975): 232–237. For a longer discussion, see Chapter Five.

15. "The Pitfalls of Polling," *Columbia Journalism Review*, May/June 1972, pp. 28–34.

16. "Primary Nonsense," *Harpers*, January 1972, pp. 41–44.

17. "The State of Wallace," *Newsweek*, October 13, 1975, pp. 36–37; "Wallace's Last Hurrah?" *The New York Times Sunday Magazine*, January 11, 1976, p. 14+; and "Party of One," *Atlantic*, October 1975, p. 26+.

18. "The Truth about John Connally," *Texas Monthly*, November 1979, pp. 156–161+; "Connally: Coming on Tough," *The New York Times Sunday Magazine*, November 18, 1979, pp. 37–39+.

19. For examples of early coverage on Republican George Bush see "George Bush Comes On," *Newsweek*, December 3, 1979, pp. 66, 69; "Early Bird on the Wing," *Newsweek*, December 11, 1979; "Optimistic Bush 'Fired Up'; Feels Drive 'Is Moving'," *New York Times*, November 23, 1979; and "Bush On The Move," *The New York Times Magazine*, February 10, 1980, pp. 20–23+.

20. Graber, *Mass Media and American Politics*; Thomas Patterson, *The Mass Media Election* (New York: Praeger, 1980); Doris Graber and Young Yun Kim, "Media Coverage and Voter Learning During the Presidential Primary Season," (Paper delivered at the 1977 Annual Meeting of the Midwest Political Science Association, Chicago, Illinois, April 21–23, 1977). For an analysis of news coverage at the national conventions, see Cliff Zukin, "A Triumph of Form over Content: Television and the 1976 National Nominating Convention" (Paper delivered at the Annual Meeting of the Midwest Political Science Association, Chicago, April 1979).

21. See, for example, "Kennedy Resigned to Media Focus on Family instead of Issues," *Washington Post*, March 25, 1980, p. A3; and "Ambushed by the Media," *Village Voice*, December 31, 1979, p. 1.

22. One study of the 1972 preconvention season reported that network newscasts gave 72 percent of preconvention coverage to campaign "hoopla," 20 percent to candidate issue statements, and only 8 percent of the time to candidate qualifications. See Thomas Patterson and Robert McClure, *The Unseeing Eye: The Myth of Television Power in National Elections* (New York: Putnam, 1976), pp. 34–42. See also Graber, *Mass Media and American Politics*, pp. 169–189; Graber and Kim, "Media Coverage and Voter Learning," and Graber, "Press and TV as Opinion Resources in Presidential Campaigns," *Public Opinion Quarterly* 40 (1976): 285–304.

23. See also Donal Matthews, " 'Winnowing': The News Media and the 1976 Presidential Nomination," pp. 55–78, especially p. 64, and William Bicker, "Network Television News and the 1976 Presidential Primaries: A Look from the Networks' Side of the Camera," both in *Race for the Presidency*, James David Barber, ed. (Englewood Cliffs, N.J.: Prentice-Hall, 1978), pp. 79–110.

24. Theodore White, *The Making of the President 1972* (New York: Atheneum Publishers, 1973), pp. 80–83.

25. For the preprimary poll standings, see "Massachusetts Vote a Bonus to Reagan," *New York Times*, March 3, 1980, p. D9.
26. For the preprimary standings see "Campaign Notes," *Washington Post*, February 9, 1980, p. A3. For an analysis of the Maine caucus returns see "Carter Holding Slim Early Lead in Maine Voting," *Washington Post*, February 11, 1980, p. A1; and "Carter Takes Lead at Maine Caucuses," *New York Times*, February 10, 1980, p. A1.
27. For an example, see "Warm-Up for the Primaries," *New York Times*, December 18, 1979, p. B14.
28. "Reagan Winner in N.C. Primary; Carter Is Victor," *Washington Post*, March 24, 1976, p. A1.
29. This "rule" may be a carryover from primaries of the brokered convention era. Then, incumbents seldom lost primaries, and those who did tended to drop out—as did Truman in 1952 and Johnson in 1968.
30. "Bentsen May Quit; Carter and Harris Lead in Oklahoma," *New York Times*, February 9, 1976, p. 1.
31. Party activists, however, have not yet succeeded in finding any way to reduce the field of contenders before the primaries and caucuses. In 1976 and 1980, Democratic or Republican activists experimented with several strategies—including a series of debates among the candidates, straw votes at state conventions or fund-raising dinners, and endorsements by party clubs. None of these plans succeeded in focusing support around a single candidate.
32. "Shakeout," *The New Republic*, February 21, 1976, pp. 7-10.
33. Graber, *Mass Media and American Politics*, p. 183.
34. For other accounts, see "Captives of Melodrama," *The New York Times Sunday Magazine*, August 29, 1976, p. 6+; "TV's Newest Program: The 'Presidential Nominations Game'," *Public Opinion*, May/June 1978, pp. 41-46, and Michael Robinson, "The TV Primaries," *The Wilson Quarterly*, Spring 1977, pp. 80-83.
35. For a discussion of the preeminent position of these two papers in American journalism, see Carol Weiss, "What America's Leaders Read," *Public Opinion Quarterly* 38 (1974): 1-22.

4

THE CANDIDATES

WHAT MAKES A PRESIDENTIAL CANDIDATE?

Traditional Tests for the Nominee

During the brokered convention system, the regulars judged a would-be nominee both on his policy or patronage promises and on his political background. The regulars apparently used several rules of thumb to decide what candidates would be ideal nominees. Writing in 1959, Sydney Hyman identified nine such "tests" for a good candidate.[1] An ideal nominee should have some elective or appointive government experience. Governors from large, two-party states were often seen as the best nominees. A nominee should be acceptable to most of the nation's major economic groups, be a Northerner from English and Protestant stock, boast a happy family life, and hail from a small town.

True, not every nominee passed each test—in 1960, for example, John Kennedy was Irish and Catholic and hailed from Boston in normally Democratic Massachusetts. Yet under the brokered convention system the regulars usually chose a nominee who passed most of these nine standards.[2] Any aspirant who failed many of the tests was not seen as likely to carry the general election.

Time and the passing of the brokered convention system have not made Hyman's nine tests totally outmoded. A candidate who failed most of the nine tests would likely have difficulty winning a popular following. Yet the new nominations system requires a candidate to take a more active role than ever before in seeking the nomination. Two tests for the system of popular appeal are described below: the credentials test and the test of personal commitment. The first is a loose description of what a candidate should *be*; the second describes what a candidate should *do*. These two tests do not explain which candidate will actually win the nomination, but they do describe what a candidate should be and do to organize a credible bid.

The Credentials Test

To win the nominations, a candidate must, first of all, convince a core of donors and activists that his candidacy can be taken seriously. To do so, a hopeful normally needs to boast some government experience sufficient to give his candidacy an aura of legitimacy. While the credentials test is no longer a particularly rigorous one, a candidate without a record of high-level government service is still unlikely to organize a credible bid.

During the brokered convention system most serious contenders were drawn from the ranks of senators and governors. Interestingly, this pattern still holds in the system of popular appeal. About three-fifths of 41 serious contenders between 1972 and 1980 have been senators, former senators, governors, or ex-governors. About a fifth have been House members, and a few have been incumbents or have held some other government post.[3]

Senators are still well positioned to make a bid. Journalists, donors, and political activists are all likely to take their bids seriously. They serve a six-year term, allowing long periods for campaigning, and they can also claim a statewide success record in previous campaigns. Senators who choose to make bids will be aided by extensive staff, national visibility, and experience on multiple Senate committees.[4] Individual donors and interest group PACs may well decide that an influential senator is a good campaign investment, since even a senator who fails is likely to remain in the Senate. An attentive Senate member is well placed to develop or seize upon a major dramatic issue, thereby capturing national media attention and making the senator a welcome guest speaker at local party dinners and fund-raisers.

The list of presidential contenders drawn from the Senate is a lengthy one. Thirteen senators or former senators have announced a bid in recent years—just over a third of all the serious candidates.

They include Senators McGovern, Humphrey, Jackson, Muskie, and Hartke in 1972. In 1976, Senators Bentsen, Bayh, Church, and (again) Jackson made a bid; Senator Byrd also ran as a favorite son. In 1980, Senators Kennedy, Dole, and Baker ran. In addition, former Senators McCarthy and Harris also made bids, in 1972 and 1976, respectively.

Although U.S. representatives are not as well positioned as senators, several have recently made bids, including Representatives McCloskey, Ashbrook, Chisholm, and Mills in 1972, Udall in 1976, and Crane and Anderson in 1980. Representatives have several problems that a senator usually does not in organizing bids. They cannot usually claim to represent large, diverse constituencies; they are unlikely to win much early media attention or national exposure; and they are seldom much in demand as speakers at party dinners or other functions. A representative may feel uncomfortable about neglecting his district, even if it is a supposedly "safe" seat. A representative also sits on fewer committees and specializes more narrowly than a senator, supervises a smaller staff, and finds that House colleagues are less tolerant of headline seekers.

Conventional wisdom holds that presidential aspirants are seldom congressional insiders. In fact, however, several recent contenders have held high-ranking House or Senate posts. Senator Jackson chaired the Interior and Insular Affairs Committee, Senator Kennedy the Judiciary Committee, Senator Hartke the Veterans Affairs Committee, and Wilbur Mills the House Ways and Means Committee. Senator Baker made his bid while serving as Senate Minority Leader, and Senator Byrd ran as a favorite son while he was Senate Majority Whip. With the rising number of subcommittees and more permissive norms toward presidential ambitions, more top-ranking Senate and House members may organize future bids.[5]

Although present or past members of the Senate and House account for the largest bloc of recent aspirants, most members of Congress never make a bid. For many members of Congress, their commitment to a congressional career precludes making a race; some may also consider themselves too young or too old, hail from an unlikely state, or be up for reelection in the nominations year and unwilling to risk their seat. Others may suffer from a past scandal or from a personal liability, which causes them to eschew a race.

Governors and former governors are the next most frequent challengers, accounting for a quarter of all the bids since 1970. These include two bids apiece by Reagan, Wallace, Sanford, and

Brown, as well as a bid by Carter and Shapp. Their bids have come both from large two-party states (California, Pennsylvania) and from small, one-party states (Alabama, Georgia, North Carolina).

Governors or former governors face both liabilities and advantages in organizing a bid. On one hand, a sitting governor is usually bogged down in the home state with time-consuming and probably insoluble problems and harried by state legislators and bureaucrats. Most state capitols are far from the media centers in Washington and New York. Since law or political custom usually limit a governor to two terms, a governor's political base is seldom very secure.

On the other hand, governors are not wholly without some advantages. They may justifiably claim administrative experience. They now often travel abroad in search of trade ties and investments for their states; these travels may later establish a claim—however tenuous—to foreign policy knowledge. Local customs and a governor's personal popularity permitting, the state bureaucracy and local businesses may be tapped for early campaign funds and staff.[6] A governor may also avoid becoming closely tied to major, divisive national issues on which senators and House members must take positions.

First-term presidents and vice-presidents also enjoy a sizeable advantage. A president or vice-president receives massive amounts of media exposure and can choose from numerous speaking invitations. An incumbent can distribute or withhold some federal grants—or at least threaten to do so—and use White House invitations, State Department briefings, and presidential telephone calls to woo the press, local politicians, donors, and key volunteers. In 1980, for example, President Carter fully used the advantages of his incumbency to shore up his renomination bid.[7]

A few other candidates have also mounted serious bids in recent years, including several with records of high-level government service such as Shriver (a former ambassador), Connally (a former Treasury Secretary as well as a former governor), and Bush (former CIA chief and envoy to China). At least two present or former big-city mayors, such as Yorty (Los Angeles) and Lindsay (New York City), have also tried. So has an occasional interest group advocate, such as McCormick, an antiabortionist.

The necessity for early, active campaigning discourages some otherwise qualified aspirants. A Supreme Court justice would find that the Court precluded early organizing.[8] A cabinet officer may have wider contacts and a larger staff than a senator or representative, but political loyalties and the lack of an independent base would probably block his ambitions.[9] Finally, corporate executives and university presidents are sometimes touted, although in recent years none have succeeded in putting together a strong bid.[10]

The Test of Personal Commitment

The credentials test alone cannot adequately predict who will run for the party's nomination or who will actually win the nod. Many public figures boast an adequate set of credentials but nonetheless do not make a bid. In 1974, for example, at least half a dozen Democratic governors enjoyed as good a set of credentials as a then-obscure outgoing Georgia governor, Jimmy Carter. In 1978 and 1979, several high-ranking Democrats considered challenging President Carter, but only Senator Kennedy and Governor Brown actually did so.[11]

To a very large degree a serious presidential bid is now based on a candidate's willingness to undergo a grueling campaign schedule, to shelve family and personal comforts, and to foresake other career interests for a year or longer before the first primary. During this time a candidate must build a personal ad hoc organization of donors, staff, and volunteers.

Few potential candidates are willing to undertake this personal commitment and to invest so much of their own time and ego. That few have a stomach for nonstop campaigning is not necessarily surprising. Most candidates describe the demands of the nominations race as repetitious, physically exhausting, and emotionally numbing.

In 1980, just as in 1976 and 1972, many candidates fell short on the test of personal commitment. Some prospective candidates explored the possibility of running but dropped their efforts when the demands became clear. Others made a half-hearted or belated effort or counted on endorsements to carry them to the nomination. Some deluded themselves into thinking that prestige in Congress, the attention of the media, or favorable early poll ratings could substitute for their personal efforts. In the new system of personal appeal, though, there is no substitute for a candidate's complete personal dedication—some might even say obsession—to the nominations race.

THE IMPORTANCE OF EARLY PLANNING

Early planning by a candidate is more critical now than ever before. Only by building a campaign organization long in advance of the first caucus or primary can a candidate cope with the demands of an ever-longer preconvention season, the increasing numbers of primaries, and the inadequate spending limits. An early start allows a candidate to chart an adequate strategy, woo volunteers, and build a base of donors for the upcoming contests.

Deciding to Run

During the brokered convention system, a candidate might not declare his candidacy until just before the first primary or even until the primaries were already underway. In 1960, for example, John Kennedy announced his presidential bid on January 2, before the March 8 New Hampshire primary. In 1968 Hubert Humphrey declared his intention to run on April 27, 1968, after incumbent Lyndon Johnson had withdrawn earlier in the primary season. In a few instances a candidate even waited until the convention opened, as did Adlai Stevenson in 1952. Before the formal announcement, a candidate might undertake some traveling, political bargaining, and a limited amount of fund-raising, but full-scale campaigning long before the primaries was not common nor was it clearly necessary during the brokered convention system.

In the new nomination system, by contrast, a candidate's efforts at fund raising, organization building, and strategy planning more often begin long before the first primary or caucus. Some candidates now make their formal announcement very early; for 1980, Representative Crane did so even before the 1978 congressional elections. Others, such as Carter, Kennedy, and Reagan in 1980, waited until the end of 1979 to announce formally.[12] The timing of the formal announcement notwithstanding, candidates increasingly begin organizing as long as two or three years before the early state contests.

A candidate's early planning typically begins with informal discussions between the candidate and past supporters, staff, family, financial supporters, and advisers. If a candidate decides to "test the waters," then a more elaborate campaign effort becomes necessary. A senator might at first simply step up his traveling and speaking schedule with more visits to the key primary states. Or a hopeful might accept a post that would thrust him into the political spotlight and increase his visibility. In 1974, Georgia's outgoing governor Jimmy Carter accepted the post of Democratic National Committee campaign chair, a job that took Carter to numerous states in support of the party's state and local candidates.[13]

While some candidates try to campaign from their present

office, others now form a separate campaign organization even
before formally announcing their candidacy. Two new types of
early campaign organizations include exploratory committees and
candidate-centered political action committees (or PACs). An exploratory committee permits a candidate to explore making a bid without
committing himself to a formal announcement. A personal, candidate-
centered PAC allows a candidate to solicit money and spend it for
personal travels, donations to other candidates, and a staff. Although
forming a PAC may, in fact, be a tacit declaration of candidacy,
monies so spent need not count against the new spending limits for
the nomination season—a legal distinction that makes these PACs
increasingly attractive to potential candidates.[14] Candidate PACs
are discussed in the section on fund raising later in this chapter.

As candidates campaign earlier and earlier and as they form a
variety of preannouncement organizations, the distinction between
declared and potential candidates grows increasingly blurred. Little-
known candidates may declare a year or two before the first primaries
in hopes of winning publicity. Better-known candidates usually
wait longer before making a formal announcement, but they may
nonetheless begin to campaign through draft committees, exploratory
committees, and PACs. Whether the formal announcement comes
early or late, though, a candidate must begin organizing long before
the early contests to have any hope of carrying off the nomination.

Staffing the Campaign

A senator, representative, or governor who decides to make a
presidential bid will find that his own office staff cannot meet the
increasingly rigorous demands of the new nominations race. Instead,
a candidate must now build a separate campaign organization from
top to bottom. A full-blown campaign may, in time, grow to considerable size. During the 1980 primaries, the Carter–Mondale staff
reportedly numbered 354 paid staff members, with a monthly payroll
of $400,000. The Bush campaign staff included 248 workers at
over $100,000 monthly, while even the much smaller Anderson
campaign included 60 staffers at $50,000 monthly.[15]

Heading the campaign organization is the campaign manager,
often chosen for a long-term involvement with the candidate. For
1980, Carter chose Robert Strauss to head his renomination drive;
Strauss had earlier served as national chairman of the Democratic
Party and worked with Carter on trade and inflation policy and as a
special ambassador for Middle East negotiations. Kennedy chose

in-law Stephen Smith, and Reagan picked John Sears, his strategist from 1976.[16]

Below the top campaign slot, others will be recruited. A pollster is usually added early in the campaign.[17] Some pollsters serve as top campaign advisers, as did Gerald Rafshoon for Carter in 1976 and in 1980; in other campaigns, pollsters may be relegated to a technician's role, depending on the individual candidate's attitudes. In either case, few candidates would be temerarious enough to campaign very long without a pollster. In addition, one or more speech-writers turn out an increasing number of campaign addresses. Issues advisers, an advisory committee of prominent supporters, advance men, secretaries, a finance chair, a direct mail consultant, accountants, bookkeepers, and a press agent are all now familiar positions in the new presidential campaign organization.

The importance of reaching large audiences causes candidates to focus on media advisers. Ad consultants help design the radio, newspaper, and television stops that often consume a quarter or more of the candidate's budget. For 1980, for example, Senator Baker hired Bailey-Deardourff as his ad agency. Some media consultants help polish the candidate's personal image, as did Robert Goodman, a prominent political consultant, for George Bush.[18]

In the field, too, a candidate's organization will expand. Most staff workers spend their time in the key primary and caucus states, recruiting local volunteers and directing strategy. At the local base of the campaign organization are the volunteers who make up the numerical bulk of the organization. Volunteers contact their own friends and local political workers, compile lists of potential voters or caucus attenders, and organize meetings and rallies for the candidate. In most cases the volunteers begin by working out of their own homes during their spare time to organize phone banks and door-knocking efforts as well as other routine campaign tasks. Although few are paid and the media usually give them little attention, many volunteers eventually work full-time in the campaign before their state's primary or caucus.

An adequate organization is too extensive and too complex to be assembled quickly. A hopeful who waits too long will probably find that the leading consultants and the most enthusiastic and skilled volunteers are already working for a rival and that money cannot be raised quickly enough. In the new system of popular appeal, the importance of building a strong campaign organization long in advance of the first primary and caucus contests cannot be overstated.

Financing the Campaign

The Campaign Finance Cycle

Candidates raise and spend their funds in three distinct phases. The first of these includes the period before the candidate's first primary or caucus race. The second runs through the candidate's first few contests. For the handful of candidates who survive the early primaries, the last phase continues through the remainder of the nominations race.

In the first phase the candidate's major expenses include assembling a staff, traveling to solicit volunteers, opening national and state headquarters, and planning a media campaign. Expenses during this period vary greatly. A candidate who makes a low-key bid may spend less than a million dollars. If a candidate spends two years or longer at building a campaign, though, the costs may be much higher. By the start of 1980, Republican hopeful Connally had already reported spending over 8 million dollars in pursuing his bid, while Reagan reported laying out nearly 7 million dollars. Among the lowest spenders, on the other hand, were Dole, at about three-quarters of a million dollars, and Anderson, who reported spending just under half a million dollars. On the Democratic side, Carter reported expenditures of about 4.8 million dollars, while the late-starting Kennedy camp had already spent nearly 3.5 million dollars.[19]

Given the tighter new spending limits, some candidates have sought to avoid counting early expenses against their total limit by forming a personal candidate-oriented PAC. If a candidate has not officially declared or openly approved a campaign effort, expenses incurred through a PAC do not count against the FEC limits. A personal PAC allows a candidate to fund his own travels and to make donations to other party candidates, as well as to build up a campaign staff. Before the 1980 season, several candidates formed a personal PAC, including Reagan's Committee for the Republic, Bush's Fund for Limited Government, Dole's Campaign America, and Connally's Citizen's Forum.

Some of the PACs may raise and spend a considerable amount of money. In 1978, the Reagan effort spent about 4.5 million dollars, while the Connally PAC spent 720,000 dollars.[20] While the PACs did make some contributions to other party-endorsed candidates, most of the money spent went directly for the candidate's own travel expenses and for staff salaries and operating expenses.

The second phase of a candidate's fund-raising and -spending cycle comes during the first few primary and caucus efforts. Since most candidates drop out after their initial races, this period, in reality, also marks the end for most candidacies. During this phase most candidates spend as much as possible, right up to the state-by-state spending ceilings. In doing so, they exhaust their campaign treasuries, leaving their coffers bare just as most of the primaries loom ahead.

Candidates spend freely in the first primaries for several reasons. The outcome of the early primary and caucus contests is often uncertain, the field of contenders large, voter attitudes unstable, and the effect of a poor early showing ruinous. Fortunately for most candidates, the early races tend to be mostly in small states with the lowest spending limits. In 1980, the spending ceilings for the first major contests were $489,882 in Iowa, $294,400 in Maine, New Hampshire, and Vermont, and $1,001,667 in Massachusetts. By contrast, the spending ceilings for the largest states were $3,037,737 and $2,030,182 in the New York and Pennsylvania mid-season primaries and $3,880,192 for California's season-end primary.[21]

If a candidate survives the first handful of primaries and caucuses —and only a few do—then the third phase continues through the remaining state contests and through the national convention. At this point few candidates can continue a race without having enjoyed some successes in the early contests. Because most campaigns rely heavily on individual donations (and the accompanying federal matching funds), continuing the campaign depends on attracting a continued flow of donations throughout the primary season. If a candidate falters in the early races, though, mass mailings and other receipts will soon dry up. By contrast, if a candidate has been judged favorably by the media, then donors will be encouraged to continue giving, multiplying the candidate's available funds.

The impact of a favorable early media verdict on fund-raising success was apparent in 1980 just as in earlier years. Illinois Republican Congressman John Anderson's campaign provides a good illustration. In 1980, before his strong early showings in the Vermont and Massachusetts primaries, Anderson had collected only $150,000 from individual donors. Afterwards his fund raising soared: in February Anderson took in $426,000 and in March over $2 million.[22] Anderson's experiences resembled that of many other candidates in 1972, 1976, and 1980. After the early primaries, campaign money follows the winners.

Sources of Campaign Funds

Candidates rely more heavily on individual donations than on any other sources. Individual donations outrank all other revenue sources and account for well over nine-tenths of all the monies collected, aside from government matching funds. Donations from corporate, labor, or special interest group PACs (which may range up to $5000 in amount) account for less than a tenth of the funds recently raised by would-be nominees.[23]

Early campaign funds usually come from a candidate's previous backers, from sympathetic individuals and groups, and from home-state or home-region donors. For his 1976 race, for example, Carter began in August of 1974 with $40,000 from a small number of Georgia backers.[24] In making his 1980 bid, Connally attracted much of his early money from the Texas banking, oil, real estate, and legal interests, just as Texas Senator Bentsen had four years earlier.

While these early, often locally collected funds provide "seed" money, they are not sufficient to finance even a modest campaign. Most candidates expand on this base through fund-raising committees and through direct mail appeals to a larger audience of small donors. The first mailings of a direct mail effort may do no more than break-even financially, but donors who do respond are added to a list to be recontacted later. In 1980, an early mailing for Senator Kennedy reportedly sent out as many as a million pieces, receiving returns from about 15,000 persons. Direct mail experts such as Morris Dees (for McGovern in 1972, Carter in 1976, and Kennedy in 1980) or Richard Viguerie (Wallace in 1976, Crane and Connally in 1980) advise the candidates and target lists of potential donors.

New limits on the size of individual donations put pressure on the candidates to find ever more diverse sources of campaign donations to replace the "fat cats" of earlier years. Televised fund-raising appeals or newspaper or magazine ads reach selected audiences. A telethon may prove a useful way to tap an audience, particularly for the well-known candidates or those with an appeal to a specific group. In 1976, Jimmy Carter conducted a five-hour Georgia telethon with several celebrities, raising a reported $325,000. In 1980, Connally, too, turned to a nationwide telethon and reported raising $1.5 million in gifts or pledges.[25]

Fund-raising dinners and receptions tap wealthier donors—those who can contribute $100, $500, or $1000. These functions, which usually feature the candidate or top campaign figures, may raise large sums of money quickly and bolster the campaign treasury. In 1980, the Carter campaign raised $500,000 on one midwestern tour by campaign manager Robert Strauss and over a million dollars on a California swing by Mrs. Carter.[26] Other candidates, too, held meet-the-candidate fund-raisers, often adding prominent business figures, state and local politicos, and celebrities as sponsors or entertainment.

Campaign fund-raisers have devised a variety of other techniques. Concerts by performers such as Jane Fonda, Helen Reddy, Linda Ronstadt, Chicago, and the Eagles raised large sums for California Governor Brown. In 1980, the Kennedy campaign solicited artwork by prominent artists such as Andy Warhol, Robert Rauschenberg, and Lowell Nesbitt. When sold, these works provided a sizeable amount for the hard-pressed Kennedy campaign at a time when Kennedy's appeal to individual donors had slackened.[27] Since the FEC does not count the artist's or performer's time and talent against the $1000 donation limits, these fund-raising practices are likely to become increasingly common in future campaigns.

Choosing Issues

During their preprimary planning, the candidates decide which issues or themes to stress in their speeches and media advertising. In most cases a candidate singles out just one or two key issues or themes to emphasize. Since relatively few voters apparently know much about the candidates before the nominations season begins, choosing issues is a critical campaign decision. And, aside from the mechanics of campaigning, a candidate's key campaign theme may be about all that most voters ever learn about that candidate.

Most candidates choose a theme tied to their past public record. They do so for several reasons: personal commitment, interest group ties, and political experience with that issue. In 1976, for example, Senator Jackson reemphasized his commitment to Israel and his hard-line views on national defense, issues developed during his Senate career. Few candidates can avoid running on their political record, even if it involves issues that are not currently helpful to their national campaign. In 1976, for example, Texas Senator Bentsen could not avoid explaining his stands on gas and oil deregulation, although that issue was unlikely to help his candidacy.

A few candidates enjoy greater leeway in choosing a campaign focus than the others. A little-known candidate without a visible national political profile is largely unencumbered by past controversies. In 1974, for example, Carter was still largely unknown even to the attentive public and, as a result, had an unusual leeway in setting the tone of his campaign.

Most candidates focus only on one or two key issues or themes, even if they endorse dozens of policy papers. Their appeals need not be wholly issue-oriented. Many candidates stress personal qualities and images as much as their issue positions. Precisely worded policy promises are usually avoided. In 1976, for example, both Carter and Ford stressed the importance of restoring trust and confidence in government and of running an "open" administration. In that year, Bayh emphasized his competence as a politician. Udall stressed both his environmental record and his endorsements by prominent Americans such as Archibald Cox, a former Watergate prosecutor.

Four years later, the same pattern reappeared. Bush stressed his integrity and his experience in government ("a president we won't have to train"), Connally his leadership traits ("leadership for America"), and Anderson his candidly expressed political views ("the Anderson difference"). Howard Baker focused on his trust-worthiness, Carter on his record as a peacemaker and on his personal honesty, and Kennedy on his claims to legislative skills and leadership.

The candidates' focus on personal images at the expense of issues is readily apparent in their campaign advertising. Most candidates work hard at developing a warm personal image. For the candidates this may be a rational choice, since the media often focus on the candidates' personal traits at the expense of issues coverage and since voters and caucus-goers apparently evaluate candidates as much on their personal qualitites as on their issue promises. The candidates' own focus on personal traits, in turn, reinforces the behavior of the media and of the voters.

Choosing a campaign theme or issue appeal is a difficult decision and one that cannot be made with much certainty of success. Sometimes political events change rapidly, as in 1980 when foreign crises unexpectedly erupted in Iran and Afghanistan just before the primary season. Or a candidate and campaign advisers may err in their estimate of the public's interest in an issue. Candidates frequently fail to develop an appeal that attracts a broad spectrum of volunteers or voters. In 1976, for example, Lloyd Bentsen emphasized his abilities as manager but found that that theme excited few voters. In 1980, John Connally's early image as a hard-nosed bargainer lacked much appeal outside high-level corporate and financial circles.

A candidate may also fail to articulate issues even if he does have some with wide potential appeal. In 1980, Senator Kennedy's late-starting and poorly organized bid failed, among other ways, to articulate clearly the differences between himself and President Carter. Kennedy did not clearly settle on any potentially popular issues, such as health care or the cost of fuel, until the media had already focused on his personal and family problems, on foreign crises, and on his own inept campaign performance. A candidate who does not provide a clear focus for his own campaign will find that the media or an adversary will provide one—inevitably to his own disadvantage.

Just as most candidates are not free to disregard their past political records, neither are they free to switch themes very quickly. Once a dominant theme has been chosen, the candidate's campaign literature, advertising, and speeches tie him to that choice. Openly disavowing a key campaign theme would be difficult, if not politically impossible, for most candidates. Instead, a candidate may downplay an issue or begin to stress new themes as the campaign wears on, thereby enlarging on earlier appeals and attracting new groups of voters. In early 1976, Carter stressed honesty, openness in government, and government reorganization, but by the midprimary season he increasingly emphasized more traditional Democratic themes of jobs, housing, and social services.

Planning Strategy

Early in the organizing stages, a candidate should also settle on how much staff effort, campaign money, and personal time to allocate to each state primary and caucus. Strategic planning presents considerable problems for most of the candidates, since the basic decisions must be made when a candidate's own resources are usually very limited and when the plans of other candidates are still unclear. At the same time, once a basic strategy plan has been fixed, it is extremely wasteful to scrap it in favor of another approach. If an early devised campaign strategy is overhauled during the primaries and caucuses, scarce campaign resources, such as the staff's organizing time, funds, volunteer efforts, and the candidate's own time, will be lost.

Candidate strategies in recent two-candidate races can be described more easily than can strategies in multicandidate contests. In a two-candidate race, both candidates aim to win a majority of the delegates, and both usually compete in almost all the states. One study of the 1976 Ford–Reagan race found that both candidates apparently used similar decision rules to assign priorities to the primaries and caucuses.[28] Both Ford and Reagan invested heavier efforts in the early primaries and caucuses, aiming not only to win delegates but also to gain favorable media verdict for the remaining contests. Both gave more attention to primaries than to caucus-convention states, and both targeted the larger states with the biggest blocs of delegates. If several primaries were held on the same day, both Ford and Reagan strove to win at least one primary. Both spent more time in states where the outcome was expected to be close. Delegate-allocation rules also affected their strategies; Ford's expected loss in the California winner-take-all primary, for example, caused him to avoid that primary although its large delegate bloc would otherwise have merited more attention.

While aspirants in two-candidate races appear to follow these principles, rational planning is not the only determinant of the candidates' state-by-state strategies. The scarcity of campaign resources, limited information about voter attitudes, hunches about an opponent's intentions, the press of deadlines, and simple mistakes also affect strategy choices. In 1976, for instance, the Reagan camp decided to write off the New York, New Jersey, and Pennsylvania primaries, apparently on the (mistaken) assumption that officially uncommitted delegates might later support Reagan. The pressure of filing deadlines and of tight campaign funds was also a factor in that ultimately costly decision.[29] Four years later, Senator Kennedy's poor early showings and his dwindling campaign funds led his managers to write off almost all the South and much of the Midwest. While the decision may have been a necessary one given Kennedy's plight, the result was to concede so many delegates that Kennedy's candidacy became, at best, a long shot.

In multicandidate races the candidates' strategies vary more widely and cannot be described so simply. Some candidates in recent years have focused their time and resources on the early primaries and caucuses, hoping for a strong showing that would provide momentum for the later contests. Other candidates, though, apparently assumed that the race would not produce an early front-runner and chose another strategy. Some have chosen to enter only a handful of states. In 1976, Senator Jackson focused on the large Northern industrial states with their large delegate blocs, writing off several early contests (in Iowa and New Hampshire) as well as much of the South and Midwest. In that year, Texas Senator Bentsen targeted several Southern states in a regional strategy.

Other candidates skipped the early primaries and caucuses in favor of the midseason or late contests. In 1976, California Governor Brown and Idaho Senator Church followed this strategy, evidently expecting that the early contests would produce a standoff. Still other candidates have ignored the primaries altogether, depending on a deadlocked convention or on a "draft" movement. In 1976, Minnesota Senator and former vice-president Humphrey avoided the primaries, although he hinted that he would be available if the party desired to draft him and several times edged toward an active candidacy. Four years later, former president Ford also avoided organizing an active campaign; Ford waited until after the early 1980 primaries to encourage a draft-Ford effort, which ultimately failed to spark much enthusiasm in GOP ranks.

Admittedly, even the best-laid strategies may fail in the execution. Much also depends on the media's interpretation of primary and caucus returns, voter reactions and turnout, the size of the field and the fragmentation of the vote, the strategies of other hopefuls, as well as the turn of unexpected events. While there is no certain strategy guaranteed to win the nomination, some strategies appear to be more promising than others. An optimal strategy for either a two-candidate or a multicandidate race concentrates the candidate's resources on the initial round of primaries and caucuses. A candidacy that fares well there will benefit from the media's naming of an early front-runner and from the public's tendency to follow the media's early verdict. After the early contests, the optimal strategy concentrates a candidate's resources on key state primaries to provide frequent victories and to eliminate rivals. Media exposure and a winner's tug on primary voters and caucus-goers must largely suffice to carry the nonpriority states. The well-advised candidate will write off only a handful of states where the prospects are poor and where delegate-allocation rules do not ensure a share of the delegates.

In its basic outline this strategy was pioneered by George McGovern in 1972 then repeated by Jimmy Carter in 1976. Both McGovern and Carter targeted their limited resources into the key early states, then relied on momentum to carry them through the rest of the mid- and late-season primaries. Both McGovern and Carter wrote off only a few states where their prospects were worst or where favorite sons might later deliver the delegates anyway. Both McGovern and Carter enjoyed an early favorable media verdict out of proportion to the demonstrated vote-getting strength.

By 1980, most of the candidates seemed to understand the utility of this strategy, although they made other serious planning flaws. In the crowded GOP field and in the Democratic contest of 1980, most (but not all) candidates focused their personal efforts and resources on the early caucuses and primaries instead of waiting for the later contests, planning a one-region strategy, or waiting for a "draft" movement.

The Frequency of Flawed Planning

One might expect that most candidates would recognize the new campaign realities in the system of popular appeal. A review of the several nominations campaigns from 1972 through 1980, however, shows that the major candidates have repeatedly made major errors in planning their strategies.

The most frequent error is beginning the campaign too late. Waiting too long is an error that inevitably leads to myriad other problems. A candidate who begins full-scale organizing and campaigning only a few months before the first caucuses and primaries will probably find that the best workers and consultants are already committed, that a grass-roots organization cannot be built in very many states, and that advertising, polling, and fund raising cannot be carried out efficiently under such hurried circumstances. A candidate who delays organizing will also find it difficult, if not altogether impossible, to meet all the state filing deadlines and to satisfy the complicated state-by-state ballot access and petition-gathering requirements. As a result, a late-starting candidate will probably fail to win a spot on several state primary ballots, forfeiting a chance at those delegates.

The failure to begin all-out campaigning sufficiently early occurred in the 1980 nominations race just as in earlier years. Many candidates evidently misunderstood the need for early grass-roots organizing and delayed their efforts until a few months before the Iowa and New Hampshire contests. Waiting too long to begin full-scale planning seems to be especially common among members of Congress. In 1980, several senators, including Baker, Dole, and Kennedy, attended to their Senate duties at the expense of full-scale campaign organizing, as did House member Anderson. Predictably, each suffered as a result. By trying to build a campaign too late, each was forced to spend cash instead of relying on volunteers, and each failed to build up strong local organizations. Each failed to recruit the best-placed local political talent for his slates or—in Anderson's case—failed to qualify for the ballot in several critical states.

Other strategic flaws, too, were apparent in 1980. Several candidates continued to shift their campaign plans and reshuffle their staff right up to and during the first primaries. Senator Baker and former Treasury Secretary Connally, for example, never appear to have settled on or stuck to a clear plan for targeting the state races.

Some candidates also targeted highly unlikely states. Connally ignored the early Iowa caucus and the New England primaries, committing only enough money and last-minute campaigning time to be counted among the losers. Instead, he concentrated his resources on South Carolina's GOP primary, a theretofore little-noticed contest that fell after the first round of better-covered contests. Senator Kennedy focused attention on the Iowa caucuses as the first critical contest with Carter; by doing so, Kennedy focused attention on a state where his forces were poorly prepared and where success was far less likely than in his native New England.

Several candidates failed to control their campaign costs, thereby complicating their cash-flow problems. The Kennedy, Connally, and Reagan campaigns offer clear examples of poorly controlled spending. Some candidates also failed to develop a clear issue appeal or a personal appeal. Brown, Baker, Dole, and Kennedy never appeared to develop a clear-cut campaign image or else changed their campaign pitch during the nominations season itself.

Flawed campaign practices may be traced to several causes. Some candidates may not understand the need for full-scale organizing several years before the first primary. Political duties may prevent a senator, governor, or representative from giving full time to building a campaign organization. The tiring, unpleasant, and routine campaign chores necessary to build a strong campaign may cause some candidates to delay their efforts. Or, some candidates may be unwilling (or unable) to make a firm commitment to run until after the midterm election or until even later.[30]

Flawed planning may also result for other reasons. The presidential nominations race is a unique contest, quite unlike a typical one-state senatorial or gubernatorial race. Unlike a state primary race, the presidential nominations contest is on a nationwide scale, continues over several months of nearly continuous primaries and caucuses, and must be conducted under far tighter fund-raising and -spending rules. As a result, a candidate who simply attempts to replicate his last successful statewide campaign, writ larger, is likely to find that game plan to be inadequate. In 1980, for example, Connally's campaign fixed upon a free-spending, media-focused approach. While that approach is typical of successful Texas campaigns, its high costs are not well adapted to the new nominations system.

Other candidates simply mimic an earlier successful nominations campaign from the brokered convention system. In 1972, Senator Muskie relied on the endorsements of top party leaders instead of grass-roots organizing. Muskie's efforts resembled the successful race of Vice-President Humphrey in 1968. Between 1968 and 1972, however, the nominations rules had changed drastically, and Muskie failed to replicate Humphrey's earlier success. In 1980, Senator Kennedy's long-delayed start may have been influenced by his two brothers' similarly late starts in 1960 and 1968.

The frequency of badly flawed campaign planning may also be due, in part, to the rapidly changing rules of the race. The McGovern–Fraser reform rules were announced only shortly before many candidates began their planning for 1972. The new campaign finance laws were first implemented in 1976, and untimely delays in matching fund payments that year obscured their effect. Later, the inflationary spiral in campaign costs outpaced the increases in the spending limits, in effect reducing the spending ceiling. Between 1968 and 1980, the number of primaries nearly doubled, and states continued to change their primary dates and delegate-allocation rules with a rapidity that might well bewilder even the most observant candidate or campaign manager. It is not, therefore, especially surprising that many of the candidates failed to adjust to the new campaign rules and realities. It may well take several more nominations contests—even under reasonably stable rules—before the candidates and their managers adjust campaign practices to meet the new system's demands.

CANDIDATE BEHAVIOR DURING THE PRIMARIES

The Early Contests

Candidates begin the primary–caucus season under widely differing circumstances. Some hopefuls stand much higher in the polls than others. Some have substantial treasuries and many volunteers, while others are running only a bare-bones campaign. Some candidates have organized in many of the states while others have targeted all their resources into the first few contests.

Most candidates commit the bulk of their campaign resources to their first contests. As a result, during the first half dozen (or even fewer) primaries and caucuses, most candidates completely or nearly exhaust their campaign treasury, their staffs' planning, most of their volunteers, and their own personal energies. Just ahead, though, loom more than two dozen primaries and even more state caucuses and conventions.

Momentum

Consider, now, the position of the early starting candidates. By this time the media have evaluated the early caucuses and primaries according to the rules already described in Chapter Three. In most instances the media will already have projected an early front-runner and will have begun to dwell on the other candidates' misfortunes. The public, in turn, will also begin to respond to the media's judgment. The national polls may not yet show much movement, but spot polls in the upcoming primary states will begin to show serious erosion from the losers. Individual donors and PACs will begin giving more generously to the projected front-runner, and, as they do, federal matching funds will swell.

For the candidate who runs well in the early contests, campaign resources will grow to meet the demands of the upcoming primaries and caucuses. Donors and volunteers will be attracted to a winner. Both state and national polls should show an upswing. Governors, members of Congress, and mayors will become more eager to endorse the likely party nominee. The media will grow more complimentary, endowing the winner with a superficially attractive image; magazine covers, network news broadcasts, and front-page stories will convey the front-runner's smiling visage.

For a candidate who is judged poorly by the press, though, the omens are gloomy. Polls will show an erosion of public support as the candidate's less-committed supporters move toward the media-designated front-runner. New donors and volunteers will be hard to attract. The media will grow less attentive and less complimentary. The candidate's staff will grow uneasy, and resignations are likely to follow. Crowds will grow small and discouraging, phone banks may be unmanned and canvassing unfinished. The candidate's personal energies and those of his family and advisers are likely to be drained. The increasing scarcity of resources will soon force the poorly judged candidate to write off more and more state contests to conserve dwindling campaign funds, thereby forfeiting more and more delegates. As this happens, the spiral of failure will worsen, causing even further erosion in the campaign. Most losing candidates are unwilling to continue their race very long under these adverse conditions and most soon drop out.

The Multicandidate Race

The dynamics of the new nomination system soon begin to take their toll on the field of contenders, especially in a multicandidate race. The media-designated front-runner will emerge very early and will assume an increasingly commanding position. The disparity in campaign resources will grow as the other candidates are unable to replenish their treasures or their supply of volunteers. While this basic pattern may be obscured by late-entering challengers or by scattered upsets during the later state primaries and caucuses, the lack of equilibrium in the candidates' campaign resources will almost inevitably become more and more pronounced.

In each of the multicandidate races of the last decade, we find the same pattern: the nominee has emerged early in the contest and never lost the early advantage. In the 1980 Republican race, Reagan's strong early primary showings left his opponents in such poor shape that only Bush stayed in the race after the Wisconsin contest. By then Bush's challenge was limited to only a handful of states. In the 1976 Democratic race, the crowded early field was also quickly reduced. Most of the contenders dropped out early in the season, and by the middle primaries Carter clearly dominated the contest. In 1972, a similar pattern appeared: McGovern surged very early, and most of the other candidates dropped out after a half-dozen or even fewer efforts. McGovern's major surviving opponent, Humphrey, was so badly strapped for volunteers and campaign funds that he was unable to compete effectively in the remaining primaries.[31]

The emergence of the nominee early in the competition does not necessarily mean that the front-runner will have the race wholly to himself. In each of the three races just described, the front-runner lost some primaries to the surviving rivals or to late-entering candidates. Nor could the front-runner prevent his opponents from organizing "stop" movements, rules or credentials challenges, or last-minute dark-horse challenges at the national party convention. Yet in each multicandidate race the front-runner made the same early surge and never lost the advantage.

The Two-Candidate Race

Momentum also plays a part in two-candidate races although its effects are not so pronounced. While the front-runner also enjoys a sizeable advantage in a two-candidate race, the weaker candidate need not necessarily be forced from the race or even weakened as much as in a multicandidate race.

Momentum is not as strong a factor in two-candidate as in multicandidate races for at least four reasons. First, both candidates in a two-candidate standoff are likely to be better known at the onset. As a result, their respective poll strength and ability to woo volunteers and donors are less subject to change even if they suffer a few early setbacks or win some victories. In both the recent two-candidate races, neither the 1976 Ford–Reagan nor the 1980 Carter–Kennedy polls varied as widely as did the polls in multicandidate contests.

Second, both the Democrats and the Republicans are now sufficiently bifurcated, especially along regional lines, that even the weaker candidate can still reasonably hope for periodic primary victories. By concentrating his resources on the most favorable states and writing off the most unfavorable ones, the weaker candidate can almost certainly produce occasional upsets, thereby stalling (if not overcoming) the front-runner's momentum. Third, new delegate allocation rules now approximate proportional representation; as a result, both candidates can expect to win sizeable numbers of delegates. Fourth and finally, either candidate may feel enough responsibility to a personal constituency or cause to continue the race well past the point at which his nomination is a realistic prospect. The weaker candidate might desire to use his bloc of delegates and his personal influence to influence the party's platform or to force concessions on the vice-presidency.

A review of recent two-candidate races demonstrates that momentum is not as great a factor there as in multicandidate races. In 1976, Ford won several early primaries, but Reagan's strength in the South and the West kept Reagan in close contention throughout the contest. Neither Ford's nor Reagan's campaigns ever collapsed, nor were either Ford or Reagan ever able to pull far ahead in the delegate count. The 1980 Kennedy–Carter showdown likewise produced an early advantage for Carter, but by writing off many states and by concentrating his resources on a few primaries, Kennedy managed to win a number of primaries and stay in the race. Both Kennedy and Reagan continued their challenge until the national party convention.

Dropping out or Staying in the Race

Throughout the nominations race, each candidate must constantly reassess whether to drop out or to remain in the race. Sometimes these decisions might appear to result from idiosyncratic, personal motives—some candidates, it might seem, are simply more dedicated and tenacious than others. Yet, on the whole, the candidates' decisions to drop out or to remain in the race can be described with notable precision.

The decision to drop out or to stay in the race depends on two factors: first, each candidate's public opinion poll standings, and second, each candidate's media verdict. Initially weak candidates (those with an initial poll rating of under 10 or 15 percent) usually need suffer but a small negative verdict in their first few efforts before they drop out of the race. A candidate who is relatively strong in the early polls (say, at 15 or 20 percent or higher), or a candidate who rises to that level early in the primary season, will be likely to remain in the race almost indefinitely regardless of his media verdict. Any candidate, of course, who wins a favorable media verdict will almost certainly continue the race regardless of his initial poll standings.

Since all but a handful of aspirants begin with a low poll rating, little national name recognition, and scanty campaign resources, an early and unfavorable media verdict is likely to finish them off. And, as Chapter Three has suggested, the media will inevitably give most of the candidates the early unfavorable verdict and this will, in effect, kill their chances. As a result, most of the candidates soon drop out of the race and the size of the field of contenders rapidly narrows.

Figure 3.1 to 3.3, earlier, illustrate this general pattern. Most candidates in a multicandidate field drop out after only a few efforts. The only candidates who continued in the race for very long were those who had been very strong initially or those who had won a favorable media verdict. As a result, the field usually quickly narrowed to two candidates, with one contender enjoying a sizeable (and increasing) advantage over the other.

Empirically, the media's verdict and the candidates' own poll standings are excellent predictors of the decision to remain in the race or to drop out. For 32 major candidates who ran in one or more caucuses or primaries between 1972 and 1980, the decision to remain in the race or to drop out was accurately predicted by these two indicators in 131 of 152 instances—an 86 percent accuracy level. These data are further described in Appendix C.

The Conventions

The last primary or state convention does not necessarily mark off the end of the nominations struggle. Some candidates may still be unwilling to concede to the front-runner without a final fight. In other cases, especially in multicandidate races, the front-runner may not have quite the required delegate margin to ensure the nomination and will need to win over delegates from the ranks of uncommitted, favorite-son, and now-failed blocs. In 1972, for example. McGovern counted only 1293 of 1509 delegates needed after the last round of state primaries and conventions.[32] In 1976, Carter could depend on only 1091 of the 1505 necessary delegate votes immediately after the last round of state primaries.[33] Although the leading candidate is unlikely to be denied the nod, the nominations struggle frequently drags on up to or even through the convention itself.

At this stage, the front-runner will need to ensure his nomination by wooing the uncommitted delegates and by calling for unity within the party. By now, the front-runner's resources should be enormously stronger than those of his remaining rivals, and, barring some disaster, he should prevail. His active rivals have been publicly defeated in the primaries, and, at least in a multicandidate race, most have formally dropped out, making it difficult for them to resurrect their candidacies. The media will already have focused attention on the front-runner, and as a result the polls should show a sizeable lead. With the vice-presidential post and the party platform as leverage, the front-runner should be able to win over many of the holdouts, isolating the hard-core opposition. Now in an undeniably stronger position, the front-runner may well argue that denying him the nomination would wreck the party's chances in the upcoming election. Not surprisingly, no front-runner has yet failed to consolidate his nomination.

Although their chances of stopping the front-runner are, at best, remote, the remaining candidates need not concede defeat. Since the national party conventions follow the last primaries by several weeks, the opponents of the apparent nominee have ample time to plan a rules fight, a dark-horse candidacy, a draft movement, or a "stop" (the front-runner) effort. Since these maneuvers provide drama and excitement as well as an air of uncertainty, the media will probably provide wide coverage to these efforts, futile as they are likely to be. In 1972, conservatives, labor supporters, and disgruntled party regulars mounted a stop-McGovern movement, seeking to reallocate the California winner-take-all delegation. In 1976, stop-Carter forces rallied briefly, but their movement collapsed even before the convention opened. Again in 1980, stop-Carter and pro-Kennedy forces sought to undo a new party rule binding delegates to their previously declared candidate. In the same year, the anti-Carter forces floated several names that anti-Carter delegates might rally at an "open" convention, including Vice-President Mondale, Secretary of State Muskie, New York Senator Patrick Moynihan, New York Governor Hugh Carey, and Washington Senator Jackson.

None of these last-minute moves has yet succeeded, and, barring bizarre circumstances, none is likely to. Unlike the brokered convention system usually there is no longer a likely but untried candidate to rally around to stop the front-runner, and by the time of the convention most of the active opponents will already have failed in the primaries and been forced from the race. Since the party regulars have now lost their control of blocs of delegates, it is increasingly difficult for anyone to shift the required numbers to block the front-runner. For the isolated individual delegate, joining the front-runner's coalition is a more logical move than joining a holdout effort.

Even if the convention's decision is a foregone conclusion, the nominee, and the party's managers and its other candidates are still likely to make it an impressive spectacle. Aside from writing the party platform and conducting other routine party business, the national convention marks the end of the intraparty struggle and opens the fall campaign. Neither the presidential nominee nor the party's other candidates will want to project a divided image or to lose a well-televised opportunity to denounce their foes and to rally the party faithful. Not surprisingly, both parties seek to provide suspense—or at least to add color and viewer appeal for their conclaves—by adding balloons, bands, streamers, standards, spotlights, a boisterous gallery, celebrity appearances, and other festivities to keep the media fixed on their meetings. In this the party managers will be aided by the media, especially the networks, whose huge outlays for convention coverage cause them to seek out and play up eccentric delegates, minor conspiracies, and platform squabbles in a constant search for excitement. All the drama aside, though, the national conventions are no longer particularly important in deciding the nomination; rather, they formalize and legitimize the work of the preceding primary and caucus contests.

SUMMARY

The new nominations race places enormous demands upon the candidates and their organizations. To compete effectively in the growing numbers of openly contested primaries and caucuses, a candidate must begin fund raising, assembling an extensive campaign staff, building a grass-roots organization, and targeting key states earlier than ever before. A review of recent campaigns, however, reveals that most aspiring nominees have not successfully adjusted their efforts to these new campaign realities.

Most candidates deplete their initial campaign treasuries and exhaust their organizations during their first few primary or caucus races. To continue a full-scale campaign after the early contests, a candidate must win a favorable media verdict—and the resulting poll gains, fund-raising success, and appeal to volunteers. Candidates who fail to win a favorable early judgment from the media will either be forced to conduct but a limited campaign effort or else will be driven from the contest altogether. As a result, the new nomination system usually produces an apparent nominee well before the national party convention.

NOTES

1. Sidney Hyman, "Nine Tests for the Presidential Hopeful," *New York Times Sunday Magazine*, January 4, 1959, p. 11.
2. Gerald Pomper, *Nominating the President—The Politics of Convention Choice* (New York: W. W. Norton & Co., 1966), pp. 122-133.
3. For a description of candidate backgrounds in earlier years, see William Keech and Donald Matthews, *The Party's Choice* (Washington, D. C.: Brookings, 1976). The serious contenders here include the following: in 1972, Democrats Edmund Muskie, George McGovern, Hubert Humphrey, Henry Jackson, George Wallace, Vance Hartke, Wilbur Mills, Eugene McCarthy, Shirley Chisholm, Terry Sanford, John Lindsay, and Sam Yorty, and Republicans Richard Nixon, Paul McCloskey, and John Ashbrook; in 1976, Democrats Jimmy Carter, Morris Udall, Frank Church, Jerry Brown, Lloyd Bentsen, Birch Bayh, Fred Harris, Robert Byrd, Milton Shapp, Ellen McCormick, Sargent Shriver, and again Jackson, Sanford, and Wallace, and Republicans Gerald Ford and Ronald Reagan; in 1980, Democrats Edward Kennedy, Jimmy Carter, and Jerry Brown, and Republicans George Bush, Robert Dole, John Anderson, Phil Crane, Howard Baker, John Connally, and Ronald Reagan.
4. Some senators direct a very large staff indeed. Between his own personal staff and that of his committees, Senator Henry Jackson commanded 89 staffers in 1976. Jackson's staff payroll reportedly totaled nearly 2 million dollars a year. Arthur Hadley, *The Invisible Primary* (Englewood Cliffs, N. J.: Prentice-Hall, 1976), p. 22.
5. Robert Peabody, Norman Ornstein, and David Rohde, "The United States Senate as a Presidential Incubator: Many Are Called but Few Are Chosen," *Political Science Quarterly* 91 (1976): 237-258. For another view, see "Senate's Club of Failed Ambitions," *Washington Post*, March 10, 1980, p. A1.
6. In 1975, both Carter and Wallace built their early campaign staff from local or regional contacts. Carter's Georgia backers also provided an important source of donors and volunteers for his candidacy. Martin Schram, *Running for President, 1976: The Carter Campaign* (New York: Stein and Day, 1977).
7. "The Campaign," *Washington Post*, June 8, 1980, p. A1; and "Making the Opponent the Issue," *Washington Post*, June 9, 1980, p. A1.
8. Charles Evans Hughes, the Republican nominee in 1916, was the last Supreme Court justice to win a nomination. Hughes eschewed campaigning and resigned from the Court only after the Republican convention drafted him as the nominee.
9. In earlier years, though, the Cabinet was a frequent source of candidates. During the congressional caucus system the post of secretary of state was considered the stepping-stone to the White House. The last cabinet officer to win the nod was then-secretary of commerce Herbert Hoover in 1928.
10. Terry Sanford, president of Duke University, was the most recent aspirant from academia. Sanford, though, had also served as North Carolina's governor and was active in the Democratic Party. He ran in 1972 as a favorite son but was drubbed by George Wallace; later, he tried to organize a race in 1976 but dropped out shortly before the New Hampshire primary.

The last business executive nominated was Wendell Wilkie in 1940. Wilkie was a late-entering candidate who completely avoided all the primaries. For another, more recent effort to promote a business executive, see "This Man Ought to be the Next President of the United States," *Esquire*, October 1967, pp. 89-93+.

11. Outgoing Illinois Senator Adlai Stevenson III and New York Governor Hugh Carey both explored making a bid for the 1980 Democratic nomination, but neither eventually chose to do so. On the Republican side, Senators Lowell Weicker (Conn.) and Larry Pressler (S.D.) both declared a candidacy but withdrew before the first primaries. General Alexander Haig, then serving as NATO chief, also considered making a bid for the 1980 GOP nomination but never made an active campaign.

12. Representative Crane announced his bid in August of 1978. Kennedy formally announced on November 7, 1979, followed by Reagan on November 13, and by Carter on December 4. See "The Road to the White House: Getting Longer and Longer," *Congressional Quarterly Weekly Report*, June 16, 1980, p. 1169.

13. For a description of Carter's early starting campaign, see Jules Witcover, *Marathon: The Pursuit of the Presidency 1972-1976* (New York: Viking, 1977); and Martin Schram, *Running for President, 1976: The Carter Campaign* (New York: Stein and Day, 1977).

14. For a longer discussion, see James W. Davis, *Presidential Primaries—Road to the White House* (Westport, Conn,: Greenwood Press, 1980), pp. 19-26.

15. "It's More Expensive to Run for President as Inflation Takes to the Campaign Trail," *National Journal*, February 23, 1980, pp. 311-313.

16. Sears was later replaced by Reagan in a campaign shake-up after the New Hampshire primary.

17. "The Almanac of Political Pollsters: 1980," *Public Opinion*, February/March 1980, pp. 50-52.

18. "Bush Gets Lessons in Performing on TV," *New York Times*, January 12, 1980, p. 23.

19. "GOP Presidential Candidates Are Freer Spenders Than Democrats," *National Journal*, February 9, 1980, p. 248. Large differences in preprimary spending were also reported among the Democrats in 1976. Before the first primary, the largest spenders were Jackson at 3.2 million dollars, Wallace at 3 million dollars, and Bentsen at 2.4 million dollars. Carter and Udall followed, at 1.7 and 1.5 million dollars, respectively. "What It Means to the Candidates," *Time*, February 9, 1976, pp. 13-14.

20. "GOP Presidential Hopefuls Gave Plenty to Party Candidates in 1978," *Congressional Quarterly Weekly Report*, February 17, 1979, pp. 307-311.

21. "Fund Raising Doubles Since Four Years Ago," *Congressional Quarterly Weekly Report*, February 23, 1980, pp. 569-571.

22. "Candidates Must Adjust to Spending Limits," *Congressional Quarterly Weekly Report*, May 10, 1980, pp. 1244-1247.

23. *Congressional Quarterly Weekly Review*, February 23, 1980, pp. 569-571.

24. Martin Schram, *Running for President, 1976*.

25. "Connally Staff Payless Despite TV Fund-raiser," *Dallas Times Herald*, February 20, 1980, p. 2A.

26. "The Fundraising Tally," *The New Republic*, February 23, 1980, pp. 11-13; and "Rosalynn Raises $1 million," *Dallas Times Herald*, February 10, 1980, p. A19.

27. "The Artful Dodge," *Washington Post*, July 21, 1980, p. A1.
28. John Aldrich, *Before the Convention* (Chicago: University of Chicago Press, 1980), especially pp. 139–145. For a lengthier discussion of candidate strategies in recent years, see James Davis, *Presidential Primaries*, especially Chapters 4 and 8. Candidate strategies in the 1980 race are described in Steven Brams and Morton Davis, "Optimal Resource Allocation in Presidential Primaries" (Paper delivered at the Annual Meeting of the American Political Science Association, Washington, D.C., 1980).
29. Jonathon Moore and Janet Fraser, eds., *Campaigning for President: The Managers Look at '76* (Cambridge, Massachusetts: Ballinger, 1977), pp. 41–43.
30. The need to make an early commitment particularly complicates the task of a challenger to an incumbent president. Few challengers are willing to announce against an incumbent president only two or three years into the incumbent's first term; by the time the incumbent's third year is out, it might well be too late to mount a successful challenge.
31. For a longer discussion, see "A Guide to Recent Presidential Nominations," later in this book.
32. "Democratic Delegate Vote Summary," *Congressional Quarterly Weekly Report*, June 24, 1972, p. 1567.
33. "Delegate Count," *Congressional Quarterly Weekly Report*, June 12, 1976, p. 1473.

5

THE PUBLICS

CATEGORIES OF PUBLICS

During the 1970s, new reforms allowed more ordinary voters to participate in delegate selection. More states held primaries, and in the nonprimary states local caucus meetings were opened to ordinary party supporters. For the first-time, rank-and-file adults controlled the dividing and naming of the delegates.

This dramatic and sudden shift of power greatly affected the role of public opinion in the nomination contest and offered more opportunities for participation than ever before. Yet while more people now take part than in earlier years, most of them still continue to ignore the process. In recent years, only about one of every five U.S. adults have voted in a presidential primary or attended a state caucus meeting. Fewer still have given money or actively worked for a candidate.

The Inactive Public

As Table 5.1 indicates, most U.S. adults take no active part at all in choosing the nominee. About four out of every five citizens neither vote in a primary nor attend a local caucus meeting.[1] As a

TABLE 5.1: Participation in the Presidential Nominations Process, 1972–80

	1972	1976	1980
Total turnout	23,629,000	29,793,000	32,391,000
Estimated total number of U.S. adults (aged 18 or over)	139,000,000	150,000,000	160,000,000
Percent of all U.S. adults participating	17	20	20

Total population figures are rounded to the nearest million.
Source: Table 2.3 and U.S. Census Estimates.

result, most of them have no impact on the nomination except indirectly, through national public opinion polls.

In presidential primary states, only about a quarter of the voting-age public participates. In caucus–convention states, the total turnout seldom if ever exceeds 10 percent of all eligible adults.[2] Apparently fewer than half of *any* social group actively participates; neither a majority of affluent voters nor of less well-to-do voters take part. Nor do a clear majority of either union or nonunion household voters turn out.[3]

Why do so few people participate in choosing the two parties' nominees? For some there may be legal barriers: failing to register in time, for example. For others the reason may be political: the contest may seem one-sided and the outcome assured, or a favorite candidate may not be on the ballot in some states.[4] Many voters find the absence of a party label confusing; to them, choosing among several Republicans (or Democrats) is a difficult and puzzling choice. In many states voters were unable to participate until the 1970s, and preconvention participation has not yet become a habit. Others simply find politics tiresome, complicated, and remote from their daily problems and concerns.

Primary Voters and Caucus Attenders

Although most adults take no active role in choosing the nominee, the number participating actively is still sizeable. In 1972, the total turnout approached 24 million voters. Four years later, in 1976, that figure jumped to nearly 30 million, and in 1980 almost 32 million U.S. citizens voted or attended a local caucus. Those figures are about double the number—about 13 million—who participated in 1968, the last year of the brokered convention system.

While primary voters and caucus attenders differ in several ways from inactive adults, the overall differences are seldom striking. Primary voters and caucus attenders are usually somewhat better educated, better employed, and more likely to be middle-aged and white. They are also more likely to identify strongly with their party.[5]

Although primary voters or caucus attenders sometimes report different attitudes on key issues than less active adults, these issue differences are seldom very pronounced. The few available studies suggest that primary voters or caucus attenders represent fairly closely all party supporters in their candidate preferences.[6] While turnout is low, little evidence exists that voters or caucus-goers have badly misrepresented the wishes of the less active majority.

While primary voters and caucus attenders are more active than a majority of adults, their level of interest and involvement should not be exaggerated. Voting in a presidential primary is seldom a particularly taxing or demanding act.[7] Many voters are doubtlessly fulfilling a self-perceived "duty" to appear at the polls. When presidential primaries are held at the same time as state and local primaries, some voters may simply cast a presidential preference vote along with their votes in hotly fought local contests. In caucus–convention states attenders may be more interested in local or state party endorsements or in issue resolutions than in the presidential nominations race. Some caucus attenders may have come simply through curiosity, through a general sense of citizen duty, because they were brought along by a neighbor or relative, or even because they were assigned to attend as part of a high school or college class project. In short, primary voting or caucus attending, per se, need not indicate any particularly overwhelming interest in the nomination race.

The Activists

In the new era of popular appeal, volunteers are more essential than ever before. A would-be nominee relies of necessity heavily on unpaid—or, at the most, poorly paid—staffers and volunteers to do the campaign's legwork. By canvassing, telephoning, stuffing envelopes, and turning out favorable voters, volunteers help a candidate to match or exceed his preprimary polls. Typically, these volunteers are drawn from a few sources: they are likely to be perennial party activists, teachers and students, interested housewives, and sympathetic interest group members.

Some candidates inspire more volunteers than others. One notable beneficiary was challenger Eugene McCarthy in 1968; McCarthy's New Hampshire challenge to incumbent Lyndon Johnson reportedly drew more than 10,000 students.[8] Four years later, another antiwar candidate, George McGovern, likewise tapped a groundswell of volunteers. McGovern's "army" reportedly numbered 8,000 for his strong New Hampshire showing, as many as 10,000 in his critical Wisconsin victory, another 10,000 or more during his decisive California primary effort, and over 40,000 in his last-of-the-season New York primary sweep.[9] These massive volunteer efforts overwhelmed the debilitated party machines of his opponents, who were seldom able to attract a sizeable base of volunteers.

With the new, tighter spending limits, no presidential candidate can now afford to pay all his campaigners. Even full-time campaign organizers may receive no more than pocket money for their labors. While the activists' motives are varied, for most volunteers the attraction lies in the candidate's personal appeal or policy promises. McCarthy and McGovern inspired antiwar activists; Jimmy Carter appealed to many volunteers through his regional ties and personal charm; Ronald Reagan tapped a network of long-active Republican conservatives. In most cases, issues are the main motivation and grass-roots activists are usually more liberal (in the Democratic Party) or more conservative (among the Republicans) than are less active party supporters.[10]

The Donors

New fund-raising laws barring large individual donations (those over $1000) forced the candidates to reach out to new sources of campaign monies, especially to small donors. These small donors are usually reached through mass mailings, telethons, private receptions with the candidate, or through broad-based fund-raising committees.

Despite increasing candidate efforts in recent years to contact more and more donors, relatively few U.S. residents actually contribute money to any of the presidential campaigns. Only about one in every ten reported making *any* political contribution at all in recent years; by no means were all these donations to prospective presidential nominees. In 1976, one study reported that about 600,000 contributions were reportedly made to one of 15 major GOP and Democratic contenders; the average donation was about

$35. If this estimate is reasonably correct, then only about .4 percent of all adults in the United States contributed directly to any of the presidential hopefuls.[11]

Aside from direct individual contributions, a final source of campaign funds involves the "silent donors"—taxpayers who check off $1 or $2 (on a joint return) on their federal income tax form. After the checkoff form was revised in 1974, about one of every four taxpayers marked the checkoff. In so doing, these taxpayers established a sizeable fund—about $94 million by 1976 and about $136 million for the 1980 primaries, conventions, and general elections. In 1976, federal matching funds paid out to the contestants totaled about $24 million before the convention; by comparison, the fifteen major contenders in either party raised about $40 million in private funds. In 1980, ten qualified candidates received about $30 million during the primaries. For the candidates, these taxpayer-designated funds have at least one considerable advantage over privately raised funds: federal matching funds entail no political obligation and make no demands upon a candidate. Once certified, the federal matching funds simply arrive automatically.[12]

The Party Regulars

Since 1970, the influence of top party leaders over delegate selection has dwindled. Since both parties' rules now require open competition for delegate posts, top party leaders can no longer simply appoint themselves and their supporters as delegates. Forced to compete with insurgents, the proportion of top party officials and elected office holders serving as delegates has dwindled sharply. In 1968, for example—the last year of the brokered convention system—two-thirds of all Democratic U.S. senators served as delegates or alternates. In 1972, only a third of all Democratic senators won delegate seats, and by 1976 the proportion fell to about one in five.[13] To stem the steady decline in the numbers of top-ranking office holders and party officials at the national convention, the Democratic Party allowed states to add an extra 10 percent of their convention delegates, with a special priority given to top elected office holders and party leaders. Nor did top-ranking GOP leaders retain their prereform influence. In the hotly contested Ford-Reagan battle of 1976, insurgent Reaganites dumped pro-Ford party leaders in several states. In 1980, victorious Reagan backers pressured several GOP senators and governors into endorsing Reagan in return for delegate posts.

While the top party leadership has fared poorly in recent

delegate contests, the national conventions are by no means populated with inexperienced amateurs. Most delegates at recent conventions boast substantial records of public service; in recent years a clear majority have held party posts, elected public office, or both. Even at the 1972 Democratic convention—a high point for insurgency— two-thirds of all Democratic delegates presently held a party office; three-quarters had or presently did hold a party post.[14] As many as two-thirds of the McGovern delegates boasted some party office-holding experience. Four years later, in 1976, two of every three Democratic delegates held some party office.[15] In the GOP, too, most of the convention delegates were seasoned party workers. In 1972, nearly all (94 percent) of the Republican delegates had presently or previously served in a party office. The Reagan delegates challenging incumbent president Ford were not much less experienced; over two-thirds (70 percent) had served in a party office, and a large majority (72 percent) had been active within the party for ten years or longer.[16]

While it is true that top state party leaders can no longer dominate delegate selection as easily as before, it is not true that political newcomers have dominated recent conventions. What has apparently happened is that the battles for delegate posts are fought among more factions of the party than ever before. Of thousands of party activists in any state, a serious challenger can almost certainly attract some to his slates even if they are not the top of the state party hierarchy. Since the candidate listed at the top of the slate matters more to primary voters than the prestige of the delegates themselves, the slates attached to a popular candidate may sweep the primary or caucus. As a result, top-ranking party leaders who back a losing candidate—for example, Muskie in 1972—may well be swept away in favor of slates composed of low-level party activists and workers.

In some ways, the party's local office holders and its grass-roots workers may well be better at mobilizing voters than are governors, state party chairmen and -women, or U.S. senators and representatives. Top-ranking party and elected officials usually spend little time in the mundane business of registering new voters, identifying likely voters, and turning out their supporters at the polls. Nor do most top-ranking politicians any longer have much patronage at their disposal with which to carry out their wishes. The real revolution in delegate selection is not that a united party organization has been overwhelmed by inexperienced outsiders. Rather, the real revolution means that low-ranking party activists, aligned with a more popular candidate, can now compete quite successfully with the party's top leaders in an open battle for the delegate seats.

The Delegates

The most studied activists are those attending the national conventions; they numbered about 4,500 in 1972 and about 5,300 in 1976 or 1980. Candidates usually slate delegates for their personal prestige, their organizing skills, or for the importance of the delegate's future (if not prior) political support. In 1976, for the first time, Democratic candidates could approve their own delegates; in 1980, the Democrats went even further by requiring candidates to vote for the candidate to whom they were pledged, at least on the convention's first ballot. Within the GOP a presidential candidate could usually, but not always, approve his own delegates to ensure the delegate's political loyalty.

While delegates are now more closely tied to a candidate than ever before, they may still bring their own concerns to the convention. Blacks, chicanos, women, union members, senior citizens, antiabortionists, and others regularly organize for the delegate-selection ballot, bargain with the candidates for delegate seats, and use their influence to wring policy pledges from the candidates.[17]

Regardless of their candidate preference, most delegates are of middle-class status or better. In 1976, for example, Democratic delegates' median income reportedly exceeded $18,000—nearly triple the national median.[18] About two-thirds of Democratic delegates in recent years have been of professional or managerial status, and about that many had at least a college degree. GOP delegates are of a similarly high social status. In 1980, about two-thirds (64 percent) of Republican delegates had a college degree, versus less than a quarter of all adults in the United States. In 1980, over half the Republican delegates reported an income in excess of $35,000 a year.[19] In their socioeconomic standing, then, the Republican and Democratic delegates were more similar than not; both groups have been overwhelmingly affluent and advantaged.

While they may come from similarly advantaged backgrounds, Democratic and Republican delegates differ enormously on their policy views. Republican delegates at recent conventions have been characterized as almost uniformly conservative on domestic issues. Most take a hard-line attitude toward criminals and political radicals, oppose school busing for integration, and frown on strikes by public employees. Within GOP ranks, the dominant cleavage is usually between the militant conservatives of the Goldwater–Reagan camp and the moderate conservatives, such as those backing Ford in 1976.[20] Self-identified liberals are by now oddities at GOP conventions; in 1980, only 2 percent of GOP delegates identified themselves as liberals. Most (58 percent) said that they were conservative.[21]

In the Democratic Party the chief cleavage lies between liberal, very liberal, or even radical Democrats, on the one hand, and those of more moderate persuasion, on the other. Self-styled conservatives are as rare at Democratic conventions as are liberals at the GOP gatherings. In recent years only 8 percent (in 1972), 4 percent (1976), or 6 percent (1980) of Democratic delegates identified themselves as conservative or right-wing. McGovern's successes in 1972 brought more liberal Democrats to the convention than ever before; in 1972, almost half the delegates (48 percent) described themselves as left liberals or radicals. Most of the others, another 30 percent, described themselves as liberal. By 1976 and 1980, however, the pendulum had swung back to the center of the party. In 1976, nearly all the delegates described themselves as either liberal (43 percent) or moderates (another 45 percent). In another poll, about half (46 percent) of the Democratic delegates in 1980 described themselves as liberal, and about that many (42 percent) said that they were moderates.[22]

Neither the Republican nor the Democratic delegates always reflect closely the attitudes of their respective party members. GOP delegates are, on balance, more conservative than all Republican voters, even though the dwindling percentage of Republicans in the electorate are themselves more uniformly conservative than in earlier decades. Similarly, Democratic delegates are consistently more liberal than their party's rank-and-file supporters. Sometimes these differences can be very pronounced, as in 1972, when the Democratic delegates were particularly liberal. In that year, the GOP delegates more closely represented the attitudes of Democratic voters than did the Democratic delegates themselves.[23] In 1976 and 1980, however, such extreme tendencies were not apparent, and each party's supporters were better represented by their own delegates.[24]

Within both parties the delegates may differ in their attitudes toward the role of the convention. Some delegates feel that taking a strong, uncompromising issue stand is the convention's key test. Other delegates argue, instead, that a successful convention's first job is to nominate an electable ticket and to unify the party around the platform; to these delegates, issues are of secondary importance. The former are often labeled "purists" or sometimes as "amateurs," and the latter as "professionals." Many delegates, of course, take a middle ground, agreeing that both issues and winning elections are high priorities.

The purist notion is often ascribed to liberal, insurgent Democrats or to very conservative, insurgent Republicans. By contrast, top party leaders and elected office holders in either party more often prefer winning tickets and a united party to strongly worded platforms. While insurgents and the party regulars sometimes do differ on this dimension, these differences should not be drawn too sharply. Nor can purist versus professional attitudes be attributed exclusively to supporters of different candidates. McGovern's supporters accepted several compromises to advance his interests at the 1972 Democratic convention, and his opponents tended to develop an increasingly uncompromising posture as that convention progressed.[25] Later, at the 1976 GOP convention, nearly all (92 percent) of the Reagan delegates took a purist position, holding that the party should "appeal to voters by maintaining conservative principles." Yet a sizeable minority (38 percent) of the Ford delegates, too, agreed with that statement.[26]

BEFORE THE PRIMARIES

Long before the first state primary or caucus, pollsters begin to survey the candidate preferences of U.S. adults. In some ways pre-primary polls are quite important. Early polls set a baseline expectations for the candidates, may affect the behavior of some donors and volunteers, and may even lead a few candidates to drop out in discouragement. Yet a review of preprimary polls in recent years also suggests that most adults are neither very interested in the nominations race nor seem very knowledgeable about the candidates before the primaries begin.

Name Recognition

The simplest test for public awareness of the candidates is name recognition. Before the primaries begin, few contenders are recognized by as many as half the party's voters or by all adults. Inevitably, the most widely recognized candidates are incumbents, previous nominees or contenders, vice-presidents, or top-ranking administration officials. Table 5.2 reports preprimary name recognition for major candidates in several recent contests. As this table indicates, the best-recognized names, with few exceptions, have been aspirants with prior nomination experience. The most notable exception in the Democratic nominations race was Senator Edward Kennedy; Kennedy was, of course, the brother both of one former president and of another challenger for the nomination. Otherwise only John Lindsay (a former New York City mayor) and John Connally (former Treasury Secretary and governor of Texas), among the first-time challengers, were recognized by three-quarters or more of all adults.

Few first-time contenders scored well in the name-awareness

TABLE 5.2: Voter Recognition of Presidential Contenders and Other Public Figures during the Preprimary Season

(In percentages)

Poll Date: Group Surveyed:	April 23–26, 1971 All Adults		October 3–6, 1975 All Adults		December 7-10, 1979 All Adults	
	Candidate	Familiar with Name	Candidate	Familiar with Name	Candidate	Familiar with Name
	(Kennedy)	94	(Kennedy)	96	(Ford)*	93
	Humphrey*	94	Wallace*	93	Reagan*	92
	Muskie*	85	(Humphrey)*	91	Connally	78
	McCarthy*	78	(McGovern)*	89	Baker	65
	Lindsay	77	(Muskie)*	84	Dole*	61
	McGovern*	68	Shriver*	76	Bush	53
	Bayh	35	Jackson*	64	Percy	50
	Jackson	29	Bayh	50	Stassen*	41
			Udall	47	Richardson	36
			Shapp	31	Simon	30
			Carter	29	Helms	26
			Bentsen	24	Anderson	24
			Harris	22	Crane	20
			Sanford*	21		

* denotes a previous president or vice-president, a presidential or vice-presidential nominee, or a contender for an earlier nomination. Candidates marked in parentheses, ( ), are those not making an active bid for the nomination in the year indicated.

Source: Gallup Polls, dates indicated. Nonincumbent nominations races only indicated. Only candidates with 20 percent or higher name recognition are indicated.

127

race. In late 1975, neither Udall, Carter, or Brown (all of whom eventually reached the 1976 Democratic convention) were recognized by as many as half of all adults. In late 1979, on the GOP side, Connally and Baker were the best-recognized of the first-time contenders. Bush, by contrast, was recognized by only about half of all adults; Anderson and Crane were recognized by only about a quarter or a fifth.

Most first-time candidates must resign themselves to a low early name recognition no matter how serious their organizing efforts. Since the media seldom cover the campaign-building stage in much depth, and since organizing efforts reach few voters directly, those candidates without a high initial name recognition will seldom increase their familiarity very quickly. Most first-time candidates must wait for a strong primary or caucus showing to provide the media coverage that will make their name the proverbial household word.

Candidates and Ideology

If many voters have difficulty simply recognizing many of the serious candidates, then placing the candidates on a left–right or liberal–conservative spectrum proves even more difficult. Voters are seldom able to agree on a candidate's left–right placement before the primaries, even for well-recognized contenders.

In early 1976, for example, Senator Humphrey and Governor Wallace were recognized by virtually all Democrats. Nonetheless, Democratic voters were still unable to agree on either man's ideological posture. Only about half of all Democrats placed Wallace to the right of center. As Table 5.3 also indicates, about as many Democrats placed Humphrey right of center (37 percent) as left of center (40 percent).

For less familiar candidates, voters are apt to be completely unclear on their ideology. Very early during the 1976 primary season, Jimmy Carter's ideology was very unclear to Democratic voters. As Table 5.3 suggests, equal numbers placed Carter left of center, right of center, or reported that they did not know. Yet his rivals for the nomination were scarcely better recognized. Udall, Jackson, and Harris all received higher percentages of "don't knows" than did Carter. If Carter's image was "fuzzy" to many voters, so were the ideological profiles of his active rivals.[27]

In 1976, Democratic voters were not alone in their confusion. In early 1976, Ford and Reagan were recognized by almost all GOP voters, but only about half of all voters placed Ford and Reagan

TABLE 5.3: Voter Perception of Candidate Ideology, 1976 Democratic Contenders

(In percentages)

Candidate:	Voter Perception, Democratic Voters Only:		
	Don't Know	Left of Center	Right of Center
Wallace	18	30	49
Humphrey	17	40	37
Udall	60	24	14
Carter	30	30	33
Jackson	42	25	29
Harris	69	20	9

Source: Gallup Opinion Survey conducted between March 26 and 29, 1978. Data reported in *Gallup Opinion Index* No. 133, August 1976. Voters were handed a card with eight political positions, ranging from far left to far right, and asked to place each candidate's position.

to the right of center, and about an equal number either placed them left of center or did not know. By 1979, just before the 1980 contests between Carter and Kennedy, a clear majority of voters were also unable to agree on the ideological stance either of Kennedy or of Carter. Only half the voters placed Kennedy left of center, while a third placed him right of center. For Carter, the voters still disagreed on his ideology, just as they had in 1976; between a third and a half placed Carter either left or right of center. See Tables 5.4 and 5.5.

Candidate Personality Ratings

Before the early primaries, voters may not only be unclear about most candidates' ideological stances, but relatively few adults report any intense feelings toward the announced or potential candidates. The combined extreme responses—those indicating either "highly favorable" or "highly unfavorable" feelings—seldom exceed a quarter to a third of all the respondents. As Table 5.6 indicates, few voters are apparently intensely "locked in," either for or against a specific candidate.

Predictably, the better-recognized candidates have the largest number of highly favorable or unfavorable responses. Yet even for

TABLE 5.4: Voter Perception of Candidate Ideology, 1976 Republican Contenders

(In percentages)

	Perceptions of All Respondents:		
Candidate:	Don't Know	Left of Center	Right of Center
Ford	14	23	56
Reagan	19	25	53

Source: See Table 5.3.

TABLE 5.5: Voter Perception of Candidate Ideology, 1980 Democratic Contenders

(In percentages)

	Perceptions of All Respondents		
Candidate:	Don't Know	Left of Center	Right of Center
Carter	12	37	46
Kennedy	13	50	33

Source: *The Gallup Opinion Index* No. 172, November 1979.

the best-known candidates, never have more than half of all adults given extreme responses; more often, about a third or so of all adults indicate either highly positive or negative feelings. Candidates with a low name recognition are usually so little known to the public that they win few extreme responses at either end of the popularity spectrum. Finally, for most candidates the highly positive responses exceed the highly unfavorable responses. In recent years, only Wallace (in 1970) and Brown and Connally (in 1979) achieved the dubious distinction of winning more highly negative views than highly positive ones.

Preprimary Voter Preferences

Before the primaries, most voters apparently have little knowledge about most of the candidates and report few intense feelings toward them. It is hardly surprising, therefore, that preprimary polls favor incumbents, previous nominees, or candidates who had made an earlier bid for the nomination. Only well-recognized and long-familiar names are likely to score well in the early polls. Early polls are heavily based on name recognition. As Table 5.7 indicates, few first-time candidates can ever hope to rank among the front-runners in the preprimary polls.

With the exception of Senator Edward Kennedy, first-time challengers seldom score very well in the preprimary preference polls. In several recent contests, the early poll leaders have not even organized an active campaign; in these instances their lead is simply a reflection of their name familiarity among the voters, usually based on some previous race. In the 1976 Democratic race—an extreme instance—most of the early front-runners did not organize a campaign; only Wallace, among the five early poll leaders, made an active bid for the nomination in that year.

The Importance of Preprimary Polls

These findings might seem to indicate that preprimary polls have little impact on the nominations race. Except for incumbents and previous contenders for the nomination, few candidates are well recognized by either party's voters until the primaries actually begin. Before the state contests most voters apparently report the most familiar names as their favorite regardless of whether that candidate has actively campaigned or not. Few voters report an intense attitude toward the hopefuls, either favorably or unfavorably. Nor can voters usually agree on the ideology of even the best known of candidates.

Early polls, however, do matter in two ways. First, the media use preprimary standings to gauge the candidates' relative strength. By relying on the polls, the media name "front-runners" and "underdogs" even before the first state caucus or primary. Second, voters who hold no intense views before the primaries and caucuses are free to shift their attitudes later. As voters learn more about the candidates during the primaries and caucuses—especially about media-designated winners—the polls may shift very quickly. The absence of intensely held, well-formed early preferences helps to explain why primary winners often rise quickly in the later polls.

TABLE 5.6: **Personality Ratings for Various Public Figures before the 1972, 1976, and 1980 Primaries**

(In percentages)

Candidate	Highly Favorable	Highly Unfavorable	Total Extreme Responses
Personality Ratings in 1970:[a]			
Humphrey	22	15	37
Muskie	24	4	28
Kennedy	26	13	39
Wallace	11	30	41
McGovern	7	5	15
Personality Ratings in 1975:[b]			
Humphrey	23	11	34
Muskie	11	8	19
Kennedy	33	16	49
Wallace	20	17	37
Reagan	23	14	37
Ford	22	15	37

[a] Ratings are from October 1970, except for McGovern, whose rating is from January 1970. See the *Gallup Opinion Index*, Report No. 125, p. 100.

[b] Ratings are from October and November 1975; *Gallup Opinion Index*, Report No. 125, p. 98.

CANDIDATES, ISSUES, AND PRIMARY VOTERS

U.S. citizens may influence the nomination in two ways—first, by voting in a state primary or attending a caucus, and second, through the national polls. Although only about one of every five U.S. adults takes part in a presidential primary or caucus, these voters and caucus-goers now have more influence over the nomination than ever before.

Recent evidence, however, indicates that presidential primary and caucus results are often difficult to interpret. Voters often have

Candidate	Highly Favorable	Highly Unfavorable	Total Extreme Responses
	Personality Ratings in 1975 *(continued):*		
Carter	4	2	6
Udall	3	2	5
Bayh	4	4	8
	Personality Ratings in 1979:[c]		
Carter	19	13	32
Kennedy	39	9	48
Brown	9	11	20
Baker	8	4	12
Connally	6	12	18

[c]Ratings for Carter and Kennedy are from September 1979; ratings for Brown, Baker, and Connally are from June and July 1979.

Source: Respondents were given a card with ten numbered boxes ranging from a plus five ("for something or someone you like very much") to a minus five ("for something or someone you dislike very much"). Respondents were then asked to rate the candidate on this ten-point scale. A response of +5 or +4 was considered "highly favorable" while a response of –5 or –4 was "highly unfavorable." Data are taken from the *Gallup Opinion Index*, Report No. 125, November–December 1975; Report No. 168, July 1979; and Report No. 172, November 1979.

but limited information on the candidates' issue stands. Turnout is usually low. Voters may prefer candidates for a wide variety of reasons, and in many instances a candidate's personal qualities are more important to voters than his specific issue stands. Primary voters do not always clearly divide their votes along liberal–conservative lines. Voters may bring a wide range of specific issue concerns to the voting booth, making it difficult to interpret the results. Several candidates may split the votes of one issue, religious, or racial bloc, while another contender collects the undivided votes of another bloc. While presidential primary results typically produce "winners" and

TABLE 5.7: Preprimary Preferences of Democratic or Republican Voters among Potential or Announced Presidential Candidates, 1971 and 1975

(In percentages)

Democrats Only:		Republicans Only:	
December 16-19, 1971[a]		October 29-November 2, 1971	
Kennedy	32	Nixon*	73
Muskie*	25	McCloskey	13
Humphrey*	19		
McGovern*	5		
November 21-24, 1975[b]		November 21-24, 1975	
Humphrey*	30	Reagan*	40
Wallace*	20	Ford*	32
McGovern*	10	Goldwater*	10
Jackson*	10	Rockefeller*	6
Muskie*	7		
Bayh	5		
		December 7-10, 1979	
		Reagan*	40
		Ford*	18
		Connally	10
		Baker	9
		Bush	7

[a] Wallace not listed on the card in this survey.

[b] Kennedy not listed on the card in this survey. When listed, Kennedy received 29 percent of the Democratic vote, versus 21 percent for Humphrey and 15 percent for Wallace.

Source: Gallup Opinion Index, various dates, polling dates indicated. Poll preferences are indicated for appropriate party identifiers for the last time during the preprimary year for which the Gallup Poll asked voter preferences. Only candidates receiving 5 percent or more are listed. Candidates marked by an asterix (*) are those who had organized a previous presidential bid, or who served as an incumbent.

"losers," they do not always reveal very much about the party faithful's issue preferences.

Issue Knowledge

Before the first primaries, many voters appear unclear about the candidates' issue positions. While this confusion usually reduces somewhat as the primaries progress, many voters remain quite uncertain even during the late primaries as to the candidates' issue stands.

In one survey conducted two weeks before the first primary in 1976, for example, candidate issue profiles remained unclear to most potential voters.[28] Only on a few scattered issues were most voters apparently familiar with the candidates' stands at that time. Yet even during the last primaries of that year, considerable uncertainty remained. One national survey during the last round of primaries reported that "an average of more than half of the potential voters did not know where their favorite candidate stood on five major issues." Only a few exceptions occurred; Udall's position on civil rights, energy, and pollution for example, was clearly perceived, as was Reagan's on military spending and welfare. For most of the other candidates the voters remained unclear on many of their issue stands.[29]

Ideology, Issues, and Vote Choice

When pressed to explain presidential primary results, political analysts often resort to the notion of the liberal–conservative spectrum. By this view, voters prefer the candidate closest to themselves on a left–right spectrum. In fact, however, knowing voters' liberal-conservative leanings is not always especially helpful in predicting their choice among candidates in presidential primaries. Voters are typically unable to agree on the candidate's left–right placement, and they seldom divide their votes among the contenders very clearly along ideological lines.

In 1976, few candidates in either party drew disproportionate strength from a single ideological camp. The most notable exception was Democratic hopeful George Wallace. In an early 1976 poll, Wallace won support from 43 percent of conservative Democrats, while winning only 21 percent of moderate-to-liberal Democrats. Even for Wallace, though, these differences largely disappeared by midprimary season. By April of 1976, Wallace's support varied only between 11 and 15 percent of all three ideological groups of Democrats. Among other Democrats, few marked differences appeared when national poll respondents were divided by their liberal–moderate–conservative preferences.[30]

On the GOP side, in 1976 liberal Republicans tended to prefer Ford over Reagan, but the margin was surprisingly small. In three monthly polls conducted over the 1976 primary season, Ford ran better among liberal than among conservative Republicans but only by an average of 12 percentage points.[31] (See Table 5.8.)

The same mixed picture on ideological clarity that occurs in the national polls is also reflected by state primary voters. Two separate analyses of 1976 primary voters in 13 key states suggested that liberal, moderate, and conservative voters did not always divide their votes sharply between the candidates.[32] In all the 1976 Democratic primaries surveyed, Carter's support was the least clearly divided by ideology. Carter received 31 percent of the votes of Democratic liberals, 40 percent from moderates, and 41 percent from conservatives. In some states Carter won pluralities from moderates and liberals but not from conservatives, while in other states he took pluralities or majorities of conservatives.[33] Carter's coalition was a broad, shifting one that varied in ideology from state to state. His supporters—disproportionate numbers of whom were

TABLE 5.8: Republican Voters' Preferences, by Ideology, during the 1976 Presidential Primary Season

(In percentages)

Republican Voter Ideology	February		March		April	
	Ford	Reagan	Ford	Reagan	Ford	Reagan
liberal	59	30	82	17	54	42
moderate	58	28	70	28	70	25
conservative	48	38	60	35	51	39
Difference in Ford support, liberal vs. conservative Republicans	11		22		3	

Source: *New York Times,* April 23, 1976, 16:5.

black, less affluent, and Southern—apparently preferred Carter largely on the basis of his personal qualities and appeal.

For other Democratic candidates in 1976, their ideological support, too, was not so clearly drawn as might have been expected. Udall and Wallace, neither of whom had run very well in the primaries, were among the clearest recipients of ideological support. Udall won 35 percent of liberal Democratic voters but only 19 percent of moderates and only 13 percent of conservatives. Wallace, by contrast, won but 8 percent of liberals, 15 percent of moderates, but 26 percent of conservatives. By comparison, Senator Jackson's support showed little difference across ideological lines.[34]

On the Republican side issue-voting was somewhat more readily apparent. Ford usually ran much more strongly among liberals, split the moderate vote evenly, and lost conservative Republican voters to Reagan two to one or more. Voting differences were more marked on noneconomic issues than on economic ones.

Overall, knowledge of the voters' economic issue positions would have enabled one to predict accurately about 50 to 60 percent of the Republican primary voters' choices in 1976, and about 50 to 55 percent of the Democratic primary votes. Noneconomic issues determined about 55 to 60 percent of the GOP votes and about the same percentage of Democratic primary votes.[35] Other voters apparently decided more along personality or nonpolicy lines.

In 1980, voters again did not always divide their votes very sharply along ideological lines. In the Democratic race, Senator Kennedy usually ran more strongly among self-identified liberals than among more conservative or moderate Democratic primary voters. This pattern was not always very marked, however, and was at least occasionally reversed.[36]

On the Republican side in 1980, Reagan, predictably, ran strongest among the party's most conservative voters, but again the ideological split was less marked than one might have expected. At the start of the first caucus in Iowa, Reagan led among all factions of the party, taking 43 percent of conservatives, 41 percent of moderates, and 29 percent of self-identified liberal Republicans in a national survey.[37] Both Bush and Reagan appealed most strongly to the party's conservative wing, although Bush apparently eventually inherited many moderate and liberal GOP votes once the field had dwindled to a two-man contest.

Specific issues often serve as better predictors of vote choice than does the liberal–conservative spectrum. Even if most candidates do not seem to differ clearly in their ideology, voters may perceive a few key issue differences. Candidates are more likely to stress a few specific issues or themes in their campaign debates, advertising, and personal appearances. Similarly, the media often focus on one or two key issues in campaign coverage.

When both (or all) of the candidates focus on the same issue, voters may more easily divide their votes along that policy line. In the 1976 New Hampshire primary, few issues clearly differentiated Ford from Reagan voters. On detente, however, GOP voters who opposed it chose Reagan 60 to 36 percent, while those favoring detente picked Ford 54 to 43 percent.[38] Later, in the Florida Republican primary, Ford won 61 percent of GOP primary voters favoring detente and two-to-one among those optimistic about the economy. By contrast, those pessimistic on the economy favored Reagan by a similar two-to-one margin.[39]

Four years later, in the 1980 GOP primary in New Hampshire, a few issues also clearly divided Reagan and Bush voters, among them the Equal Rights Amendment. In one poll, only about a quarter (28 percent) of Reagan voters favored the amendment, while a clear majority (62 percent) of Bush voters did. On other issues, though, the differences in voter preferences between the candidates were less pronounced.[40]

Candidates may also enjoy a markedly different appeal to special interest groups. Often a candidate with long-standing ties to an interest group or a racial, ethnic, regional, or religious bloc stresses those issues, thereby linking his campaign closely to that voter bloc. Appealing to a large or active bloc in a low turnout primary may strengthen a candidate's chances of carrying the race.

In 1972, for example, Hubert Humphrey consistently won large majorities of black voters on his long-term civil rights commitments. In the Wisconsin, Michigan, and Pennsylvania Democratic primaries Humphrey took two-thirds to three-quarters of black voters. Only in California's late primary could McGovern cut into Humphrey's heavy minority group support.[41] By contrast, McGovern typically scored very well among young voters. In the California primary, for example, McGovern won up to three-quarters of the 18-to-24 year old primary voters.[42]

Four years later, Senator Jackson—who made his criticism of detente and support for Israel key campaign issues—ran far better among Jewish voters than among all other Democrats. In the 1976 Florida primary, for example, Jackson won two-thirds of the votes of Jewish Democrats, although he won only 24 percent of the overall Florida primary vote.[43] In the same Florida primary, by contrast, Carter won a 34 percent plurality victory but took three-quarters of the black vote over his two antibusing rivals, Wallace and Jackson.[44]

While issue or demographic blocs are often more helpful in explaining primary vote choice than the liberal–conservative notion, several problems also arise. Not all voters, of course, fall into the same voter bloc—issue or demographic blocs vary from state to state; even within a single state several core groups may exist, each with a different key issue. While some blocs focus on national issues, others are more concentrated in a particular state or region.[45]

Because multiple issue groups may exist within a single state, presidential primaries seldom serve as an issue referendum on any single issue. The 1972 Democratic primary in Florida, for example, was widely billed as a busing referendum. Yet busing was only one of several key issues frequently cited by primary voters. In one statewide poll, over half the Democratic primary voters cited the Vietnam war as a key concern, and about half also mentioned the economy. School busing and crime were mentioned by about four to ten voters.[46]

Overall, no single issue appears to have dominated either the 1972, the 1976, or the 1980 primaries. Rather, presidential candidates won their votes by appealing to a series of more narrowly concerned issue publics and by winning other votes through their personalities and personal appeals.

Candidates and Personalities

Some contenders are as well known for their personal qualities or their personalities as for their specific positions on issues. Voters apparently rely heavily on a candidate's personal qualities and experience in office when choosing among the hopefuls. Traits such as leadership, honesty, morality, candor, or a candidate's long-time experience in office are often reported by voters in explaining their vote choice. These tendencies are most apparent when two or more candidates seem similar one to another on major issues, or when one or more candidates stress their personal qualities instead of specific issue pledges.

Data from the 1970s suggest the importance of a candidate's personal qualities. Late in the 1976 primaries, for example, one survey reported that over half (57 percent) of U.S. residents chose their favorite candidate more on the basis of personal qualities than on specific issue positions.[47] Another survey—of the 1972 New Hampshire primary—reported similar results. In that well-publicized contest personal attributes (such as honesty or leadership capabilities) were rated as more important by the voters and proved to be better predictors of vote choice than were issues.[48]

Personalities and personal qualities were again important in the 1980 race, particularly on the Democratic side. Massachusetts Senator Kennedy's personal misfortunes and perceived personal flaws cost him widespread support that he might otherwise have drawn, especially from liberal and moderate Democrats. At one point in the 1980 race, up to a third of the Democrats surveyed said that Kennedy's personal life made them unlikely to vote for him.[49]

Some candidates draw more heavily on the basis of personal qualities or their government experience than others. In one study of the 1972 Democratic primary in Pennsylvania, two-thirds of Humphrey supporters pointed to government experience as Humphrey's strongest attribute. By contrast, two-thirds of McGovern voters cited some specific issue in explaining their vote choice.[50]

Similarly, studies throughout the 1980 Democratic contest demonstrated the importance of personal qualities for voters who chose President Carter. Throughout the 1980 primaries, sizeable numbers, albeit minorities, of voters named honesty and integrity as the most important factors in their choice. Among these voters Carter handily led Kennedy. In the Pennsylvania Democratic primary of 1980, for example, one of every five Democratic voters identified honesty or integrity as among the most important reasons for their vote choice; among these voters Carter easily defeated Senator Kennedy, by a margin of five to one. By contrast, another one of every six voters in that primary cited leadership qualities as critical to their choice; here, Senator Kennedy led two to one.[51] Throughout most recent contests, personalities and personal qualities have cut across the liberal–conservative dimension of voter choice.

A Model of Voter Choice

How, then, do presidential primary voters choose among the candidates? Primary voters do not completely neglect issues in their vote choice. Yet recent data suggest that primary voters seldom have very complete information about the candidates' issue stands. Voters seldom rely on global evaluations such as the liberal–conservative continuum. Primary voters often misunderstand candidates' issue stands, judge the candidates on their personal qualities, or resort to a single issue or an interest group cue in judging the candidates.

One simple model holds that most primary voters prefer "short cuts," or at least find these necessary in choosing among the potential

nominees. Few voters go to the trouble of ranking their own preferences on a long list of issues, then determining each candidate's
stands, and choosing accordingly. Nor can most voters apparently
rely on a global dimension such as the liberal–conservative spectrum.

Instead, the typical voter's decision making seems much
simpler.[52] Voters appear to search only long enough to find a candidate who appeals to them on a key issue or personality trait. Or
some voters may find that there is only one candidate who does not
offend them. A voter who perceives a particularly appealing candidate, or one who finds all but one candidate objectionable, then
chooses that contender. For most voters these decisions require
only a minimal effort at information collecting; the nightly newscast,
the morning newspaper, or word-of-mouth will usually suffice.

A Note on Nonprimary States

While few studies are available on the motives of caucus-goers
in the nonprimary states, limited evidence does suggest that they
have a variety of motives for attending other than the presidential
nominations contest.[53] Many may do so through habit or through
party loyalty, to support a favorite interest group, to back a state
or local candidate, or merely through a sense of civic duty or even
curiosity.

In the nonprimary states, caucuses and conventions often
provide the organizational basis for the local and state party. Party
officers may be chosen; issues and resolutions are debated and a
party platform eventually written; fund-raising drives, registration
efforts, and even, in a few places, social functions are planned. All
these activities may also attract attenders to the local caucus meetings.

In some nonprimary states special interest groups promote
caucus attendance, sponsoring resolutions, manning telephone
banks, and making personal requests to voters to encourage caucus
attendance. Interest groups in several states organize to elect delegates
to the district and state party conventions and, later, to the national
party conventions to lobby on their behalf. In 1976, for instance,
North Dakota's Democrats divided into several issue subcaucuses at
their party convention: a liberal issue group, a pro-life group, an
agricultural group, an education caucus, and a labor faction. Again
in 1980, Democrats in that state showed that issues were critical in
the party caucuses; over half the delegates selected to the state convention were uncommitted and, in addition, over a quarter were
selected from a variety of issue caucuses. In several other states,
such as Utah, Iowa, and Minnesota, as well, issue blocs now appear

to be equally as or even more important than presidential candidate factions at party caucuses and conventions.

In some states, as in Minnesota and Utah, party conventions also endorse state and local candidates before the state primary. Or the caucus–convention process may actually nominate candidates subject to a challenge primary—as in Delaware or Connecticut. Here, candidate supporters may turn out to support their favorite state and local candidates.

In some states party business may dominate the caucus–convention agenda. In Washington in 1976, the Democratic state convention passed a new party charter. In Mississippi, the long-standing split between the "regular" (conservative, states' rights) Democrats and the "loyalist" (integrated, national party) faction was patched over when both groups attended the same meetings in 1976. In other states, battles for party officers and national committee members may dominate a sizeable part of the state convention's agenda—as among the Connecticut and Minnesota Democrats in 1976.

DURING THE PRIMARIES: THE NATIONAL POLLS

Most U.S. adults participate in the nominations race only passively—by holding an opinion reflected in the national polls. National public opinion polls, such as the Gallup Poll, the Harris Poll, or the *New York Times*-CBS Poll, survey a public four-fifths of whom never vote in a primary or attend a local caucus. Nor, apparently, can most adults identify the candidates' stances on many of the issues, agree on the candidates' liberal–conservative placement, or report any intense personal feelings toward the candidates.

Under these conditions it is hardly surprising that the polls may shift markedly. An analysis of recent contests shows that poll shifts are neither haphazard nor random. Instead, changes in the national polls occur in a regular, highly predictable pattern. Most often, the polls follow the media's verdict. Media-designated winners gain in their poll standings, while media-designated losers find that their polls fall off.

The polls appear to respond primarily to the media's verdict. Before the first primaries and caucuses, potential voters divide their preferences among the active candidates and among inactive but familiar names. At this point many reported opinions are but weakly held; others report no opinion at all. Few U.S. voters seem to be irrevocably "locked in" to any particular candidate.

During the first primaries and caucuses, the nominations race captures wide public attention for the first time. The media analyze the results, projecting an early front-runner and focusing attention on the declared leader. As a result, donors, interest group officials, volunteers, and party workers may shift their loyalties. So, too, do the mass of less active U.S. residents begin to change their preferences. Not surprisingly, the mass public shifts in the same way as do the activists. While the rate of change may vary, the same tendency recurs: the public moves toward winners.

The tendency for polls to follow primary and caucus winners is readily apparent when the media's verdict is compared to public opinion polls. Figure 5.1 presents one of the clearest examples: in this figure, Carter's 1976 poll standings are contrasted with his media-designated verdict throughout the 1976 preconvention season, illustrating one of the strongest patterns of polls following the media's verdict. Initially, Carter was the favorite of only 4 percent of Democratic respondents. As he scored well in the early primaries, his poll standings steadily improved, until he finished the primary season as the favorite of over half of all adult Democrats.

Other candidates who were initially little known show similarly strong relationships between the candidates' media verdict and poll standings. Figure 5.2 shows the media verdict and poll standings for McGovern in 1972. Like Carter, McGovern found that his poll standings followed his favorable media verdict. George Bush, too, found his polls strongly related to his primary and caucus showings in 1980. After an early surge in Iowa and Puerto Rico, Bush moved ahead in the polls from 6 percent to 24 percent. After his New Hampshire losses, though, his polls fell to half their highest levels. The relationship between the media verdict and the polls for Bush in 1980 are shown in Figure 5.3.[54]

While the relationship between the media verdict and the polls is not as strong for better-known candidates, the same pattern does recur from year to year and from contest to contest. A candidate who is judged to run well in the primaries and caucuses will probably surge in the polls. These relationships are measured and reported in greater detail in Appendix D.

Lags in the Polls

While media-designated winners improve their poll standings, the process is not always a simple, continuous one. Even a well-publicized primary victory does not always bring an immediate surge in a candidate's poll standings. Neither does a single poor primary showing always cause an immediate falloff in a candidate's polls.

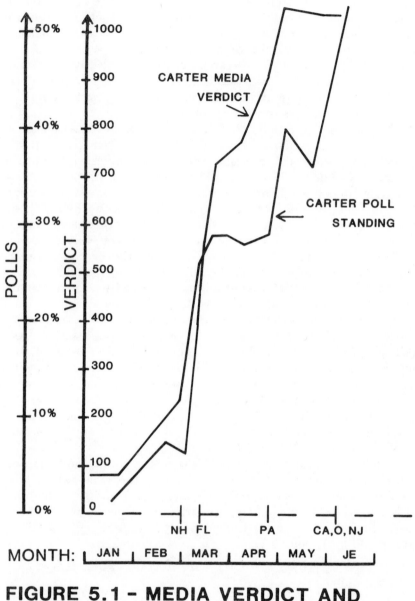

FIGURE 5.1 - MEDIA VERDICT AND POLL STANDINGS FOR CARTER, 1976
(POLL SOURCE: THE GALLUP POLL)

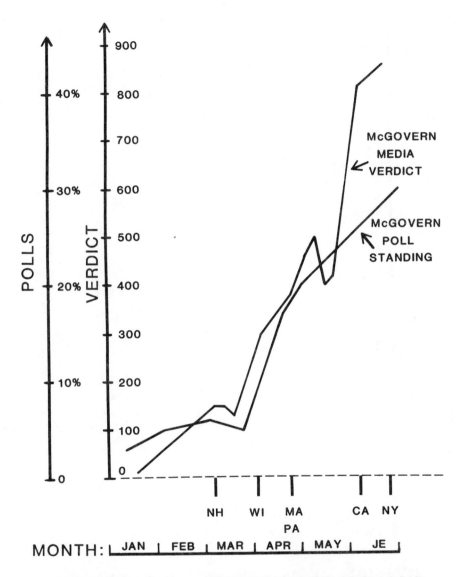

POLLS

VERDICT

900
40% — 800
700
30% — 600
500
20% — 400
300
10% — 200
100
0 — 0

McGOVERN
MEDIA
VERDICT

McGOVERN
POLL
STANDING

NH   WI   MA   CA   NY
                PA

MONTH: | JAN | FEB | MAR | APR | MAY | JE |

FIGURE 5.2 - MEDIA VERDICT AND POLL STANDINGS FOR McGOVERN, 1972
(POLL SOURCE: THE GALLUP POLL)

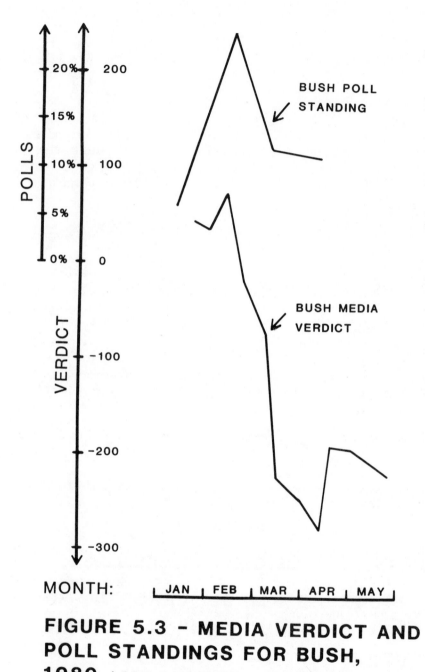

POLLS

VERDICT

20% — 200

15%

10% — 100

5%

0% — 0

−100

−200

−300

BUSH POLL
STANDING

BUSH MEDIA
VERDICT

MONTH: JAN | FEB | MAR | APR | MAY

FIGURE 5.3 – MEDIA VERDICT AND POLL STANDINGS FOR BUSH, 1980 (POLL SOURCE: NEW YORK TIMES/ CBS POLL)

Polls do react to primary and caucus success (or failure), but the changes are often characterized by lags and delays.

Lags or delays in poll shifts may result either from a candidate's behavior or because of delays in the public's reactions. Many candidates do not contest each state primary or caucus, but rather compete only in selected states. At times a candidate may fare well in one state, but then skip several subsequent races. If this happens, that candidate may find that his poll ratings climb immediately after his victory, but then level off or even sag back to the earlier level during the period of inactivity.[55] The polls rise most steadily, immediately, and dramatically when a candidate scores several primary or caucus wins immediately one after another.

Lags in poll changes may also result from delays in the public's reactions.[56] Since most adults are only casually interested in the nominations race, these lags in the public's reaction are not at all surprising. If a candidate drops out or drops back to inactive or to a favorite-son status, some supporters may not understand the implications of the decision, or they may not find another candidate sufficiently appealing to justify an immediate switch. Since many U.S. citizens prefer a candidate chiefly because of name familiarity, these adults may require considerable news exposure to force them to change their preferences. Some, of course, are so intensely loyal to a particular candidate that they may resist changing, no matter how abysmally that preferred candidate fares. Others may feel so negatively toward a candidate that they are unwilling to change, no matter how successfully a disliked candidate runs in the primaries and caucuses.

Delays in poll changes, then, may result either from the candidate's own decision or from the low level of interest and information of most potential voters. Not infrequently, a candidate will rise (or fall) in the polls only to find that his poll gains (or losses) will level off until after another well-publicized primary. In 1976, for example, Carter gained steadily as a result of his early poll showings until he hit a plateau in the polls, with a rating around 30 percent. Carter's poll ratings surged again to 53 percent only after the last-of-the-season primaries, when most of his opponents conceded the nomination to him.

Early versus Late Polls

Candidates find that the polls shift more rapidly during the early primaries and caucuses than during the mid- or late-season contests. For those candidates who remain in the race from start to finish, poll changes are usually most dramatic during the first few contests.[57] The reason is not difficult to discern. During the early contests, few adults are yet saturated with news, and many are just then gaining their first information about many of the candidates. By the mid-season or late primaries, many adults have at least a little (and, probably, sufficient) information about the candidates; so informed, they are less-and-less likely to shift their preferences.

While the tendency toward voter "inertia" in the later primaries and caucuses is apparent, exceptions do occur. A spectacular primary win late in the season may still bring at least a modest gain in the polls—as for McGovern in 1972 after his double wins in the California and New York primaries. In 1976, Carter enjoyed a dramatic upsurge in the polls after the last Democratic primaries of that year virtually ensured his nomination. Appendix D measures the relationship between polls and the verdict throughout the duration of the primary season. For candidates who stayed in the race throughout the season, polls changed much more dramatically during the first half than during the later contests.

Candidate Familiarity and the Polls

Well-recognized candidates are not as likely to rise (or fall) dramatically in the polls on the basis of their primary or caucus showings as are less familiar challengers. Because of their familiarity to party identifiers, initially well-recognized hopefuls are at least partly "insulated" from rapid changes in the polls. By contrast, first-time challengers and those unknown to the public must depend more heavily on a strong primary or caucus showing to boost their polls.

A good example of this "insulation" effect occurred during the 1976 GOP contest between Ford and Reagan. In that year, neither Ford nor Reagan's poll standings varied as greatly as their primary-caucus showings. Figure 5.4 shows the Ford and Reagan media verdicts and poll standings from 1976. Four years later, the Carter–Kennedy Democratic standoff showed the same "insulation" effect. After a dramatic poll shift before the first primaries, neither Carter's nor Kennedy's poll standings ever responded much to their media verdicts.[58] Figure 5.5 shows the 1980 Carter–Kennedy media verdicts and poll standings.

Appendix D reports the different relationships between a candidate's poll standings and media verdict for well-known versus little-known candidates. As Appendix D reports, initially well-recognized candidates (Wallace and Humphrey in 1972, Reagan and

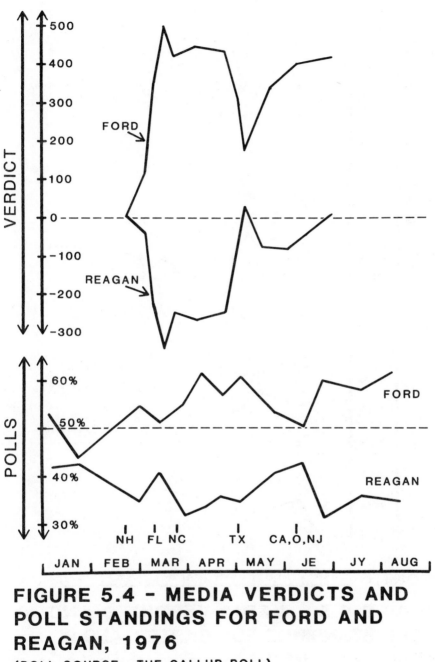

FIGURE 5.4 - MEDIA VERDICTS AND POLL STANDINGS FOR FORD AND REAGAN, 1976

(POLL SOURCE: THE GALLUP POLL)

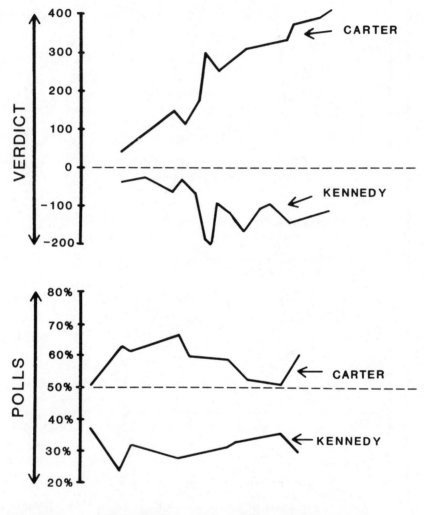

FIGURE 5.5 – MEDIA VERDICTS AND POLL STANDINGS FOR CARTER AND KENNEDY, 1980 (POLL SOURCE: THE GALLUP POLL)

Ford in 1976, and Reagan, Carter, and Kennedy in 1980) show little relationship between their verdicts and the poll standings. Initially little-known candidates, however, are almost wholly dependent on their primary and caucus showings to boost their poll ratings.

SUMMARY

Recent changes in the nomination process mean that ordinary voters can have a more significant role than ever before. These new opportunities notwithstanding, only about one of every five U.S. citizens either votes in a presidential primary or attends a local caucus; most simply ignore the process or follow it only passively.

Even the behavior of those potential voters who do not participate actively is often difficult to interpret. Although voters and caucus attenders do not wholly ignore issues, a combination of circumstances does not allow primary or caucus results to be easily interpreted. Voters choose candidates for a wide variety of reasons, among them a candidate's personality or experience in government. Few voters seem particularly well informed on many of the candidates' issue stands. Few apparently rely on sweeping concepts such as the liberal–conservative spectrum. Instead, voters may rely on a plethora of special interests or else choose a favored candidate altogether on nonpolicy grounds.

The most consistent and overriding pattern found in recent contests is momentum. When one candidate is judged favorably by the media, that candidate takes on a superficially appealing image. Donors, volunteers, and the mass public fall behind the emerging front-runner. Since most voters are, at best, slightly informed and little attached to any candidate before the primaries, the tendency toward momentum need not be especially surprising.

Momentum virtually ensures that an apparent nominee will emerge before the national party conventions. At the same time, however, the process reveals far less about the party faithfuls' issue preferences. If the nominee receives any mandate from the nominations race, it is more likely to be a personal one or the result of the contest's inherent momentum than an issue mandate.

NOTES

1. By contrast, the turnout in the 1976 presidential election was about 54 percent of all adults. See Marlene Pomper, ed., *The Election of 1976* (New York: David McKay, 1977), p. 72.

2. Austin Ranney, *Participation in American Presidential Nominations, 1976* (Washington, D.C.: American Enterprise Institute, 1977), pp. 16, 20.

3. Richard Rubin, "Presidential Primaries: Continuities, Dimensions of Change, and Political Implications" (Paper delivered at the 1977 Annual Meeting of the American Political Science Association, Washington, D.C., August 1977).

4. When two or more candidates make a state contest a priority race by increasing their statewide spending, or when all candidates are automatically listed on the primary ballot, turnout rises, See Ranney, *Presidential Nominations, 1976*, pp. 29, 32-33.

5. Thomas R. Marshall, "Turnout and Representation: Caucuses Versus Primaries," *American Journal of Political Science* 22 (February 1978): 169-182; Herbert Kritzer, "The Representativeness of the 1972 Presidential Primaries," *Polity* 10 (Fall 1977): 121-129; Rubin, "Presidential Primaries"; Morley Winograd, *Openness, Participation and Party Building: Reforms for a Stronger Democratic Party* (Washington, D.C.: Democratic National Committee, 1978), pp. 10-23.

6. Austin Ranney, "Turnout and Representation in Presidential Primary Elections," *American Political Science Review* 66 (March 1972): 21-37; Marshall, "Caucuses versus Primaries"; Kritzer, "Representativeness"; William Morris and Otto Davis, "The Sport of Kings: Turnout in Presidential Preference Primaries" (Paper delivered at the 1975 Annual Meeting of the American Political Science Association, San Francisco, California). For an exception to this pattern, see Robert Denhardt and Jay Hakes, "The Impact of Democratic Party Reform on the South," *Journal of Political Science* 4 (Fall 1976): 36-51.

7. In the 1980 New Hampshire primary, for example, just under half the Democratic primary voters said that they had been "paying a great deal of attention to the presidential campaign." See "Polls in New Hampshire Support View of a Volatile Voters' Mood," *New York Times*, March 2, 1980, p. A1.

8. Lewis Chester, Godfrey Hodgson, and Bruce Page, *An American Melodrama* (New York: Viking, 1969), p. 79.

9. Theodore White, *The Making of the President 1972* (New York: Atheneum, 1973), pp. 99-100, 108-109, 122, 130-131.

10. David Nexon, "Asymmetry in the Political System: Occasional Activists in the Republican and Democratic Parties, 1956-1964," *American Political Science Review* 65 (September 1971): 716-730.

11. Herbert Alexander, *Financing Politics: Money, Elections and Political Reform* (Washington, D.C.: Congressional Quarterly, 1976), pp. 81-82, 248.

12. In 1976, however, disputes between the Supreme Court, Congress, and the White House over the composition of the Federal Election Commission disrupted payments during the critical New York and Pennsylvania midseason primaries.

13. Winograd, *Openness, Participation and Party Building*, p. 18.

14. Jeane Kirkpatrick, *The New Presidential Elite: Men and Women in National Politics* (New York: Russel Sage Foundation, 1976), pp. 10-11.

15. John Jackson, James Brown, and Barbara Brown, "Recruitment, Representation and Political Values: The 1976 Democratic National Convention

Delegates" (Paper delivered at the 1977 Annual Meeting of the Southwest Political Science Association in Dallas, Texas), p. 11.

16. Thomas Roback, "Recruitment and Incentive Patterns among Delegates to the 1972 and 1976 Republican National Conventions" (Paper delivered at the 1977 Annual Meeting of the American Political Science Association, Washington, D.C.), Table Six.

17. For a discussion from 1972, see Denis Sullivan, et al., *The Politics of Representation: The Democratic Convention* 1972 (New York: St. Martin's Press, 1975), pp. 44-65.

18. Winograd, *Openness, Participation and Party Building*, p. 19.

19. "Bush First Pick among GOP Delegates as Reagan's Running Mate," *Dallas Times Herald*, July 10, 1980, p. A13.

20. Thomas Roback, "Political Attitudes among Republican Leaders: The Case of Delegates to the 1972 National Convention" (Paper delivered at the 1974 Annual Meeting of the American Political Science Association, Chicago, Illinois) and "The Role of Women and Blacks in the Republican Party: Attitudinal Perspectives of National Convention Delegates, 1972 and 1976" (Paper delivered at the 1978 Annual Meeting of the Southern Political Science Association, Atlanta, Georgia); John Soule and James Clarke, "Amateurs and Professionals: A Study of Delegates to the 1968 Democratic National Convention," *American Political Science Review* 64 (September 1970): 888-898.

21. "A Platform as Vehicle for Unity," *New York Times*, August 13, 1980, p. B1.

22. Jackson, et al., "Recruitment, Representation, and Political Values." See also *New York Times*, August 13, 1980, p. B1.

23. Kirkpatrick, *The New Presidential Elite*, pp. 312-313. For an earlier discussion, see Herbert McCloskey, Paul Hoffman, and Rosemary O'Hara, "Issue Conflict and Consensus among Party Leaders and Followers," *American Political Science Review* 54 (June 1960): 406-427.

24. *New York Times*, August 13, 1980, p. B1.

25. Denis Sullivan, Jeffrey Pressman, and F. Christopher Arterton, *Explorations in Convention Decision Making* (San Francisco: W. H. Freeman, 1976), pp. 22-25.

26. Roback, "The Role of Women and Blacks," Table One.

27. Two weeks before the 1976 primary season opened, the *New York Times*-CBS Poll reported a similar confusion about candidate issue stands. In the February 2-9, 1976, survey, 23 percent of the sample viewed Wallace as a liberal, 17 percent as a moderate, 34 percent as a conservative, and the rest (26 percent) were undecided. Carter was known to 28 percent of Democratic voters, about three times the recognition level of Udall and about equal to Jackson's recognition level. Carter was seen as a liberal by 22 percent, a moderate to 37 percent, a conservative to 22 percent, with 19 percent uncertain. On several major issues—including race relations, detente, and abortion—Carter's views were not clearly understood by most voters. See "Polls Find Voters Judging '76 Rivals on Personality," *New York Times*, February 13, 1976, p. 1.

28. Ibid.

29. "Polls Find Public Is Hazy on Candidates," *New York Times*, June 4, 1976, p. A12.

30. "Reagan Votes Are Held Similar to Those for Carter," *New York Times*,

February 26, 1976, p. 18; "Impact of Florida Vote," *New York Times*, March 10, 1976, p. 1; "Reagan, Wallace Facing Key Tests," *New York Times*, March 21, 1976, p. 1.

31. "Ford Says Reagan's Position on Canal Could Lead to 'Blood Bath' in Panama," *New York Times*, April 23, 1976, p. 16.

32. David Gopoian, "Issue Voting in the 1976 Presidential Primaries: A Comparative State Analysis" (Paper delivered at the 1979 Annual Meeting of the Southern Political Science Association, Gatlinburg, Tennessee); and Garry Orren, "Candidate Style and Voter Alignments in 1976," in *Emerging Coalitions in American Politics*, Seymour Martin Lipset, ed., (San Francisco: Institute for Contemporary Studies, 1978).

33. Orren, "Candidate Style," Table One, pp. 140–141.

34. Ibid.

35. Gopoian, "Issue Voting," Tables 6, 8, 22, 23.

36. "Polls in New Hampshire," *New York Times*, March 2, 1980, p. A1; "Late Surge for Underdogs," *New York Times*, April 23, 1980, p. A1; and "An Uneasy Electorate," *New York Times*, June 4, 1980, p. A1.

37. "Reagan Increases His Lead among Republicans," *Chicago Tribune*, December 20, 1979, Section 3, p. 3.

38. "Reagan Votes Are Held Similar to Those for Carter," *New York Times*, February 26, 1976, p. 18.

39. "Impact of Florida Vote," *New York Times*, March 10, 1976, p. 1; "Reagan, Wallace, Facing Key Tests," *New York Times*, March 21, 1976, p. 1.

40. "Polls in New Hampshire," *New York Times*, March 2, 1980, p. A1.

41. "Democrats Seek NY Backing in Primary Today," *New York Times*, April 6, 1976, p. 1; "Survey Shows Penn. Backed McGovern Because of Heightening of War," *New York Times*, April 26, 1972, p. 29; "Survey Contrasts 2 Front-Runners," *New York Times*, April 27, 1972, p. 1; "Wallace Off the Critical List: Sweeps Primary in Michigan and Wins Handily in Maryland," *New York Times*, May 17, 1972, p. 1; "Times Study: Debate Hurt McGovern," *New York Times*, June 8, 1972, p. 1.

42. "Times Study," *New York Times*, June 8, 1972, p. 1; "Times Survey: Defections in Party Face McGovern," *New York Times*, June 9, 1972, p. 1.

43. "Impact of Florida Vote," *New York Times*, March 10, 1976, p. 1.

44. *New York Times*, March 10, 1972, p. 1; "Muskie Comes in 1st and Humphrey 2nd in Labor Poll Here," *New York Times*, March 11, 1972, pp. 1, 33.

45. In the 1972 California Democratic primary, for example, ecology and the environment ranked among the top voter concerns, although those issues had not been so important elsewhere. See "Times Study," *New York Times*, June 8, 1972, p. 1.

46. "Florida Study Finds War Topped Busing," *New York Times*, March 17, 1972, p. 16.

47. "An Uneasy Electorate," *New York Times*, June 4, 1976, p. A12.

48. Daniel Williams, et al., "Voter Decision-Making in a Primary Election: An Evaluation of Three Models of Choice," *American Journal of Political Science* 20 (February 1976): 37–49.

49. "Chappaquiddick and Its Devastating Political Effects," *New York Times*, March 22, 1980, p. 89.

50. "Survey Shows Penn. Backed McGovern," *New York Times*, April 26, 1972, p. 29.

51. "Late Surge for Underdogs," *New York Times*, April 23, 1980, p. A1.
52. Williams, et al., "Voter Decision-Making," tests three models of voter choice. The simplest model simply requires voters to eliminate candidates one by one, until only one acceptable candidate remains. Voters may use personal attributes as well as a candidate's issue stands in judging among the candidates. This simple model closely resembles the descriptions of presidential primary voters discussed earlier in this chapter.
53. Data on various state caucuses and conventions were gathered from a content analysis of state newspapers during the 1976 caucuses and conventions, and from a more limited review in 1980. Analysis of coverage generally began just before the first-level (usually precinct) GOP or Democratic caucuses and continued through the state party conventions.

    Papers, cities, and states analyzed include the *Daily Oklahoman* (Oklahoma Cita, Oklahoma); *The Clarion Ledger* (Jackson, Mississippi); *The Hartford Times* (Hartford, Connecticut); *The Star-Tribune* (Casper, Wyoming); *The Kansas City Times-Star* (Kansas City, Missouri); *The Minneapolis Star* (Minneapolis, Minnesota); *The Bangor Daily News* (Bangor, Maine); *The Wichita Eagle* (Wichita, Kansas); *The Des Moines Register* (Des Moines, Iowa); *The Honolulu Star Bulletin* (Honolulu, Hawaii); *The Salt Lake City Tribune* (Salt Lake City, Utah); *The Burlington Free Press* (Burlington, Vt.); *The State* (Columbia, South Carolina); *The Forum* (Fargo, North Dakota); *The Great Falls Tribune* (Great Falls, Montana); *The Times Picayune* (New Orleans, Louisiana); *The Evening Journal* (Wilmington, Delaware); *The Anchorage Times* (Anchorage, Alaska); and *The Seattle Post-Intelligencer* (Seattle, Washington).
54. The marked shifts in national polls are also found, often to an even greater degree, in available statewide polls. In the 1980 Republican contest, for example, many available state polls showed that voters fluctuated widely in their attitudes toward the candidates, especially at the start of the primary season. In particular, George Bush's early successes in Iowa and Puerto Rico set off a rapid surge in many polls. After Bush faltered badly in New Hampshire and in subsequent primaries, though, his boomlet in several state polls rapidly collapsed. In New Hampshire, for example, Bush won only 8 percent in a September 1979 poll of Republican and Independent voters, but after the Iowa caucuses he surged (momentarily) to a 45 to 36 percent lead over Reagan. Similarly, in a Florida poll Bush surged to a 42 to 29 percentage lead after the Iowa results, only to fall behind again, 26 to 42 percent, after his New Hampshire setback. Other state polls for Illinois and Massachusetts showed equally sharp swings. For polls on New Hampshire, see "Dramatic Reversal of Fortune in New Hampshire," *Washington Post*, February 28, 1980, p. A1; and "Polls in New Hampshire," *New York Times*, March 2, 1980, p. A1. For polls on Massachusetts see "Poll Puts Bush, Reagan Even," *Dallas Times Herald*, February 3, 1980, p. 2A; "Poll Has Bush Way Ahead," *Dallas Times Herald*, February 10, 1980, p. A19; and the *Dallas Times Herald*, March 4, 1980, p. 2A. For statewise polls in Florida, see "Bush Passes Reagan's Lead in Florida, Poll Shows," *Washington Post*, February 4, 1980, p. A2; "Loss by Reagan to Bush of a Southern State Seen," *New York Times*, February 18, 1980, p. D6; "Florida GOP Primary Now Seen as 2-Man Race," *New York Times*, March 1, 1980, p. A9; "Bush Buoyed by Late Polls," *Washington Post*, March 8, 1980, p. A1; and "Reagan: Administration Harasses Cuban

Exiles," *Washington Post*, March 10, 1980, p. A5. For polls on Illinois' GOP primary, see "Campaign Notes," *Washington Post*, February 5, 1980, p. A3; "Illinois Shapes Up as a Fight Between Reagan, Anderson," *Washington Post*, March 13, 1980, p. A1; and "GOP Game: Will Ford Deal Himself In," *Washington Post*, March 6, 1980, p. A4.

55. In 1976, for example, Jackson skipped the Ioawa caucuses and the New Hampshire primary, then ran in the Massachusetts, but not the Vermont, primary. Jackson ran in Florida, but then skipped Illinois and North Carolina, reentered the battle in New York's primary, but skipped the same-day Wisconsin primary. Jackson also ran in the Pennsylvania primary, his last race before dropping out. For Jackson, the Massachusetts win sparked a rise in the polls that later faded during Carter's wins in Florida, Illinois, and North Carolina.

56. This effect may be treated as akin to the bandwagon effect often observed during the brokered convention system for top party elites. See William Gamson, "A Theory of Coalition Formation," *American Sociological Review* 26 (June 1961): 373–382; and "Coalition Formation at Presidential Nominating Conventions," *American Journal of Sociology* 68 (September 1962): 157–171.

57. For another study that reports similar results see James Beniger, "Polls and Primaries," in *Presidential Primaries*, by James Davies (Westport, Conn.: Greenwood Press, 1980), pp. 111–133.

58. While the Carter-Kennedy poll standings changed relatively little during the 1980 primaries, a sharp reversal did occur just before the 1980 primaries began. In a Gallup Poll conducted between October 12 and 15, 1979, Kennedy led, 60 to 30 percent. After that date, public opinion reversed itself and by January 25–28, 1980, Carter had gained a similarly impressive lead, 63 to 24 percent. See *The Gallup Opinion Index*, Report #175, February 1980, pp. 18–19.

6

THE ERA
OF POPULAR APPEAL

THE NEW NOMINATIONS SYSTEM

Nearly two hundred years have passed since the first president of the United States was selected. From that time to the present, enormous changes have occurred in the manner in which U.S. politicians have won the right to be considered seriously for the presidency. During the early 1800s, would-be presidents won nomination through a caucus of their party's congressmen. Later, top party leaders and candidates bargained for the nomination at the national conventions. During the 1970s, a third nominating system emerged: the system of popular appeal.

Different nominating systems are compared in Figure 6.1, with the continuum reflecting differences in the control that top party leaders and elected officials have held over the nomination. At the top of the continuum are the early nominating systems that originally gave party leaders and elected office holders (the regulars) virtually complete control. Toward this end of the continuum fall the congressional caucus system and the early brokered convention system. Further toward the center falls the brokered convention system after the advent of presidential primaries in the early 1900s. Still further toward the bottom of the spectrum falls the new era of popular appeal. In the current system, party regulars and the party's top-ranking office holders have much less control over the party's nominee.

As Figure 6.1 indicates, the past two centuries of politics in the

NO DIRECT ROLE FOR THE PARTY'S RANK-AND-FILE. TOTAL CONTROL BY TOP PARTY LEADERS OR ELECTED OFFICEHOLDERS.

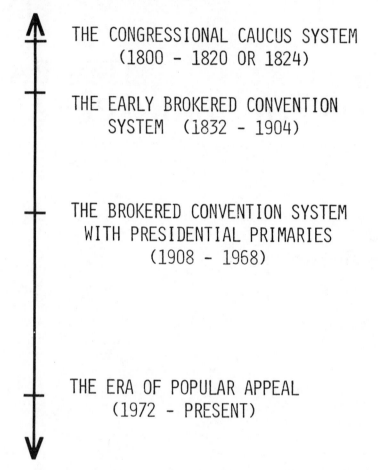

THE CONGRESSIONAL CAUCUS SYSTEM
(1800 - 1820 OR 1824)

THE EARLY BROKERED CONVENTION
SYSTEM (1832 - 1904)

THE BROKERED CONVENTION SYSTEM
WITH PRESIDENTIAL PRIMARIES
(1908 - 1968)

THE ERA OF POPULAR APPEAL
(1972 - PRESENT)

DIRECT CONTROL BY THE PARTY'S RANK-AND-FILE. NO SIGNIFICANT ROLE FOR THE PARTY'S REGULARS.

FIGURE 6.1 - A COMPARISON OF NOMINATION SYSTEMS

United States show a continued movement down the spectrum, from a nominations system in which the party regulars once held a virtual monopoly over the nominations to one in which their role is now quite limited. At the same time, the role of the party's grass-roots activists and rank-and-file voters has steadily expanded.

Figure 6.1 also indicates that the shifts in nominating systems have not been steady and incremental, year by year. Rather, when nominating systems collapse and are replaced, the change is usually relatively sudden. The congressional caucus system was abandoned in the early 1820s and was replaced nearly a decade later by the brokered convention system. Later, after 1968, the brokered convention system itself completely collapsed and was replaced during the 1970s by the system of popular appeals. Both the congressional caucus system and the brokered convention system fell apart under the stresses of an immediate political crisis, a long-term erosion of popular support, divisions among political elites themselves, and a shift in power and control within the party system.

In the new nominating system, presidential hopefuls win the party nod through a series of open appeals to the party voters. The role of top party regulars is now very minimal. The new nominations contest is played over a series of openly contested state primaries and caucuses. Unlike earlier years when the party regulars spoke for the voters, party supporters now vote directly on candidates and delegates. The media, not the party regulars, now stand between the candidate and the voter.

The system of popular appeal has other important characteristics, too: a focus on individual, not collective goals; the fragmentation of power; and an inherent tendency toward momentum. In the new system the candidates, the media, and the public each focus primarily on very individual, private goals. Now, no single player or set of players much considers the collective welfare either of the parties or of the nation. The concept of collective welfare is too ephemeral to be useful in understanding the new nominations contest.

Nor can either the media, the public, or the candidates, acting alone, normally control the nominations outcome. Power and control are now spread so broadly that meaningful coordination is difficult, if not altogether impossible, to achieve. The new nominations system is better characterized as a wholly impersonal process, showing little evidence of coordination among top party leaders, candidates, delegates, or voters. Openness, fluidity, and impersonality are critical dimensions of the new system.

In most cases the nominations race is characterized by a high level of momentum. Momentum results from the individually oriented behavior of the media, of voters and caucus-goers, of donors, and of the presidential candidates themselves. During the state primaries and caucuses, most of the aspiring nominees fail and, publicly discredited, they drop out of the race or else fall back to such a weak position that the front-runner's nomination is virtually assured. This natural tendency toward momentum occurs not as a result of collective planning or from the deliberate intentions of any of the participants, but as a result of the interactions of very individually oriented participants and of the new rules.

ALTERNATIVE VALUES IN THE NOMINATIONS CONTEST

New rules, which gave more control over delegate selection to voters, caucus-goers, and activists ended the brokered convention system. These recent changes are not simply new demands, unique to the late 1960s and the early 1970s. Rather, demands for more openness and for grass-roots control over the nominations process reflect one side in a long-standing dispute over the proper way to nominate and elect candidates.

At the risk of oversimplifying decades of controversy, two competing, fundamentally different visions exist in U.S. politics as how best to conduct nominations and elections. Each school interprets political reality and the democratic experience differently. Each makes a different recommendation about how to nominate candidates. While both schools are democratic—in that each relies directly or indirectly on voters as a source of legitimacy—they disagree on how best to represent the voters and on what role an ordinary voter should plan in nominating the candidates.

The Progressive Vision

Since the late 1800s, Progressives have argued that a candidate should win nomination by appealing directly to the party's voters. Progressives would deny the party's top-ranking elected office holders and its organizational leaders control over choosing the candidates. To the Progressives, the party regulars are merely a barrier between the party's voters and its candidates.[1]

The Progressives and their latter-day successors, the participatory democrats, argue that the party regulars have not adequately represented the party's ordinary voters. These critics of the party regulars often focus on demographic representation, pointing out that until recently few young persons, women, or racial minorities have served as delegates at the national party conventions.[2] Nor were poor or working-class party supporters often well represented at party conventions dominated by the regulars. Progressive reformers argue, even further, that the party regulars also neglected the issue concerns of these groups. Instead, the regulars are more likely to focus on patronage and personal favors in picking the party's nominee.

Direct, personal involvement by voters in primaries or caucuses fulfills yet another goal of Progressives and participatory democrats: developing political skills and building loyalty to the party. Direct involvement by ordinary voters is seen as bringing benefits not only to the representative process, but also to the individuals who participate and to the political parties.[3]

Finally, many Progressives also emphasize the importance of a direct, popular mandate for the executive. At the core of the Progressive argument lies an implicit reliance on the president as a focal point in national politics. This argument contends that the executive should have a mandate separate from the Congress and from state politicians. If top office holders and party leaders control the nominating of the president, then the executive will be forced to restrain his own initiatives to court favor with the party regulars. By contrast, an independent mandate from the voters will "energize" the executive. Even if the Congress is bogged down in defending parochial local interests, a president chosen directly by the voters can rely on a personal mandate to press for his program.[4]

The Progressives' argument for direct popular control over nominations can be traced back to the late 1800s and early 1900s, when they established the first direct primaries. In state politics, direct primaries allow voters to nominate the party's ticket directly. In national politics, primaries permit the party's voters to choose national convention delegates who favor a specific candidate. While the early pressure generated by the Progressives was lost during the 1920s, the same arguments reappeared decades later during the reforms of the 1960s and 1970s. This time, however, the Progressives and participatory democrats were more successful in transforming presidential nominating politics.

The Party Regular Position

Defenders of the party regulars disagree with each of the Progressives' arguments. The regulars argue, first, that they can better represent the party's rank-and-file identifiers than can delegates chosen through presidential primaries and caucuses, and second, that an overreliance on direct popular participation gives an advantage to well-organized, but ideologically extreme, candidates. Finally, the party regular position focuses on restraining, not "energizing," the executive.

The regulars dispute the Progressives' argument that grass-roots participation is the only adequate way to represent the party's supporters. In presidential primaries, only a small percentage of the party's supporters usually turns out, and even fewer voters attend precinct caucus meetings. Even worse, the regulars argue, those who do participate are often more ideological and extreme than the party's rank-and-file supporters.[5]

As a result, the regulars argue, presidential primaries and caucuses often overrepresent the support of more extreme candidates, thereby misrepresenting party sentiment. By contrast, the party regulars take a longer-range perspective on the nominations, emphasizing compromise and the coalitional nature of the party. The party's organizational leaders and its top-ranking office holders are more likely to choose a nominee from the party's center, not from its extremes, and to choose a nominee who will be more broadly acceptable to the average party supporter.[6]

The party regulars extend their argument one step further. Because they see an open nominations procedure as easily dominated by more extreme amateurs and activists, they fear that the resulting nominee may be unable either to rally the party's regular supporters or to attract the independent and crossover voters necessary to win a general election and, as a result, may suffer a disastrous defeat in the general election. To the regulars, the new nominating system has a built-in bias toward nominating candidates who are too extreme to unify the party, and it is, as a result, prone to "natural landslides," elections in which the ideological candidate is badly trounced. To the regulars, Goldwaters and McGoverns are by no means atypical and unexpected events. Rather, the new nomination system is prone to extremist candidates and frequent debacles at the polls.[7]

Unlike the Progressives, the party regular school emphasizes the need to restrain the president. Defenders of the regulars argue that a party's rank-and-file adherents cannot effectively bargain with and restrain a president, once elected. Only the party's regular leaders and its elected office holders can restrain potential excesses and abuses by the president. By removing the control of the regulars over presidential nominations, the party organization can no longer play a role in preventing presidential abuses such as those of the Nixon campaign committee (CREEP) and the Watergate violations.[8]

Without the support of the party's regulars, the regulars argue, a president can also not govern effectively. A president who wins a mandate directly from the voters may not develop the rapport nor the skills at compromise and conciliation needed to work with Congress, the governors, and the bureaucracy. A nominations process that ignores the parties and elected office holders, argue the regulars, is poor preparation for an effective government during a president's term in office.[9]

THE FUTURE OF PRESIDENTIAL NOMINATIONS

During the early and mid-1970s, the party regulars were denied control over the nominations process and relegated to a minor role in the process. During that time, Progressive reformers and participatory democrats succeeded in changing the rules to achieve most of their major goals: openness, grass-roots control, and direct appeals by candidates to voters. In undoing the brokered convention system, modern-day reformers ushered in the new system of popular appeal.

The recent success of the progressive and participatory democratic schools of thought has not, however, prevented widespread criticism of the new nominating system. Critics have proposed a variety of possible changes, from minor alterations to a complete overhaul of the system. Four proposals or groups of proposals for change are reviewed briefly below. These include proposals for regional primaries, proposals for a greater role for the party regulars, proposals to adjust various minor perceived flaws in the process, and proposals for a national primary.

Regional Primaries

Several proposals address the proliferation of presidential primaries and propose grouping the primaries by region. Although McGovern–Fraser Commission members apparently did not desire more presidential primaries at all,[10] the numbers of primaries did increase dramatically—from 17 states holding at least one party primary in 1968 to 37 states in which at least one party held a presidential primary in 1980. Since each state may now choose its own caucus or primary date, several states may hold their primaries on or about the same date. If these states are far distant one from another, a candidate may be forced to travel long distances to campaign in each state.

Noting the strains placed on the presidential candidates, some members of Congress have offered legislation to substitute regional primaries for the current state-by-state format. One plan offered by Oregon's Senator Robert Packwood proposes five regional primaries, held a month apart, over a five-month period. A federal commission would list each major candidate in each regional primary. The order of the primaries would be chosen by lot, and delegates would be awarded to candidates by proportional representation.[11]

While none of the several regional primary plans now pending in Congress has made much progress toward passage, several states have coordinated their own presidential primary or caucus dates with nearby states. As a result, a few smaller regional primary groupings have appeared. In 1980, for example, Massachusetts and Vermont both held primaries on March 4, following the February 26 New Hampshire primary. Alabama, Florida, and Georgia held a same-day primary on March 11, 1980, which followed the South Carolina GOP primary on March 8. North Carolina and Tennessee both scheduled primaries on May 6, 1980, while Arkansas and Kentucky, as well as Nevada and Idaho, slated primaries on May 27. Several other state parties or legislatures considered coordinating primary dates in 1980 but eventually did not do so.

Regional primaries may very well ease the burden on the candidates by saving them travel time, funds, and energy. Yet unless almost all the states were grouped into a handful of regional primaries —as in the Packwood plan—the move toward regional primaries would do little to alter the basic features of the new nominations system. The most important features of the new system—its openness, grass-roots control, direct appeals by candidates to voters, and its momentum—would be little changed by requiring regional primaries.

More Control for Party Regulars

Another set of proposals aims to increase the control that top party leaders and elected office holders hold over the nomination. Defenders of the party regulars argue that the regulars best represent the less active and less articulate majority of party supporters and urge that top party leaders be guaranteed some share of the delegate seats.

To be sure, these proposals are tantamount to a quota of sorts for the party regulars. Yet many critics of the new nominations system argue that this quota would be more than justified by the improved quality of representation at the national convention. Most proponents argue for a relatively modest share—10 or 15 percent—of the delegate seats to be reserved for the regulars. Others, however, argue for even higher quotas for the regulars—that up to a quarter,[12] 40 percent,[13] or even a majority[14] of the delegate seats be reserved for the regulars.

In 1980, the Democrats took a modest step in this direction. For that convention the Democrats allowed each state to expand its delegation by 10 percent to add delegates from the ranks of party officials and high-ranking elected office holders. Priority was given to Democratic governors, state party chairs and vice-chairs, and U.S. senators and representatives. The added delegate seats, however, were to be divided by candidate preference in the same proportion as the publicly chosen delegates.[15]

Adding delegate seats for the party regulars increases their visibility at the conventions. Yet plans such as the 1980 Democratic one do little to reassert the control of the regulars over the nomination. Three reasons might be offered to explain why the more modest of these proposals would have but a minimal effect on the nominations process.

First, under a plan like the Democratic Party rules for 1980, party leaders and elected officials win their seats as individuals. The party regulars so chosen would still be unable to appoint and direct large blocs of delegates. Under the 1980 Democratic rules, the regulars are dependent for their seats upon the publicly elected delegates and upon the candidates themselves. Under these conditions it is unlikely, if not altogether impossible, for the regulars so chosen to organize a bloc of delegates and negotiate with the candidates.

Second, unless the balance between the candidates is unusually close, it is unlikely that seating a small number of regulars would change the balance of delegates between the leading candidates. Not all senators, governors, state party chairs, or big-city mayors necessarily share the same candidate preference. It is more likely that the regulars would simply reflect the same balance found among the publicly elected delegates.

Third, appointing a small share of the delegates from the regulars' ranks would probably do little to slow momentum toward a candidate who ran well in the state primaries and caucuses. Unless a very large share of the delegates—perhaps half or more—were selected ex officio, the media would probably continue to focus on the primaries and caucuses, just as they already do. The momentum found in present races would probably not be much lessened.

Unless a proposal were enacted to guarantee the regulars a very high share of the delegate seats—perhaps half or more of all the seats—these proposals should probably be characterized as "window dressing." Even if the regulars win more visibility at the conventions, plans such as the 1980 Democratic one would not guarantee them control over the nomination. Only if a large share of the delegate seats were automatically guaranteed to national committeepersons, state party chairs and vice-chairs, governors, U.S. senators, representatives, and big-city mayors would these proposals undo the basic features of the system of popular appeal. Any proposal in which that many delegate seats were guaranteed to the regulars, however, would probably stand little chance of acceptance by either of the national parties at present.[16]

"Cleaning Up" the System's Flaws

Many separate proposals advocate small changes in the nominations process. Individually these proposals would have but a modest impact on the nominations system; none would undo the basic features of the system of popular appeal. Five such changes include proposals to eliminate crossovers, to extend proportional representation in the division of delegates, to change the manner in which vice-presidents are named, to relax the fund-raising and -spending restrictions, and to change the focus of media coverage. Together these proposals illustrate how broad are the suggested changes in the nominations system. They also indicate, however, that individual changes of this type are not likely to undo the system of popular appeal.

One proposed change involves eliminating crossover voting in presidential primaries. In several primaries in 1976 and 1980, crossover voters—Republicans voting in a Democratic primary, or vice versa—may have reversed the outcome or changed the relative standings of some candidates. In 1980 the Democratic Party sought to bar crossover voting in individual states that did not already do so but relented at least in one state after the Wisconsin legislature refused to comply.[17] Efforts to eliminate the last instances of crossover voting are likely to continue.

A second unresolved issue involves proportional representation in the division of delegates. Democratic Party rules for 1980 required proportionality in delegate division, and in most states the Republicans, too, operated under rules requiring or approximating proportionality. A few states, however, still clearly deviated from proportionality, as did the Illinois Democrats and the Texas Republicans in 1980, for example. On the Republican side only the

California Republicans continued to operate under a statewide winner-take-all rule, despite efforts of an anti-Reagan faction to divide the delegation proportionally. Challenges to nonproportional delegate-allocation rules have already begun to appear in state and federal courts, and more cases are likely to appear in the future.[18]

Still other proposals for reform address the manner in which vice-presidents are chosen. Some critics argue that the presidential nominee should have more time to consider his running-mate—a change that might be achieved by allowing a few extra days between the presidential and vice-presidential balloting at the convention or else by nominating the vice-president at a later meeting of the national party committee. Another proposal would require a presidential nominee to list several acceptable running-mates, perhaps as many as three to fives names, and deliver this list in a sealed envelope to the convention chair. After the presidential nominating vote, the sealed envelope would be opened and the delegates would be free to vote on the vice-presidential nominee.[19]

A fourth set of proposals would relax the donation and spending limits now imposed by federal law. Many critics note that a steadily rising inflation has, in fact, reduced the real amount of money that individuals can contribute and candidates can spend far below the levels required for an effective national campaign. These critics would allow individuals to give more than the present $1000-per-donor limit and would also allow aspiring nominees to increase their overall spending levels.

A fifth set of criticisms focuses on the media. Many media critics urge newspapers and television to lessen their emphasis on polls, primary results, and the mechanics of campaigning and to focus instead on the issues involved in the campaign. To achieve this end, the media might assign reporters to specific states or to groups of states ("zone reporting") instead of to particular candidates. These changes might help prevent reporters from being "coopted" by a candidate's organization. The media might also rely more heavily on issues specialists in covering the campaigns.[20]

Reviewing these many diverse proposals suggests two conclusions. First, the agenda of reformers is a broad one. All the features of the new nominating system are not yet firmly fixed, and efforts to change some parts of the rules will continue in the contests ahead. On the other hand, not all of these minor changes would do very much to alter the system's most basic features. The system of popular appeal would probably accommodate most or all of them without being fundamentally altered.

The National Primary

A final proposal for change considered here involves a national presidential primary. In this plan, the present state-by-state system of primaries and caucuses would be replaced by a single national presidential primary held across the nation on the same day. In one such proposal, candidates would enter the national primary by filing petitions in 17 states, with signatures collected in each state equal to 1 percent of that state's turnout in the last presidential election. If no candidate won more than 40 percent of the vote on the first round of voting, a runoff would be held between the two top vote-getters to decide the nomination.[21]

A national primary would change some but not all the key aspects of the era of popular appeal. Remaining would be the openness and easy entry by would-be nominees, the direct appeals by contenders to voters, direct control by voters over the outcome, and a reduced role for the party regulars. The major change from the present nominations system would be to end or at least to alter significantly the importance of momentum: the process whereby candidates who run well in the early contests gain more and more resources for the later state primaries, caucuses, and conventions. Instead of a series of primaries and caucuses lasting over five months, a single nationwide primary (or perhaps one primary with a runoff) would decide the nomination.

The actual effect of adopting a national presidential primary, however, is less certain. Supporters of a single national primary argue that it would replace the hodgepodge of state primaries and caucuses with a single presidential primary, thereby simplifying the process. In fact, adopting a national primary might well provoke party activists and regulars to organize before the primary to build support for their favorite. Party activists in an increasing number of states already sponsor straw polls to endorse presidential contenders—as they did in Iowa, Maine, Florida, New York, and California before the 1980 primaries, for example. A national primary might simply provoke the activists to move the momentum game even earlier, to a pre-primary round of state, regional, or national party conventions and conferences.

Whatever its merits or flaws, the national primary scheme enjoys considerable popularity among the mass public. Gallup Polls have shown a steady, sizeable majority favoring the plan since the 1950s. In one recent poll, two-thirds (66 percent) of those interviewed favored a national primary, while only about a quarter of the respondents (24 percent) opposed it.[22] That large majorities of the public favor this idea is not very surprising, since a national primary would simplify the nominations contest and would resemble the direct primaries already found in most states for state and local nominations.

Although public opinion polls consistently show approval for a national primary, few political activists or party leaders favor the plan. Among party leaders, the national primary plan has been roundly criticized for a number of perceived flaws. Its critics argue that a national primary would be to the advantage of well-known figures at the expense of less well-recognized challengers. It might cause the field of candidates to swell, fragmenting the vote and necessitating a runoff. Crossovers might still be possible in states like Wisconsin, which do not require party registration. A national primary, with or without a runoff might still lead to the nomination of a more extreme candidate, making the task of unifying the party even more difficult. Finally, its critics charge that a national primary might give a final setback to the already weakened party organizations.[23]

Proposals for a national primary are not new: President Woodrow Wilson proposed a national primary as early as 1913. Plans for a national primary, however, have made little headway in Congress, and a single, nationwide primary does not appear likely any time soon, despite its widespread public support. A review of changes in nominating systems suggests that mass public opinion support alone is not sufficient to usher in a new system of nominating politics. A political crisis, a failure of confidence in the present system, and demands by a large section of the political activists also are necessary. At this writing, it is not apparent that the future system of popular appeal is likely to collapse within the immediate future.

SUMMARY

Since the earliest days of choosing presidents of the United States, the process of selection has undergone great changes. Whenever the party system was based on two major parties, each has found some way of narrowing the list of candidates to just one contender per party. At least three major nominations systems have appeared in American history. Each system has had regular features, and each has endured for a certain time period. After 1968, the brokered convention system gave way to the system of popular appeal.

As each earlier system gave way to the next, the controlling elites were displaced by other elites. In the system of popular appeal, top party leaders, elected office holders, and large donors were replaced by a much broader group of voters and caucus-goers, grass-roots volunteers and activists, small donors, and the media. In the new system power and control are spread more broadly than ever before.

While the system of popular appeal appears to have stabilized during the late 1970s, it is by no means universally accepted or praised. Critics have proposed a host of possible changes. Some of these are relatively minor, but others would greatly change the nominations system. Proposals that would give the party regulars a majority of delegate seats might serve to return nominating politics to its pre-1968 features. Proposals for a national primary, by contrast, might provide for even more direct popular control and participation.

While a host of proposed changes have been offered by its critics, the system of popular appeal seems likely to endure, essentially unchanged, for the immediate future. In the past, more than grumbling by the displaced elites and some widespread but unorganized sentiment for change have been necessary to undo an entrenched nominating system. A political crisis, a sharp erosion of public confidence, and an erosion of the support of the dominant elites have also been required to make an abrupt change from one nominations system to another. At this writing there is little evidence that these conditions exist. For the time being, at least, the system of popular appeal seems likely to continue.

NOTES

1. For a discussion of Progressive logic, see James Ceaser, *Presidential Selection: Theory and Development* (Princeton, N.J.: Princeton University Press, 1979). For examples of Progressive or participatory democratic arguments, see George McGovern, *Mandate for Reform—A Report of the Commission on Party Structure and Delegate Selection* (Washington, D.C.: The Democratic National Committee, 1970); James Sundquist, *Dynamics of the Party System* (Washington, D.C.: Brookings, 1973), p. 307; and Robert LaFollette, *Autobiography* (Madison, Wisconsin: Robert LaFollette, Co., 1913).

2. McGovern, *Mandate for Reform*, pp. 11, 27-30.

3. For an extended discussion see Carole Pateman, *Participation and Democratic Theory* (Cambridge, Cambridge University Press, 1970). See also John Saloma and Frederick Sontag, *Parties: The Real Opportunity for Effective Citizen Politics* (New York: Vintage, 1973); and Benjamin Ginzberg and Robert Weissberg, "Elections as Legitimizing Institutions," in *Parties and Elections in an Anti-Party Age*, Jeff Fishel, ed. (Bloomington, Indiana: Indiana University Press, 1978).

4. Ceaser, *Presidential Selection*, Ch. 4, 6.

5. Jeanne Kirkpatrick, *The New Presidential Elite: Men and Women in National*

Politics (New York: Russel Sage Foundation, 1976); and "Representation in the American National Conventions: The Case of 1972," *British Journal of Political Science* 5 (1975): 265-322; Coalition for a Democratic Majority, *Toward Fairness and Unity for '76* (Washington, D.C.: Coalition for a Democratic Majority, 1974).

6. Ceaser, *Presidential Selections*, Ch. 6; Everett Ladd, Jr., with Charles Hadley, *Transformations of the American Party System* (New York: W. W. Norton & Co., 1978), Ch. 7; Denis Sullivan et al., *The Politics of Representation* (New York: St. Martin's Press, 1974), p. 34. For a contemporary discussion, see "Bring Back the Polls," *The New Republic*, March 22, 1980, pp. 5-8.

7. Ladd and Hadley, *Transformations*, pp. 306-319; Austin Ranney, *Curing the Mischiefs of Faction* (Berkeley, California: University of California Press, 1975), pp. 102-103.

8. Ceaser, *Presidential Selection*, pp. 7, 309-343.

9. Michael Krasner, "Why Great Presidents Will Become More Rare," *Presidential Studies Quarterly* 9 (Fall 1979): 367-375.

10. Austin Ranney, "Changing the Rules of the Nominating Game," in *Choosing the President*, James David Barber, ed. (Englewood Cliffs, N.J.: Prentice-Hall, 1974), pp. 73-74.

11. "Presidential Primaries: Proposals for a New System," *Congressional Quarterly Weekly Report*, July 8, 1972, pp. 1650-1654.

12. Richard Watson, *The Presidential Contest* (New York: John Wiley & Sons, 1980), p. 103.

13. Tom Wicker, "The Elections: Why the System Has Failed," *The New York Review of Books*, August 14, 1980, pp. 11-15.

14. Interview with Austin Ranney, in "Primaries '80: Once Again the System Worked, Sort Of," *New York Times*, June 8, 1980, p. E2.

15. Morley Winograd, *Openness, Participation and Party Building: Reforms for a Stronger Democratic Party* (Washington, D.C.: The Democratic National Committee, 1978), p. 50.

16. For a discussion of delegate attitudes toward recent party rules changes, see John Jackson, "A Decade of Reform: The Perspective of the Democratic Delegates" (Paper delivered at the 1979 Annual Meeting of the American Political Science Association, Washington, D.C.) and "The Future of the American Party System from the Perspective of the Party Elites" (Paper delivered at the 1979 Annual Meeting of the Southwestern Political Science Association, Ft. Worth, Texas).

17. "Court in Wisconsin Backs Open Primary," *New York Times*, January 20, 1980, p. 15.

18. "Ruling May Alter GOP Delegate Picks" *Dallas Times Herald*, June 22, 1980, p. 13.

19. William Keech and Donald Matthews, *The Party's Choice*, (Washington, D.C.: Brookings, 1977), p. 248; and "Republicans Study Convention Change," *New York Times*, November 25, 1979, p. 28.

20. See the proposals by F. Christopher Arterton, "The Media Politics of Presidential Campaigns," in *Race for the Presidency*, Barber, ed., pp. 51-54. See also Keech and Marber, *The Party's Choice*, p. 248; and Watson, *The Presidential Campaign*, pp. 103-104.

21. "Presidential Primaries," *Congressional Quarterly Weekly Report*, July 8, 1972, pp. 1650–1654.

22. *The Gallup Opinion Index*, Report #174, January 1980, pp. 19–20.

23. For criticisms of the national primary plan see Alexander Bicket, *Reform and Continuity: The Electoral College, the Convention, and the Party System* (New York: Harper and Row, 1968), pp. 37–39; Saloma and Sontag, *Parties*, pp. 71–72; Judith Parris, *The Convention Problem: Issues in Reform of Presidential Nominating Procedures* (Washington, D.C.: Brookings, 1972), pp. 172–177.

A GUIDE TO RECENT PRESIDENTIAL NOMINATIONS

THE 1972 REPUBLICAN CONTEST

The Events

Of recent nominations races, the 1972 Republican contest produced the least controversy. Incumbent GOP President Nixon easily bested two little-known U.S. representatives—California's Paul McCloskey and Ohio's John Ashbrook. By the New Hampshire and Florida primary, Nixon had ensured his renomination.

Before the earliest primaries, Nixon dominated all his party's early polls, and neither of his rivals were able to make gains. In late fall, 1971, the Gallup Poll reported that 73 percent of GOP voters preferred Nixon, with 13 percent for McCloskey, and another 14 percent undecided. Later, just before the New Hampshire primary, Nixon won 84 percent support from Republican voters nationwide, compared to McCloskey and Ashbrook, who won only 5 percent apiece.[1]

Nixon not only won strong, early poll support, but also gained widespread support from GOP state and congressional leaders, led the fund-raising efforts, and dominated the news coverage of the GOP race. Together, McCloskey and Ashbrook were only able to raise about 1.2 million dollars for their challenges, and both ran short of funds early in the contest.[2] Hampered by a shortage of funds and volunteers, McCloskey concentrated his efforts on New Hampshire. Ashbrook focused both on New Hampshire and Florida.

Bolstered by the publicity of his visit to China in late February, Nixon swept the March 7 New Hampshire primary, winning 68 percent of the vote. McCloskey, who had earlier cited a benchmark of 20 percent of the New Hampshire vote as a minimum to stay in the race, gained just 20 percent of the GOP vote total, and Ashbrook won about 10 percent.[3] Three days later, on March 10, McCloskey withdrew, citing a lack of funds, and returned to California to campaign for reelection to his House seat.[4]

Later, in the March 14 Florida primary, Nixon won a second strong victory, taking 87 percent of the GOP primary vote to Ashbrook's 9 percent. While Ashbrook later made scattered efforts, including a 10 percent showing in the late California primary, he never posed a serious threat to Nixon's renomination effort, and for the rest of the preconvention season media attention focused largely on the Democratic race. The limited press coverage of the GOP noncontest focused on disputes over the GOP convention site, the vice-presidential nomination, and the then-little-noted arrests of five men at the Watergate headquarters of the Democratic National Committee, on June 17.

Significance

Although the GOP contest was settled early in 1972, it was not without significance. The race showed the importance of momentum: Nixon's early wins thwarted his rivals' momentum and effectively ended their challenge. It also showed the ability of incumbent presidents to dominate media attention, especially through foreign policy initiatives or crises. Nixon's eight-day visit to China in February and his May conferences in Moscow with Soviet leaders focused national attention on foreign policy. Few contenders except an incumbent can dominate media attention except by their primary wins. Nixon's success in ignoring his rivals during both general and the preconvention contests would be imitated later by Ford's "rose garden strategy" in 1976 and by Carter's reluctance to campaign openly during the Iran and Afghanistan crises in 1980.

The 1972 contest, however, suggested a false unity within Republican ranks. The apparent harmony among GOP ranks dissolved four years later into open warfare between conservative and moderate Republicans. The Nixon fund-raising and -spending scandals also later provided a strong impetus for the tighter fund-raising, -spending, and -reporting provisions that applied to all the candidates by 1976.

THE 1972 DEMOCRATIC CONTEST

A Crowded Field

As the 1972 Democratic race began, no clear front-runner had emerged. Rather, early polls showed Democrats split among several leading candidates and a host of outsiders.[5] While Maine Senator Edmund Muskie won considerable media attention as the early front-runner, his nomination was far from assured.

Each of the major Democratic contenders traced their claims

and their popular followings back to the tangled events of 1968. Senator Muskie, the early poll leader, had gained favorable notice for his 1968 vice-presidential race. Former nominee Hubert Humphrey, now a Minnesota Senator, had nearly won the presidency that year despite a hard intraparty split. Well-known and well-liked by most party regulars, Humphrey eventually decided on another run at the presidency. South Dakota's Senator George McGovern had served as a last-minute liberal stand-in for assassinated challenger Robert Kennedy; thereafter, he continued his work as chair of the Democratic Party's rules reform commission. Alabama Governor George Wallace returned to the Democratic Party after a third-party bid in 1968. Massachusetts Senator Edward Kennedy was perceived by many as a possible successor to his two brothers, John and Robert. The accident at Chappaquiddick in July of 1969 and family problems, however, persuaded the senator to avoid the 1972 race. Former Minnesota Senator Eugene McCarthy—the early challenger to incumbent president Johnson in 1968—also reasserted his candidacy.

These contenders were joined by a large field of other candidates. Washington Senator Henry Jackson organized a race, as did former New York City mayor and Republican-turned-Democrat, John Lindsay. New York City black congresswoman Shirley Chisholm announced a bid, as did her House colleague, Ways and Means Chair Wilbur Mills. One Indiana senator, Birch Bayh, announced, then dropped his bid, to be followed by Indiana's other Democratic senator, Vance Hartke. Former Oklahoma senator and Democratic National Party Chair Fred Harris, along with Wisconsin Senator William Proxmire, considered making a run but dropped out before the early primaries. Finally, former North Carolina governor and Duke University President Terry Sanford organized a home-state effort as a Southern moderate to challenge Wallace.

Not only was the field of hopefuls large, but the rules of the race were new. The new McGovern–Fraser Commission rules were circulated in April 1970, but only adopted in February 1971 by the Democratic National Committee. Few of the would-be nominees evidently understood the new party rules, which provided more access for average Democrats, stripped top party regulars of their control over delegate selection, and—perhaps unexpectedly—produced more primaries than ever before.

Few candidates apparently planned for the rigors of the new nominations game. Most waited until a year before the contests—or even later—to begin their fund-raising efforts, to complete their planning, and to start campaigning. As a result, few campaigns were well prepared for the strains of the nominations race. Only McGovern displayed his knowledge of the new rules by planning early, building a loyal cadre of donors and volunteers, and focusing on the early state primaries and on the nonprimary states.[6]

The Preconvention Season

After early but inconclusive caucuses in Arizona and Iowa, media attention focused on the traditionally important New Hampshire primary. Since New Hampshire was in Senator Muskie's native New England and since early state-wide polls showed him an easy winner, a Muskie victory was expected. McGovern, however, focused his personal attention and volunteers—up to 8,000 by one count—on the state, while Muskie spent little time campaigning there. New Hampshire primary results hinted at the first signs of Muskie's weakness. Muskie ran first, but garnered only 46 percent of the vote. McGovern ran a surprisingly strong second, at 37 percent, with the remaining votes divided among several minor candidates and write-ins. Although the showing was not a clear loss for Muskie, neither was it an impressive showing. As a result, McGovern gained credibility and some momentum, while Muskie faced increased pressure to produce a clear victory.

One week later, the March 14 Florida primary, however, produced a clear win only for Wallace, who led a crowded field with 42 percent of the vote.[7] Humprey ran second, with 19 percent of the vote, Jackson third with 14 percent, and Muskie a weak fourth with but 9 percent of the vote. Though Muskie partially recovered with a victory against McCarthy in the Illinois preference balloting, his campaign began to look considerably weaker in the upcoming, now critical, Wisconsin primary.

Returns from the April 4 Wisconsin primary began to narrow the field. By this time many candidates were running short of funds. Nationally, Humphrey has passed Muskie as the poll leader, 30 percent to 22 percent, with Wallace running third, at 17 percent. Wisconsin's returns provided McGovern with a clear claim as a major contender. Again concentrating his personal efforts, his limited funds, and his volunteers in the state, McGovern led the crowded field with 30 percent of the vote. Aided by GOP crossovers, Wallace finished second, at 22 percent, edging out Humphrey at 21 percent. Muskie ran but a poor fourth, at 10 percent. Lindsay dropped out of the race on election night, the victim of continued poor showings.

The next round of primaries fell in major Northern industrial states: Pennsylvania and Massachusetts on April 25 and Indiana and Ohio on May 2. These key state primaries further narrowed the race to a three-candidate race, between Humphrey, McGovern, and Wallace. After dividing his energies between Pennsylvania and Massachusetts, Muskie ran poorly in both and dropped out. Jackson dropped out after the Ohio primary. Humphrey ran first in Pennsylvania, with 35 percent of the vote, while McGovern won a clear victory in Massachusetts, with 53 percent. In Indiana, Humphrey edged Wallace 47 to 41 percent, while Ohio returns produced a virtual tie between Humphrey (41 percent) and McGovern (40 percent).

Although the primary states gained most of the media coverage, many states chose their delegates through open caucuses and state conventions. There, McGovern forces continually fared better than expected, as small but active groups of liberals and antiwar Democrats battled with the yet smaller, often poorly organized, and less dedicated regulars and conservatives. In Southern caucus states, McGovern actually ran better than Wallace, who had failed to understand and organize in the nonprimary states.[8] As a result, McGovern gained a strong bloc of delegates to add to his primary state totals.

In the next primaries, the three leaders—Humphrey, McGovern, and Wallace—consolidated their strength. Wallace won handily in Tennessee, with 68 percent of the votes, then bested home-state favorite-son Sanford in North Carolina, 50 to 37 percent. In Nebraska, McGovern led Humphrey, 41 to 34 percent; on the same day, Humphrey ran ahead of Wallace in West Virginia, 67 to 33 percent.

Just before the Maryland primary, Wallace suffered an assassination attempt that left him paralyzed. The shooting, in a Laurel, Maryland shopping center, overshadowed the strong showings by the Alabama governor, who ran first in the May 16 Maryland primary with 39 percent of the vote. Aided by GOP crossovers and antibusing sentiment, Wallace also led the field in Michigan, with 51 percent.

With Wallace hospitalized, the race narrowed to McGovern and Humphrey. During the remaining primaries, McGovern's momentum, stronger organization, and superior fund-raising efforts paid off. McGovern won in Oregon, then outlasted Humphrey in California's winner-take-all primary, to add 271 convention delegates to his total. McGovern also won in New Mexico and in South Dakota the same day as the California primary. Bolstered by his momentum, one week later McGovern also swept New York's complicated districted delegate race, thereby gaining at least 250 delegates to add to his total.[9]

Late season victories provided McGovern's final momentum,

providing him with a winner's image, a surge in the polls, and a solid base of delegates. As a last-ditch effort, Humphrey tried to persuade the Democratic Convention to divide the large California delegation. McGovern forces, however, won a floor vote and demonstrated their control over the convention. Both Muskie and Humphrey withdrew just before the official balloting, leaving McGovern a certain winner.

Significance

The 1972 Democratic contest was the first in the new era of popular appeal not obscured by an incumbent or a dominant front-runner within the party. Neither social scientists nor practicing politicians immediately understood the new system—until a then-obscure Georgia governor repeated McGovern's feat four years later.

Why did so few politicians, journalists, or academics understand the transition? In part the reason may be that the new rules were partly, but not wholly, in force in 1972.[10] The new rules, so widely misunderstood, left unanswered the question of whether McGovern's success was due to the new rules or to the peculiar misfortune and ineptness of the regulars.

The 1972 race was also complicated by the large field of candidates. In the early and midseason primaries, the field was crowded and few races allowed a clear head-on race. Candidates often ran on personality appeals. Until the late primaries, issue differences between the candidates were evidently not very clear to many voters.

The McGovern victory demonstrated the importance of momentum, early planning, a nationwide effort, and grass-roots organizing. Overall, the McGovern campaign set a model for later "underdogs" to follow. Four years later, Carter followed McGovern's earlier campaign—focusing on early planning, in-depth grass-roots organization, and an emphasis on momentum. Eight years later many, but not all, the contenders followed the same formula.[11]

THE 1976 GOP CONTEST

The Reagan Challenge

The 1976 Republican race opened with an unusual feature: two "front-runners." The first was the incumbent, Gerald Ford; unlike any other incumbent in U.S. history, however, Ford had never before been elected to a national office, either as president or vice-president. Instead, he had been appointed to the vice-presidency after Spiro Agnew resigned in disgrace, then ascended to the presidency after Richard Nixon, too, resigned under threat of impeachment.

The second hopeful was an unusually strong challenger, former California governor Ronald Reagan. Reagan, a favorite of the well-organized GOP conservatives, had mounted a late challenge to Nixon in 1968, then spent several years on speaking tours. Strong among the GOP activists, Reagan also boasted a strong base among the party's voters. Late in 1971, Reagan either led or tied Ford in the polls of party supporters, although by the New Hampshire primary Ford had regained the poll lead.[11]

New rules for the 1976 contest further confused the race. Several additional states adopted first-time primaries, forcing both candidates to a more open race than ever before. Fund-raising was more difficult, as large donations were banned for the first time. Later, during the mid-primary season, matching funds were cut off, leaving Reagan, in particular, strapped for funds.[12] Finally, the GOP did not require proportional representation, and in California and in the caucus–convention states both Ford and Reagan backers used winner-take-all tactics to seek extra delegates.

Both the Ford and Reagan camps had problems in understanding and applying the new rules and campaign realities. Ford came to the White House with no experience in running national—or even state-wide—races and no recent experience in running against a strong primary challenger. Nor did Ford boast a loyal core constituency among grass roots activists or a clear plan for winning the nomination.[13] Reagan, on the other hand, found himself unable to contest several key primary states—such as New York, Pennsylvania, Ohio, New Jersey, West Virginia, Maryland, and Wisconsin—effectively. As a result, Ford's support among party regulars gained him easy victories and large numbers of delegates in those states.[14]

The Preconvention Race

Early attention focused on the GOP primary in New Hampshire. Reagan put forth a major effort in the small state, aided by an active organization. Early polls showed him leading, and his own local managers predicted a win. When the returns were counted, however, Ford eked out a narrow lead of 49.4 percent to 48 percent, with fewer than 1600 votes separating the two. While the margin was not an especially impressive one for an incumbent, Ford had surged ahead, no matter how narrowly, and turned back Reagan's predictions of an outright win. By those standards, it appeared at least something of a victory for the besieged incumbent.[15]

In the next major primary, in Florida, Ford again enjoyed a narrow victory, 53 percent to 47 percent, again upsetting the earlier poll predictions. That race, along with victories earlier in Massachusetts and Vermont and later in Illinois, gave Ford new momentum. Speculation grew that Reagan might soon be forced from the race.

Reagan, however, surprised his opponents by upsetting Ford in the North Carolina primary after openly criticizing the president on detente and other foreign policy issues. After that upset, Reagan withdrew to California for more planning, ignoring the next round of contests in Wisconsin, Pennsylvania, and Washington, D.C., all of which Ford won. But Reagan's strength showed in the upcoming Georgia, Texas, and Indiana contests in early May, and, as a result, Reagan again stopped Ford's momentum and bolstered his own showing.

Later primaries yielded mixed results, and the regional split within the party was readily apparent. Reagan scored well in the South and West, winning in Nebraska, Arkansas, Idaho, Nevada, Montana, South Dakota, and the California winner-take-all delegate primary. Ford carried the traditionally moderate GOP states in the Northeast and Midwest, leading in West Virginia, Maryland, Michigan, Kentucky, Oregon, Tennessee, Rhode Island, New Jersey, and Ohio.

The seesaw battle continued through the late round of state conventions. Because the GOP allowed winner-take-all rules for dividing delegates, both camps resorted to strong-arm tactics in search of a few more delegates. As the last delegates were chosen, no more than 100 delegates separated the two contenders. While Ford led the delegate count, both sides wooed uncommitted delegates with unfailing enthusiasm.

The battle continued through the national party convention. Reagan advisers continued to try to provoke a Ford blunder and added one new challenge after another. Reagan designated Pennsylvania Senator Richard Schweiker as his vice-presidential choice, then tried to force the Ford camp to name their own choice. Ford refused and won a tight convention vote that demonstrated his slight, but apparently stable, delegate lead. Later, the Ford camp chose not to battle an apparently critical platform plank on Ford's foreign policy approach. Ford then won the nomination by the narrow margin of 1187 to 1070 delegate votes.

Significance

The 1976 GOP contest showed the special dynamics of a race between two strong candidates. Although the state and national polls did respond to early primary wins, neither Ford nor Reagan could generate sufficient momentum to force his opponent from the race.

The 1976 Republican race suggested that nominations races with two strong candidates are the least likely to produce an early winner. In this case, both sides are relatively strong. Both may draw on a pool of volunteers and a strong regional base. If both candidates are persistent and determined to remain in the race, neither may be forced out.

The strong two-candidate race differs from a multicandidate contest. In the two-candidate race, both candidates may have surpassed the organizational threshold to remain through many state primaries. In the multicandidate race, many of the hopefuls are so weak that a few early losses will force them from the contest. In the two-candidate race, both candidates are likely to have a stronger financial base; in more crowded races, few candidates enjoy such strength. In a two-candidate race, both candidates are likely to have a regional core; in more crowded races, the candidate backings will be more confused.

In other respects, too, the 1976 Republican race demonstrated the impact of the new rules on the regulars. No major favorite sons or stand-ins appeared. In several states, local leaders who favored the losing candidate were humiliated. In the West, for example, Reagan backers often denied delegate seats to pro-Ford party regulars. In short, the contest focused on the presidential contenders; local party officials and elected office holders fared well only by pinning their efforts to a major, serious contender.

The Ford–Reagan contest, also showed the importance of new fund-raising rules. Neither side could count on large donations, which had often been the basis of past Republican candidacies. Instead, each was forced to solicit more small donations. Unfortunately for Reagan, his efforts were disrupted by the conflict over the Federal Election Commission's composition midway through the primaries.

Finally, the 1976 contest indicated the utility of the presidency in campaigning for reelection. Ford was able to delay paying campaign expenses, dominate the national news, and woo uncommitted delegates from the White House. As an incumbent, Ford could count on a host of federal officials to campaign for him, as well as the probable loyalty of the national party organization. These advantages are considerable and suggest that a sitting president is difficult to dislodge, even under new rules that equalize and limit spending and open the delegate selection process.

THE 1976 DEMOCRATIC RACE

The Early Field

A unique feature of the 1976 Democratic contest was that most of the early poll leaders were never active candidates at all. Of the seven candidates who won more than 5 percent in the last Gallup Poll of 1975, only three organized for the race: Washington Senator Henry Jackson, Alabama Governor George Wallace, and Indiana Senator Birch Bayh. The other four poll leaders—Senators Edmund Muskie (Maine), Edward Kennedy (Massachusetts), Hubert Humphrey (Minnesota), and George McGovern (South Dakota)—had previously mounted a candidacy but did not in 1976.[16]

As in 1972, the Democratic field was crowded. Jackson and Wallace led the early polls and fund-raising, but neither was strong enough to discourage a large field of first-time challengers. Texas Senator Lloyd Bentsen organized a well-funded bid; Idaho's Senator Frank Church also joined the race in the later primaries. The several candidates from the Senate were joined by Arizona's U.S. Representative Morris Udall, a candidate with a record of environmental and reform causes.

Not only congressmen, but also governors and ex-governors joined the field. California Governor Jerry Brown, Pennsylvania's Milton Schapp, and former governors Terry Sanford (North Carolina) and Jimmy Carter (Georgia) all organized a challenge. So, too, did former Oklahoma senator and ex-party chair Fred Harris, former vice-presidential nominee and Kennedy in-law Sargent Shriver, and antiabortionist activist Ellen McCormick. Rounding out the field was the year's only favorite son, Senate Majority Whip Robert Byrd of West Virginia.

The plethora of candidates fueled speculation that the primaries would not produce a nominee at all and that the convention would eventually turn to a compromise candidate. The most-mentioned name as a compromise nominee was long-time Democratic leader Hubert Humphrey. Humphrey refused to bid actively for the nomination, although he led the polls throughout most of the preconvention season and did little to quash speculation that he would accept the party's nomination, if offered.[17]

The Preconvention Season

The candidates adopted a variety of different strategies. Senator Jackson targeted the big Northern industrial states: Massachusetts, New York, and Pennsylvania among the early primary states. Former Georgia governor Carter focused his efforts on the early primary and caucus states to win momentum. California Governor Brown and Idaho Senator Church waited until the mid- and late primaries, hoping for a strong late showing that would impress a deadlocked convention. The strategies of several other candidates—Shapp, Bentsen, Shriver, and Wallace, for example—were never very clear.[18]

The first contests were in nonprimary states: Iowa, Mississippi, and Oklahoma's caucuses. Major media attention focused on Iowa, where a theretofore unknown Carter had committed his major energies and had led an earlier straw poll at a party fund-raiser. Joined by several challengers, Carter led the caucus results, winning 28 percent of the delegates, to Bayh's 13 percent, with 10 percent for Harris.[19] Later, Carter ran second to Wallace in Mississippi's caucuses and tied the former Oklahoma senator in that state's local meetings. Bentsen, who ran poorly in both states despite major spending, many endorsements, and a media campaign, dropped back to a favorite-son status in his home state's primary.

While Iowa's results and Carter's early efforts in New Hampshire won him media attention, no clear front-runner had yet emerged. The New Hampshire field was crowded, with Carter squaring off against Udall, Bayh, Harris, and Shriver. Wallace and Jackson avoided the Granite State race. When the votes were counted, Carter again led, with 28 percent of the vote and 14 of 17 delegates. Udall ran second, with 23 percent; Bayh finished third.

Carter's lead, although far from a clear win in the crowded field, immediately won him major media attention. He won front covers from the major news-weeklies, *Time* and *Newsweek*, and news coverage from television and newspapers. Jackson's plurality win in the next major primary in Massachusetts won him far less media attention, despite Jackson's gaining more delegates than had Carter in the latter's New Hampshire win.

The next major primaries, in Florida, Illinois, and North Carolina, confirmed Carter's emergent strength. In Florida, Carter topped both Wallace and Jackson, with 34.5 percent of the vote, besting the Alabama governor in a major Southern state. Later, in Illinois, Carter again led against Wallace and Shriver. Then, in North Carolina,

Carter gained an outright majority against Wallace, 54 to 35 percent, in a state where Wallace had polled a majority in the Democratic primary four years earlier. As a result, Wallace and Shriver dropped out, and Harris was little heard from again.[20] Carter's poll strength, predictably, shot up, from 4 percent before New Hampshire to 29 percent after North Carolina.

Results in Wisconsin, New York, and Pennsylvania further narrowed the field. Although hampered by a lack of matching funds, Udall, Carter, and Jackson took their campaigns to the major states.[21] In Wisconsin, Carter won a narrow lead from Udall, 37 to 36 percent, while Jackson led the same-day delegate race in New York's complicated primary but failed to win the clear majority of delegates he had earlier promised.[22] Three weeks later, in the key Pennsylvania primary, Carter surged ahead of both Jackson and Udall, winning 37 percent to Jackson's 25 percent and Udall's 19 percent. Jackson soon dropped out; Udall, who had never finished first, failed either to rally the liberal camp or to prevent the late entries of Church and Brown.

After Pennsylvania, Carter became the clear front-runner. His two major competitors, Jackson and Wallace, had been forced out, and Udall had failed to win a single primary. Others—Shriver, Shapp, Bayh, Sanford, Bentsen, and Harris—joined Jackson and Wallace on the sidelines. Humphrey delayed entering, then decided not to contest the late primaries. During the last half of the primary season, Carter ran strongly in the South and Midwest, taking the lead in primaries in Georgia, Indiana, Michigan, Arkansas, Kentucky, Tennessee, South Dakota, and Ohio. In the West and in Eastern "machine" states, however, Carter ran less well. He lost in Maryland, Nevada, California, Rhode Island, and New Jersey to latecomer Brown. He also trailed Church in Nebraska, Idaho, Oregon, and Montana. Favorite son Byrd easily outdistanced the inactive Wallace in West Virginia.

The last primaries, on June 8, solidified Carter's hold on the nomination. As expected, Brown won in California, and Carter led the preference polls but lost most of the delegates in New Jersey's complicated primary. The media, though, focused most of their attention on Ohio's primary; there, Carter won an outright majority (52 percent) to Udall's 21 percent and Church's 14 percent. Shortly thereafter, Carter gained endorsements by Wallace, Jackson, and Chicago's Mayor Daley.[23] Church dropped out, endorsing Carter, and Carter won an easy nomination at a surprisingly harmonious Democratic convention.

Significance

The 1976 Democratic race demonstrated for the second time the impact of the new rules. The large field of hopefuls found their initial entry made simple by the new rules opening the process, and by the relatively low threshold for gaining matching funds. Some challengers may also have been encouraged by new party rules that encouraged proportionality in the division of delegates. Other informal "rules"—by the media, donors, and voters—however, just as quickly narrowed the field and once again produced a front-runner long before the party's convention.

The 1976 race demonstrated the importance of momentum. In 1972, McGovern won major candidate standing with his strong showings in New Hampshire and Wisconsin. In 1976, Carter followed that performance, with a narrow but first-place finish in Iowa, then in New Hampshire and Florida. In winning his lead, Carter gained the media's attention, improved his own fund raising, picked up volunteers, and rose rapidly in the polls. After the Pennsylvania primary, both early poll leaders—Wallace and Jackson—dropped out, and the surviving "liberal" candidate, Udall, was widely discounted.

As in 1972, the role of issues and ideology was less than clear. Commentators had particular difficulty labeling Carter. In Iowa and New Hampshire, Carter ran against a field of more liberal candidates, but in Florida and North Carolina against Wallace and Jackson. In all these races, Carter won over a broad, not very ideologically oriented constituency. He gained about equal levels of support among self-styled liberals, conservatives, and moderates. Carter's open appeals for restoring trust and confidence in government won a wide backing, and his Southern background, varied credentials, and colorful family and religion went beyond the traditional "liberal versus conservative" debate. To most voters, ideologies are seldom as clear as they may seem to journalists and political scientists.[24]

Again in 1976, candidates and their advisors had apparently not counted on momentum to produce a winner. Many looked at the long string of primaries, at rules encouraging proportionality, and the large field of contenders. From these, they expected a deadlocked convention. As in 1972, many observers misunderstood the tendency of the polls, the media, and the donors to narrow the race quickly and produce a front-runner. In 1976, as in 1972—and later in 1980—that front-runner emerged by the early primaries.

The lessons of the 1976 Democratic race may have been obscured by the peculiarities of the year and by the GOP stand-off between

Ford and Reagan. The Federal Election Commission's cutoff of matching funds during the key major primaries complicated spending plans for the most of the candidates, especially in Pennsylvania. Other highly publicized disputes—Carter's "ethnic purity" remark, Wallace's health, and Jackson's antibusing appeals, for example—all took attention from one overriding fact: the 1976 Democratic race closely paralleled the model of 1972.

THE 1980 REPUBLICAN CONTEST

The Candidates

Unlike 1976, the 1980 Republican field was a crowded one. The early front-runner was Ronald Reagan, a former California governor who had first run in 1968 and who had challenged Gerald Ford in 1976. Popular with the party's right wing and well recognized, Reagan led his active rivals in the preprimary polls.[25] Former Texas governor and ex-Treasury Secretary John Connally organized a well-funded campaign drive. With his appeal to corporate donors, Connally raised more funds even than Reagan, although he ran far behind Reagan in the polls. GOP Senate Minority Leader Howard Baker also announced although Baker, unlike Reagan and Connally, delayed his drive to attend to Senate business.

Reagan, Connally, and Baker led the early polls but were joined by several other contenders. George Bush—a former Texas congressman, former GOP national chairman, former CIA chief, and former envoy to China—spent over two years building an impressive grass-roots organization. Senator Robert Dole, Ford's 1976 vice-presidential running mate, also announced his candidacy. Two Illinois congressmen from either wing of the party—John Anderson from the moderate or liberal wing, and Philip Crane from the GOP's militantly conservative faction—also made bids. A few others also entered the race or considered doing so. Two GOP senators, Lowell Weicker of Connecticut and Larry Pressler of South Dakota, both declared but dropped out before the early primaries. Former president Gerald Ford hinted at his availability, then openly encouraged a draft-Ford movement during the primaries, but eventually decided against making the effort.

The Preconvention Season

The race heated up during a series of well-publicized but nonbinding straw polls sponsored by party conventions or meetings in Iowa, Maine, and Florida. In Florida Reagan turned back a well-funded Connally challenge; Bush ran ahead at an Iowa fund-raising dinner and also upset Baker at a Maine state convention's straw poll. None of the results of these straw polls won the candidates any delegates, but the results did help Bush win credibility as a serious candidate and focused public attention on the race even earlier than usual.

As in other contests, the early caucuses and primaries were covered by the media far out of proportion to the numbers of delegates actually awarded. The Iowa precinct caucuses held on January 21 showed the importance of an early precinct-level organizing effort. Aided by his precinct organization and by a statewide televised debate—which Reagan skipped—Bush won a narrow plurality of preference votes of GOP caucus attenders. Bush's plurality was a narrow one—32 percent to Reagan's 29 percent statewide—but he had unexpectedly upset the front-runner and run far ahead of the earlier polls. Bush followed his Iowa upset with another victory in Puerto Rico's GOP primary, trouncing his major rival, Senator Baker, by a three-to-two margin.

As a result, Bush surged in the polls, rising from 6 percent in one pre-Iowa poll to 24 percent in a national poll before New Hampshire.[26] Reagan, by contrast, began to slip off the polls. While Bush's polls rose, his showings were not so much apparently based on his different issues appeal than Reagan, but more on his emergence as a winner and likely rival to Reagan in a two-candidate standoff.

Media attention focused on New Hampshire, where both Reagan and Bush had built a sizeable local organization. Reagan enjoyed a late surge just before the primary, aided by another debate controversy and by some campaign assistance from conservative groups. At another televised debate, which included Reagan and Bush, Reagan protested the exclusion of the other candidates, on camera, while Bush sat passively. Reagan was also aided by the added spending of right-wing groups who spent at least $60,000 on his behalf, as well as by constant attacks on Bush by conservative publisher William Loeb. In contrast to the preelection polls that had predicted a tight race, Reagan won handily, taking 50 percent of the vote. Bush took second place with 23 percent, and the other candidates split the rest.

The heavy publicity won by Reagan halted his slippage in the polls; by contrast, Bush's earlier momentum collapsed, and he fell to half his earlier level of support in the national polls. The surprising beneficiary of Bush's New Hampshire setback was Illinois congressman John Anderson, who won 31 percent in the next week's primary in Massachusetts and took 30 percent in the same-day, nonbinding Vermont primary. In fact, Anderson finished only second in both states, to Bush in Massachusetts (who won 31 percent) and to Reagan in Vermont (with 31 percent). The media, however, noted Anderson's unexpected strong showing and boosted him to the status of a major contender. Anderson then enjoyed his own rise in the national polls from 1 percent to 10 percent (in the *New York Times*-CBS poll), and markedly improved his fund-raising tallies.

The first few primaries and caucuses reduced the field consider-ably. Senator Baker shortly thereafter dropped out to return to his Senate duties. Senator Dole ceased his active campaign to pursue reelection from Kansas. Representative Crane made only a slight further effort, in Illinois, before he, too, conceded and dropped out.

After the New England contests, attention turned to the South and Midwest, with primaries in South Carolina (on March 8), in Florida, Georgia, and Alabama (on March 11), and in Illinois (March 18). Boosted by his win in New Hampshire, Reagan swept the Southern states, forcing out rival John Connally, who had pinned his hopes on a strong South Carolina showing. With Bush and Anderson splitting the Illinois vote, Reagan won again, taking a 48 percent plurality to 37 percent for Anderson and only 11 percent for Bush.

By this time—with only nine primaries passed—Reagan had emerged as the clear leader. Bush's campaign had lost its momentum, and he dropped back to efforts in only a very few large industrial states (New York, Michigan, Pennsylvania), in his own or his family's political home states (Texas, Connecticut), and in a few other, less conservative states (Wisconsin, Maine, Maryland, and the District of Columbia). Bush eventually won a few state primaries and ran close to Reagan in several others but dropped out even before the last round of primaries after Reagan's delegate tally indicated that the former California governor had clinched the nomination. Anderson stayed in through the April 1 Wisconsin primary but failed to defeat Reagan there and then dropped out to pursue an ultimately futile independent bid for the presidency.

Significance

The 1980 GOP contest strongly resembled the Democratic multicandidate race four years earlier. In both instances, a large initial field dwindled rapidly in size, with a front-runner emerging during the first dozen or fewer primaries. Even before the mid-primary season the eventual Republican nominee in 1980, Reagan, emerged in such a strong position that his nomination was nearly assured. The only remaining contender, Bush, was reduced to such a limited campaign that his nomination was, at most, improbable.

The 1980 Republican race also repeated other patterns found in earlier years. Winners in early contests found that their poll standings and fund-raising success improved markedly; early losers fell off in the polls and on the fund-raising circuits. Candidates who waited until just before the primaries to begin organizing seriously (such as Senator Baker), or who waited until the primaries were underway to decide whether to run (as did former president Ford) found that their delay had cost them any hope for success. The strongest candidates (Bush and Reagan) spent several years building a pool of donors, grass-roots volunteers, and a personal campaign staff.

THE 1980 DEMOCRATIC CONTEST

The Preconvention Race

Like the 1976 Republican contest, the 1980 Democratic race began with two strong and well-recognized candidates—one an incumbent president and the other a challenger well known and long popular in the party's ranks. Jimmy Carter, who had begun four years earlier as a relative unknown and an outsider, now strove for renomination and reelection as an incumbent. He was challenged by Senator Edward Kennedy of Massachusetts, the brother of one past president and of another aspirant, who had for a decade led the popularity polls among Democrats. Carter and Kennedy were joined by a third challenger, Governor Jerry Brown of California, who had made a brief run in 1976. A few other little-known candidates also declared, such as Lyndon LaRouche and former Mississippi governor Cliff Finch, both of whom received few votes and little attention. Other politicians, such as Illinois' outgoing senator Adlai Stevenson III and New York Governor Hugh Carey, apparently considered making a bid, but deferred to Kennedy.

The 1980 nomination season actually began in earnest long before the first primary or caucus. President Carter's backers began planning for the contest, raising funds, encouraging a switch in some state's primary dates, cultivating local politicians, and setting in place a grass-roots organization as long as a year before the first caucus. By contrast, Senator Kennedy delayed making a decision to run, first supporting Carter's reelection, then declaring his own candidacy in late 1979. In the interim, dozens of draft-Kennedy groups sprang up to encourage the Massachusetts senator to join the race.

Despite the efforts of draft-Kennedy groups and the senator's own announcement, Kennedy's challenge fared poorly in the period just before the early caucuses and primaries. In part, Carter's resurgence in the polls was due to foreign events. In early November of 1979, Islamic militants seized the U.S. Embassy in Iran, taking embassy officials as prisoners. Shortly afterwards, in December, the Soviets overthrew one pro-Soviet government in Afghanistan and sent in troops to prop up another regime. Americans rallied behind Carter, sending his polls soaring. In part, however, Kennedy's decline in the polls was also due to his own shaky start. Kennedy supporters in Iowa and Florida lost straw polls to the better-organized Carter camp, further eroding Kennedy's winning image. Kennedy projected poorly in several interviews and in his speeches, failing to articulate clearly the issue differences between Carter and himself.

Between November 1979, when Kennedy announced, and the next year's caucuses and primaries, Kennedy's early poll lead over Carter collapsed. In the October 1979 polls Kennedy had led 60 percent to 30 percent. Four months later, in February 1980, Carter had reversed the lead, enjoying a 61 percent to 32 percent lead—a margin that then changed very little during the remainder of the preconvention season.[27]

The early caucuses in Iowa and Maine and the New England primaries fell just as Carter's poll ratings reached their peak. Carter won an impressive victory in Iowa's caucuses, taking 59 percent of the precinct-level delegates selected—well over the 50 percent level set for a Carter victory by Senator Kennedy himself. In the February 10 Maine town caucuses Carter also took a plurality of the delegates. In New Hampshire's first primary, Carter won his third early contest, taking 48 percent of the vote to Kennedy's 38 percent. Kennedy did salvage a must-win victory in his home state's primary one week later, although Carter handily won the same-day Vermont primary.

If the first caucuses and primaries badly weakened the Kennedy effort, the next group of primaries further solidified Carter's advantage. Carter won landslide margins in three Southern primaries— Florida, Georgia, and Alabama. Then, despite a Kennedy endorsement by Chicago Mayor Byrne, Carter also swept the Illinois primary by a two-to-one margin in the "beauty contest" and took 165 of 179 delegates in the separate (loophole) delegate-selection contest.

The Kennedy camp's woes multiplied after these early setbacks. His organization was thereafter chronically short of funds; the media increasingly focused on his personal and family troubles and on his campaign woes; volunteers grew fewer; staff shakeups continued. To save their dwindling resources for a few large states, Kennedy's aides wrote off most of the South, the Midwest, the Plains states, and the West. While Kennedy did win a few later primaries—in New York and Connecticut, Pennsylvania, California, and New Jersey, among the larger states—many of his margins were narrow ones; under new party rules he did not acquire enough delegates to offset Carter's overwhelming wins in most other states. After the last primaries, Carter had won 51 percent of all the votes cast in presidential primaries to Kennedy's 38 percent; Carter also won nearly 60 percent of the delegates.

The third hopeful, California Governor Brown, also suffered from his poor early showings. After a third-place finish in Iowa, Maine, New Hampshire, and finally, in Wisconsin, Brown found himself out of funds, ineligible for further federal matching funds, short on volunteers, running poorly in the polls, and winning little serious attention from the media. As the Wisconsin votes were reported, the California governor abandoned his presidential hopes and returned to his home state.

By the April 1 Wisconsin primary, Carter had virtually ensured his nomination by eliminating one rival, Governor Brown, and reducing his other challenger, Senator Kennedy, to a long-shot prospect. While Carter increased his delegate leads, a stalled economy, a stalemate in Iran, a continued Soviet presence in Afghanistan, along with a well-publicized—if ultimately uneventful—Senate inquiry into his brother's dealings abroad, all cost Carter his earlier lead in the national polls against his apparent GOP rival, Ronald Reagan. While Carter continued to lead Senator Kennedy handily among the Democrats, Kennedy remained in the race.

Growing fears of a Carter loss in November and a standoff in several last-round primaries led to a stop-Carter effort at the national party convention. The anti-Carter forces made one last-ditch effort, attacking a new party rule that required delegates to vote for the candidate under whose name they had been chosen in the earlier primaries or caucuses. Carter's delegates remained loyal, and Carter won the test vote handily, by a 1936 to 1391 margin. Kennedy then withdrew his name and Carter was renominated.

Significance

The 1980 Democratic race suggested the instability of the national polls, even for two well-known candidates. While public opinion did not vary much during the primary–caucus season itself, national polls sharply reversed themselves during the four-month period just before the first caucuses and primaries. Even for familiar candidates, apparently, the polls may show a considerable instability.

The Carter-Kennedy contest also showed the difficulty of running against an incumbent. Any astute incumbent begins with several advantages: an easier access to the media, numerous surrogate campaigners, the availability of federal grants, the advantages of the White House to woo donors, delegates, and local politicians, and a previous experience in a national presidential campaign. While a challenger, such as Senator Kennedy, may be tempted to delay a challenge until just before the primaries, to delay that long is likely to lead to a considerable disadvantage.

Finally, the 1980 Democratic contest also illustrated the impact of early victories or losses on a candidate's chances of winning the party's nod. Kennedy's early losses in a few primaries and caucuses debilitated his organization, discouraged volunteers and donors, and forced his campaign to write off large blocs of delegates. As a result, by the end of the first few primaries, Carter had almost certainly won his renomination battle.

NOTES

1. *The Gallup Opinion Index*, Report #78, December 1971, p. 11; and #81, March 1972, p. 12.
2. Herbert Alexander, *Financing Politics* (Washington, D.C.: Congressional Quarterly Press, 1976), p. 193; Ernest May and Janet Fraser, eds., *Campaign '72: The Managers Speak* (Cambridge, Mass.: Harvard University Press, 1973), pp. 77–78.
3. The 20 percent benchmark figure for McCloskey is cited in *Congressional Quarterly Weekly Report*, February 26, 1972, p. 427.
4. McCloskey, however, allowed his name to remain on the ballot in about 10 states as an antiwar protest. *Congressional Quarterly Weekly Report*, March 18, 1972, p. 587.
5. The Gallup Poll taken in December of 1972 showed Kennedy as the first choice of Democrats, with 32 percent. Muskie trailed, with 25 percent, followed by Humphrey, at 19 percent. Wallace's name was not included on the list; McGovern won only about 5 percent of the responses. The last Gallup Poll taken just before the March 7 New Hampshire primary, however, showed Humphrey taking the lead, with 31 percent of the responses. Muskie trailed at 23 percent, then Wallace at 15 percent.
6. For a description of candidate planning for the 1972 campaigns, see May and Fraser, eds., *Campaign '72*, pp. 33–34, 41–63.
7. In Florida, all serious contenders were automatically entered by the

Florida Secretary of State, thereby producing the extremely crowded field.

8. May and Fraser, *Campaign '72*, pp. 41–43, 100.

9. Just after the New York primary, McGovern was credited with 1169.3 delegates, of the 1509 needed to win the nomination. Humphrey trailed far behind, with 472.2; Wallace, with 389. See *Congressional Quarterly Weekly Report*, June 24, 1972, p. 1513; and July 1, 1972, p. 1577. The remaining delegates were uncommitted or tied to other candidates. McGovern's late surge allowed him to lead the last preconvention Gallup Poll, with 30 percent to Humphrey's 27 percent and Wallace's 25 percent. See William Keech and Donald Matthews, *The Party's Choice* (Washington, D.C.: The Brookings Institute, 1977).

10. Democratic contenders were not restricted by the later fund-raising and -spending limits, although several did agree to a "gentleman's agreement" on limiting spending.

11. In November 1975, Reagan led Ford in the Gallup Poll, 40 percent to 32 percent, and in December, the two candidates were tied, at 45 percent apiece. Ford regained the poll lead among Republicans in January, and just before the New Hampshire primary led Reagan 55 percent to 35 percent.

12. For a description of the Reagan fund-raising problems, see Jonathon Moore and Janet Fraser, eds., *Campaign for President—The Managers Look at '76* (Cambridge, Mass.: Ballinger, 1977), pp. 19–72, especially pp. 40–43. See also *Newsweek*, April 26, 1976, pp. 20–21.

13. Moore and Fraser, eds., *Campaign for President*, pp. 38–40.

14. Ibid., pp. 71–72, 34, 40–41.

15. Reagan's early advantage in New Hampshire is described in *Newsweek*, February 2, 1976, pp. 20–23, February 23, 1976, pp. 20–21, and March 8, 1976, pp. 20–21. Reagan backer Meldrim Thompson, then New Hampshire governor, apparently claimed that Reagan would capture "well over 50 percent of the vote." This claim contradicted the Reagan camp's plans to claim victory at 40 percent of the returns. See *Newsweek*, February 23, 1976, p. 21.

16. In the Gallup Roll of November 21–24, 1975, Humphrey led, with 30 percent, with Wallace at 20 percent, McGovern and Jackson at 10 percent each, Muskie at 7 percent, and Bayh at 5 percent. When Kennedy's name was added, he topped the polls at 29 percent to Humphrey's 21 percent and Wallace's 15 percent.

17. See Moore and Fraser, eds., *Campaign for President*, pp. 79, 100–103. See also Jules Witcover, *Marathon* (New York: The Viking Press, 1977), pp. 311–316, 345–347.

18. Moore and Fraser, *Campaign for President*, pp. 64–80.

19. Witcover, *Marathon*, pp. 200–203, 212–215.

20. Sanford dropped out before the primaries began. Bayh after Massachusetts, and Shapp after Florida.

21. The Federal Election Commission was prohibited from dispensing matching funds during this period due to the failure of Congress and the president to reconstitute the commission after the Supreme Court's *Buckley v. Valeo* ruling. See the *New York Times* issues of March 24, p. 20; April 7, p. 21; April 9, p. 14; April 14, p. 1; April 17, p. 6; April 18, IV, p. 15;

April 19, p. 21; April 21, p. 18; April 22, p. 25; and April 23, p. 17, all from 1976.

22. See the *New York Times*, March 16, p. 24, and April 7, pp. 1 and 22.

23. For a description of the post-Ohio endorsements, see F. Christopher Artertor, "The Media Politics of Presidential Campaigns" in *Race for the Presidency—The Media and the Nominating Process*, James Davis Barber, ed. (Englewood Cliffs, N.J.: Prentice Hall, 1978), especially pp. 45-48.

24. See David Gopoian, "Issue Voting in the 1976 Presidential Primaries: A Comparative State Analysis" (Paper presented at the 1979 Southern Political Science Association Convention, Gatlingburg, Tennessee). Udall and Wallace were the candidates whose support varied most by the ideological leanings of the voters. By contrast, Carter's support was spread widely among the party's voters.

25. *The Gallup Opinion Index*, Report #175, February 1980, p. 20.

26. Data from the *New York Times*-CBS poll.

27. *The Gallup Opinion Index*, Report #175, February 1980, p. 18.

APPENDIX A:
Notes on Measuring
the Candidates' Media Verdict

After each primary, caucus, or state convention, news stories reporting the outcome were content analyzed to measure the reported success (or failure) of each major candidate. Only front-page column inches were counted, and a scale ranging from +2 (greatest success) to −2 (worst failure) was used. Coding ceased when the candidate withdrew or suspended his active candidacy.

The *New York Times* and the *Washington Post* demonstrated a high level of agreement in reporting the success or failure of the candidates. The level of agreement is reported below:

1972 Democrats		*1976 Democrats*	
Muskie (6)	.85*	Carter (28)	.79**
McGovern (15)	.49*	Udall (11)	.68**
Humphrey (10)	.73**	Wallace (9)	.86**
Wallace (11)	1.00**	Shriver (6)	.75*
		Harris (5)	.93*

1976 Republicans		*1980 Republicans*	
Ford (25)	.74**	Reagan (21)	.68**
Reagan (27)	.81**	Bush (19)	.76**
		Anderson (5)	.62

1980 Democrats	
Carter (23)	.86**
Kennedy (21)	.81**

Note: Only those primaries or caucuses for which both the *Times* and the *Post* offered a judgment on the candidate's performance are used in computations. Correlations indicated are Kendall's Tau.
* denotes statistical significance at the .05 level.
** denotes statistical significance at the .01 level.
Numbers in parentheses indicate the number of primaries, caucuses, or state conventions on which the correlation is based.

APPENDIX B:
Notes on Measuring
News Coverage, 1972–80

This analysis tests how fully editors of major newspapers used four criteria to determine the extent of news coverage for state primaries, caucuses, and conventions. The dependent variable is the amount of front-page postprimary (or caucus) coverage, per state, measured by the number of column inches. Four characteristics of primaries or caucuses are used as independent variables, or predictors.

The Dependent Variable

The number of front-page column inches given to reporting the outcome of each state primary, caucus, or convention was measured as the dependent variable. Coverage was measured for both major parties from 1972 through 1980. Included were text, headlines, and pictures. Such stories usually occurred the day following the primary, caucus, or convention, although in some cases coverage continued for two or more days. The dependent variable is ratio level.

The Independent Variable

Four independent variables were correlated with the dependent variable, including:

1. *The percentage of all national convention delegates from each state, per party, per year.*   This is a ratio-level variable.

2. *A state's historic importance in the nominating process.*   This ordinal-level variable was devised by counting the number of times since 1936 each state was cited as critical in forcing a major contender for the nomination to withdraw, or in establishing a contender as the front-runner. The states were trichotomized into groups of states with the greatest historic importance, states of some importance, and states that were never critical to a major candidate. Source: William Keech and Donald Matthews, *The Party's Choice* (Washington, D.C.: Brookings, 1976).

3. *The make-or-break test.*   This dichotomous variable measured whether or not any candidate faced a make-or-break test in a state primary, caucus, or convention. If the event was judged likely to establish a front-runner or to force a candidate from the race, that state was coded as critical. Source: *Congressional Quarterly Weekly Report*, issues immediately preceding each state primary or caucus. Data are available only for 1976 and 1980.

4. *The mode of delegate selection.*   States were dichotomized into caucus–convention or presidential primary states, depending on how the actual delegates were allocated.

Each independent variable proved to be statistically significantly correlated with the dependent variable (amount of coverage). The strength of relationships is indicated below in Table B.1.

Similarity of Coverage

In 1972 the intercorrelation of the dependent variable (amount of coverage) in the *Times* and the *Post* was R = .91**. In 1976, the correlation was .70**; in 1980, the correlation was .63**.

Predicting the Amount of Coverage

To test the combined explanatory power of the predictors, all four were combined into a multiple regression equation. The dependent variable was the amount of news coverage in the *Times* or the *Post*. The resulting explained variance, or R^2, is indicated below:

	R^2
1972 *New York Times* coverage	.65
1972 *Washington Post* coverage	.68
1976 *New York Times* coverage	.75
1976 *Washington Post* coverage	.51
1980 *New York Times* coverage	.51
1980 *Washington Post* coverage	.35

**Statistically significant at .1.

TABLE B.1: Correlations between Amount of News Coverage and Four Characteristics of the Presidential Nominations Process

Independent Variable	(Dependent Variable) Amount of Postprimary or Caucus Coverage In:					
	1972		1976		1980	
	Post	Times	Post	Times	Post	Times
1. Size of convention delegation						
Democratic	R = .57**	R = .60**	R = .41**	R = .46**	R = .30*	R = .54**
Republican	R = .59**	R = .61**	R = .36**	R = .41**	R = .24*	R = .46**
2. Historic importance of a state	K = .60**	K = .52**	K = .38**	K = .48**	K = .23*	K = .21
3. Make-or-break test						
Democratic	n.a.	n.a.	K = .28**	K = .20*	K = .32**	K = .32**
Republican	n.a.	n.a.	K = .24*	K = .24*	K = .36**	K = .41**
4. Mode of delegate selection						
Democratic	Eta = .59	Eta = .54	Eta = .28	Eta = .48	Eta = .26	Eta = .12
Republican	Eta = .59	Eta = .54	Eta = .28	Eta = .48	Eta = .26	Eta = .26

Symbols: R = Pearson product-moment correlation   * statistically significant at .05
K = Kendall's Tau correlation   ** statistically significant at .01
Eta = Eta correlation   n.a. not available
The number of cases equals all states and the District of Columbia, or 51.

APPENDIX C:
Candidate Behavior in the Preconvention Season — An Empirical Analysis

Chapter Four asserts that candidates decide to drop out or stay in the nominations contest based on two factors: their performance in state primaries and caucuses and their public opinion standing. To test this hypothesis, three alternative models are tested:

Model 1:   candidate performance in   candidate decisions to
            state primaries and caucuses → drop out or to remain
            (The verdict)   in the race

or

Model 2:   public opinion poll   candidate decisions
            support for, and shifts   → to drop out or to
            toward a candidate   remain in the race

Combining the two predictors:

Model 3:   candidate performance in
            the primaries and caucuses
            (The verdict)   ↘ candidate decisions
                    +   to drop out or to
            public opinion poll support   ↗ remain in the race
            for, and shifts toward a
            candidate

An Empirical Analysis

The Dependent Variable

The dependent variable is dichotomous: a candidate decides *either* to remain as an active contender *or* to drop out of the race. Dropping out is measured by a candidate's formal withdrawal or from the date a candidate declares an end to active campaigning. A candidate may make this decision after each round of state primaries, caucuses, or conventions.

The Independent Variables

Two sets of predictors are used, first separately and then jointly. The first set of variables includes three measures of a candidate's performance in the state delegate-selection races. These include the candidate's verdicts in the most recent contest(s), during the last two rounds of state contests, and cumulatively over the entire preconvention season to date.

The second set of predictors includes several measures of poll support for the candidate. Nine related variables are included here:

1. the candidate's poll changes over the current period,
2. the candidate's poll standings at the beginning of the current period,
3. the candidate's poll standings at the end of the current period or round,
4. whether the candidate is the poll leader or not,
5. if so, for how long,
6. poll changes over the previous two rounds or periods for the candidate,
7. the percentage of party identifiers who regarded the candidates "highly favorably" at the start of the primary season,
8. the percentage rating the candidate "highly unfavorably" at that time,
9. the percentage of party identifiers familiar with the candidate at the start of the primary–caucus season.

All these nine poll measurements would be known to (or could be estimated by) the candidates during the primaries and caucuses. Gallup Poll measurements are used for all the races except the 1980 GOP contest, for which *New York Times*-CBS Poll data are used.

Periods of Measurement

Each period, round, stage, or trial (all herein used synonymously) is defined as a time period begun by a poll measurement of the preferences of party identifiers. During each period one or more primaries and caucuses are held. The period terminates when another (Gallup or *New York Times*-CBS) poll is taken. Six periods were measured in 1972; ten periods in 1976. For the 1980 Democrats eight periods were measured, and for the 1980 Republicans three periods are available.

A candidate may be active throughout some or all the periods. A few candidates are active throughout all the primary–caucus season; in 1972, for example, McGovern was active for all six periods measured. Most candidates, however, were active for only part of the season before dropping out. Senator Hartke, for example, was active in 1972 only for the New Hampshire primary before he dropped out. Hence six trials or periods are available in 1972 for Senator McGovern, but only one for Senator Hartke.

For all the candidates in the 1972, 1976, and 1980 GOP and Democratic races, there were 152 periods during which some candidate actively pursued the nomination. Calculations below are computed on this base of 152 periods or trials.

A Note on Discriminant Functions

Discriminant function analysis is a special form of regression analysis appropriate for situations in which the dependent variable is dichotomous. One or more independent variables are used as predictors in developing a best-fit equation to predict the dependent variable (here: remaining in the race or dropping out). The best-fit equation then generates a prediction for each case, and the predicted outcome is compared to the actual or observed outcome. For a description of the program used see Norman Nie, et al., *Statistical Package for the Social Sciences* (New York: McGraw-Hill, 1975), pp. 434–467.

The Results

The first model outlined earlier used only the candidate's performance (the verdict) as predictors. This model correctly predicted 112 of 152 cases—or 74 percent.

The second model used only various public opinion variables. This model correctly predicted 131 of the 152 candidate decisions to drop out or remain in the race—or 86 percent.

The third model combined both public opinion and candidate performance variables. The combined model also predicted 131 of 152 candidate decisions—or 86 percent—correctly. The accuracy rate for the third, or combined, model is indicated in Table C.1.

Summary

Given the arbitrary time designation of the periods measured—which were defined by the Gallup Poll's or the *New York Times*-CBS Poll's measuring dates—the level of accuracy achieved appears very high. Data results suggest that the candidates do rely on their poll standings and on the media's verdict in deciding whether to drop out or to remain in the race.

TABLE C.1: Discriminant Function Predictions for Candidate Decisions to Drop out or Remain in the Nomination Race

	Predicted Behavior	
Actual Behavior	Remain in the race	Drop out of the race
Remain in the race	118	14
Drop out of the race	7	13

Total cases predicted = 152

Total cases predicted correctly = 131

Total errors = 21

Percentage of cases predicted correctly = 86

APPENDIX D:
The Effect
of the Media Verdict
on Public Opinion Polls

To test the impact of the media verdict on public opinion polls, the following two models were tested:

Model 1:	media verdict	→	poll changes, per period, per candidate
Model 2:	media verdict	→	overall poll standings, per candidate

The Independent Variable

The independent variable, the media's verdict, was measured in three alternative ways to reflect differing assumptions about the speed with which voter opinions react to candidate success (or failure) in the primaries and caucuses:

1. *The period verdict* is defined as the success of a candidate during each primary or caucus or each group thereof. The period verdict tests whether public opinion polls react immediately to changes in a candidate's verdict.

2. *The lagged verdict* is defined as the success of a candidate during the two periods immediately prior to the current round of primaries and caucuses. The lagged verdict tests whether the public opinion polls react in a delayed fashion to candidate success or failure.

3. *The cumulative verdict* is defined as the success of a candidate over the entire primary–caucus season to date. This variable tests the extent to which polls react to the candidate's cumulative verdict.

The Dependent Variable

Public opinion changes are measured in two ways. In the first model, poll changes are measured as the changes in a candidate's poll standing from the start to the conclusion of each period. In the second model, the dependent variable is each candidate's poll standing at the end of each period.

Periods of Measurement

Each period, round, stage, or trial (herein, all used synonymously) is defined as a period begun by a poll measurement taken of party identifiers, during which one or more primaries and caucuses were held, and concluded with another poll measurement taken of the preferences of party identifiers. See Appendix C. Measurements are made only during periods when a candidate is actively competing for the nomination.

Levels of Measurement

The media verdict, poll changes, and poll standings for each candidate are ratio-level measurements. Regression (R^2) techniques are reported here, to indicate the amount of change in poll changes or poll standings that are related to changes in the media's verdict.

The Two Models Restated

Broken into the various terms, the two models are tested below as follows:

Model 1:

$$\text{Period verdict} + \text{Lagged verdict} + \text{Cumulative verdict} \rightarrow \text{Public opinion poll changes, per candidate, per period}$$

and *Model 2:*

$$\text{Period verdict} + \text{Lagged verdict} + \text{Cumulative verdict} \rightarrow \text{Overall public opinion poll standings per candidate}$$

TESTING THE MODEL

Table D.1 indicates that the media's verdict is often a useful predictor both of public opinion poll changes and of a candidate's overall poll standings. Data in Table D.1 also indicates that the

TABLE D.1: Effect of the Media Verdict on Public Opinion Polls

Independent Variables	Dependent Variables	
	(Model 1) Poll Changes, per Candidate, per Period	(Model 2) Poll Standings at the End of Each Period, per Candidate
1980 Democrats:		
period verdict only	$R^2 = .09$	$R^2 = .37$
cumulative verdict only	$R^2 = .02$	$R^2 = .68$
lagged verdict only	$R^2 = .00$	$R^2 = .51$
period + cumulative + lagged verdicts	$R^2 = .10$	$R^2 = .71$
1980 Republicans:		
period verdict only	$R^2 = .02$	$R^2 = .43$
cumulative verdict only	$R^2 = .03$	$R^2 = .55$
lagged verdict only	$R^2 = .05$	$R^2 = .74$
period + cumulative + lagged verdicts	$R^2 = .07$	$R^2 = .86$
1976 Democrats:		
period verdict only	$R^2 = .13$	$R^2 = .18$
cumulative verdict only	$R^2 = .15$	$R^2 = .58$
lagged verdict only	$R^2 = .06$	$R^2 = .34$
period + cumulative + lagged verdicts	$R^2 = .18$	$R^2 = .61$
1976 Republicans:		
period verdict only	$R^2 = .01$	$R^2 = .01$
cumulative verdict only	$R^2 = .06$	$R^2 = .77$
lagged verdict only	$R^2 = .08$	$R^2 = .20$
period + cumulative + lagged verdicts	$R^2 = .10$	$R^2 = .85$
1972 Democrats:		
period verdict only	$R^2 = .02$	$R^2 = .01$
cumulative verdict only	$R^2 = .11$	$R^2 = .07$
lagged verdict only	$R^2 = .25$	$R^2 = .27$
period + cumulative + lagged verdicts	$R^2 = .29$	$R^2 = .31$

Note: Data were not available for the 1972 Republican contest.

cumulative and lagged verdicts are usually better predictors of a candidate's poll changes or overall poll standings than is a candidate's immediate (period) verdict alone. These data suggest that public opinion polls do react to candidate success or failure (as measured by the media verdict) but that the reaction time is usually not immediate.

Table D.1 also indicates that the strength of the relationship between the media verdict and the candidates' poll changes or overall poll standings varies from year to year and from contest to contest. The media verdict works best as a predictor of overall poll support for the 1980 Democrats and for the 1976 Democrats and Republicans but worst for the 1972 Democratic race. Overall, the media verdict appears to predict overall poll standings for the candidates better than changes in poll support during each period.

EARLY VERSUS LATE PRIMARIES

A second question tested here is whether polls shift more rapidly during the first half of the primary-caucus season than during the last half. The hypothesis here is that they do, since voters are most likely to shift preferences early in the primary-caucus season when they have less information. By the late primaries and caucuses, voters may be relatively saturated with information and may have settled on their candidate preferences.

In testing this hypothesis, only data for candidates who remained active throughout the primary-caucus season were included. Candidates included were Humphrey, Wallace, and McGovern (1972 Democrats), Ford and Reagan (1976 Republicans), Carter and Udall, (1976 Democrats), and Carter and Kennedy (1980 Democrats). The regression test was computed again for these nine candidates for the first half versus the last half of the preconvention contests. Data are indicated below:

	Dependent Variable:	
	Poll changes, per candidate	
Independent Variables	*first half*	*last half*
Period + lagged + cumulative verdict	$R^2 = .37$	$R^2 = .10$

Results indicate that the polls are more dependent on the media's verdict during the early contests than during the later primaries and caucuses. In the early contests over a third of all the poll changes can be associated with the media verdict, while in the late primaries poll changes appear little related to changes in a candidate's verdict. Results also indicate that much of the candidates' poll shifts cannot be directly linked to the media's verdict and, hence, remain unexplained.

WELL-KNOWN AND LITTLE-KNOWN CANDIDATES

A third hypothesis tested here is that the poll ratings of candidates with a high initial name recognition are less dependent on the media's verdict than are those of less well recognized candidates. Or, alternatively, the poll standings of little-known candidates are more dependent on their media verdicts than are the poll standings of better-known candidates.

To test this hypothesis, candidates were divided into those who were initially well recognized, including Wallace and Humphrey (1972 Democrats), Reagan and Ford (1976 Republicans), Carter and Kennedy (1980 Democrats), and Reagan (1980 Republicans). Less well recognized candidates included McGovern (1972 Democrats), and Carter and Udall (1976 Democrats). The explained variance, or R^2, for both groups is indicated below:

Dependent Variable

Independent Variables	Overall poll standings, per candidate	
Period + lagged + cumulative verdict	Well recognized candidates $R^2 = .14$	Less recognized candidates $R^2 = .74$

Data indicate that less well recognized candidates indeed find their poll ratings closely related to their primary or caucus success (as measured by the verdict). Better-recognized candidates are more "insulated" from poll changes based on the media verdict.

INDEX

ABOUT THE AUTHOR

THOMAS R. MARSHALL is Assistant Professor of Political Science at the University of Texas at Arlington.

Dr. Marshall has published several articles in the area of political parties, campaigns and elections, and political socialization. His articles have appeared in the *American Journal of Political Science*, the *Western Political Quarterly*, the *American Political Quarterly*, and others.

Dr. Marshall holds a B.A. from Miami University, Oxford, Ohio, and a Ph.D. from the University of Minnesota.